CW01337864

INSIDE ANDALUSIA

A travel adventure in southern Spain

By David Baird

Published by Mirador Books

"A worthy successor to the great writers, beautifully illustrated" — *Daily Telegraph.*

"Recommended" — *The Guardian.*

"Full of fervour... Once you have read it, you will want to go there too" — *The Scotsman.*

"A fine writer" — *Automobile Magazine, USA.*

"Read it from cover to cover with immense pleasure... beautifully produced" — *Island Gazette.*

"A magnificent literary work" — comment by jury which awarded *Inside Andalusia* the Vega Inclán National Tourism Prize.

"Witty, informative... makes us live intensely a very personal, closely-observed view of Andalusia" — Ian Gibson, biographer of Federico García Lorca.

First published in a large-format hardcover edition
in 1988 by Lookout Publications S.A.

Published April 1993 by Mirador Publications S.L.

Printed by Gráficas San Pancracio, S.L., Pol. San Luis. C/. Orotova 17, Málaga

ISBN: 84-88127-07-3   Deposito Legal: MA-597/1993

Andalusia's name derives from al-Andalus, which was the name the Moorish conquerors gave to the area of Spain under their control. It is believed that the word referred to the Vandals, who had ravaged Spain in the 5th century.

This book is dedicated to the people of Andalusia.
Their hospitality, readiness to help and patience made
both travel and research a pleasure.

CONTENTS

FOREWORD

D AVID Baird has two qualities essential in any travel writer worth his salt: a profound curiosity about people and places and a highly personal mode of expression. He is living proof that Buffon was right when he said that literary style "is the man himself", and those of us fortunate to know this lanky Shropshire lad find it impossible to distinguish between the man and the writer. Which is how it should be.

An essential component of the Baird style is its humour. That this man looks at life with an amused, quizzical eye was already apparent in his book The Incredible Gulf, first published in 1970, which chronicled a 10,000-mile trip around Australia's Gulf of Carpentaria. There the author not only brought vividly to life a wide range of engaging personalities ranging from buffalo-hunters, prawn-fishers and crocodile-raisers to Aborigines who, as Baird put it, "handle the controls of a bulldozer as skilfully as they throw a boomerang", but did so with a verve, a wryness and an amiability that set the book far above the average exercise in the genre.

Baird was born in the year in which the Spanish Civil War began (a subterranean influence on his future life?), and soon realized that he had travel in his blood. At the age of 23 he gave up his first job, horrified at the thought of eking out the rest of his days in a dismal office, working from nine to five with three weeks' holiday a year and a (probably insufficient) pension at the end of the whole depressing experience.

After that heroic decision his path took him to France, Spain (1959, 1960s), Canada, Mexico, Australia and finally, in 1971, Spain again, where he settled, during all of which time the list of temporary professions undertaken to keep body alive (soul was in fine fettle) would fill several pages of introduction — and hopefully will form the raw material for further books.

Baird's Inside Andalusia, which has grown out of the series thus titled that began to appear in Lookout in 1985, shows the writer at his most engaging, witty and informative, and it is difficult to doubt that in Andalusia he has now found his true home. This is no normal travel book, with systematic lists of hotels, the best places to eat and the "best" things to see. What the book does is to make us live intensely a very personal and closely-observed view of the south, Baird's view, while at the same time generating in us an intense urge to get out there and see for ourselves what the writer has seen. With Baird, as with Richard Ford, Walter Starkey or Gerald Brenan, armchair perusal is not enough, and what all *four Spain-lovers really want is for readers to toss their books aside and take to the road themselves. I am confident that such will be the reaction of those who read* Inside Andalusia. *David Baird makes us want to live more fully, to live Spain more fully, to see more and to see it more clearly (he himself would no doubt deny all this). His book is an achievement for which I am sure many people will be grateful. I certainly am.*

Ian Gibson
Biographer of Federico García Lorca

Beyond The Myth

IT is amazing how easy it is to become an expert on Andalusia. Newcomers manage the feat all the time. A month's stay is usually enough. Soon facile generalisations are pouring out faster than the Guadalquivir in flood. Since I am a slow starter, it took me a little longer. Nevertheless, within a year, I was an authority.

Then, doubts began nibbling away at my certainties. At every turn I was confronted with paradoxes and contradictions. Possibly, a degree of wisdom does come with age; these days I try to keep my mouth shut when new arrivals "explain" the place I have made my home. After nearly 20 years here, I have learned that what on the surface may appear clear-cut is often in reality surprisingly complex, that Andalusia is the last place to make snap judgements.

Clichés cling to Andalusia like a ruffled *gitano* dress to a flamenco dancer's curves (there's one for you). Richard Ford, acutest commentator of all English travellers, saw the whole of Spain last century as "a land bottled for antiquarians" and, more recently, illustrious ethnologist Julio Caro Baroja described the Andalusian village as a "living museum". Although such views still contain some truth, change has come fast to southern Spain. The "museum" now throbs to disco music while mother watches the video.

Andalusia today is in the throes of shifting from a near-medieval life-style into the uncertainties of the 20th century. That only adds to the fascination of this 87,000-square-kilometre region — about the size of Maine, twice the size of the Netherlands — with its 6.5 million inhabitants. To be sure, you can easily find the timeless stereotypes beloved by tourism publicists: matadors striding arrogantly out to flirt with death and bold gypsies exploding into dance; sensuous guitar chords shimmering through jasmine-scented summer nights. But that is only part of the picture, colourful but deceptive.

Andalusians themselves take a mischievous delight in angrily rejecting the image of the *charanga y pandereta* (literally "brass band and tambourine", meaning the frivolous stereotype) and next moment seemingly confirming it by their own actions. During the region's most popular fiesta, the Rocío pilgrimage, a young *jerezano* earnestly insists: "Don't get the wrong idea from what you see here. There is more to us than just folklore. We can be serious too, because we have poverty and anguish and injustice."

After some more wine, he confides: "Actually, we're all anarchists." Soon after, I see him whirling among the laughing revellers, dancing *sevillanas* perilously close to the campfire flames, the perfect image of the *pandereta.*

Among the tourist haunts of the Costa del Sol, you may come across a caricature of the typical *andaluz.* He wears a flat Córdoba hat and a red cummerbund and he sells carnations at exorbitant prices. Occasionally he will put on a heel-tapping, finger-flicking performance. It is good for business, but I suspect he gains a secret satisfaction from this parody. The ignorant watchers think this is Andalusia, but he knows the reality.

Andalusian humour is often black and sarcastic because, believes Seville cartoonist Emilio Rioja, of the people's poverty and oppression. It is "humour as a civilized release of desperation, of contained rage, as the start of liberation, or perhaps as the only cheap entertainment since we have nothing else."

Like many of his countrymen, Rioja objects to the popular, *gracioso* image of the typical *andaluz* as a happy-go-lucky type, overflowing with charm but basically a feckless buffoon. Stereotypes are hard to shake off, however. When 75 foreign photographers descended on Spain to portray a day in the life of the "real Spain", they named what they most wanted to picture. Gypsies, castanet-clickers and matadors easily headed the list.

"I get so angry when a false picture is given to foreigners," mutters a ham-curer in the Alpujarras. "As if we were all gypsies! There are only half a million of them in the whole of Spain. As for flamenco, the truth is it makes me nervous. I much prefer Mozart and Bach."

So what is a typical Andalusian?

"There is no such thing. By trying to generalize, you only produce another cliché," says a *sevillano.* "Look at me. Born in the heart of the city and raised here. I could no more dance flamenco than the minuet, I hate bullfights and I don't drink wine, I drink milk."

Andalusia's multi-layered history has shaped people and culture into an intricate mosaic. The land itself has surprising variety. A traveller comes across strawberry fields and gritty desert; bleak, inaccessible hamlets and urban sophistication. The native of Jaén, who like his province is almost Castilian in his severity, is very different from a man from Cádiz, who is renowned for his high spirits. To a pig-farmer from the forested uplands of Huelva, desiccated Almería could just as well be Algeria. Judged by their complexions, some Andalusians could have stepped from a nomad's tent, others from a Viking galleon.

This book attempts to show some of this diversity. If it awakens the reader's curiosity, it will be worthwhile. If it gets just a little under the skin of Andalusia, it will be an achievement. If it solved the enigma of the Andalusian character, with all its apparent contradictions, it would be a miracle.

Anthropologists, historians, sociologists, writers who have examined the region have given birth to a multitude of theories about the Mediterranean's oldest people, juggling paradoxes with imaginative but mixed results. Of some of these paradoxes, the Andalusian merely comments with a shrug, "Only an *andaluz* would undertand this." That incites the non-native either to conclude he is dealing with a very shallow culture or with one of oriental inscrutability.

A northern Spaniard, Javier Castroviejo is a scientific observer, a biologist and zoologist. But after many years in Andalusia (if he were English, by now he would have been knighted for his part in protecting the Coto Doñana nature sanctuary), Javier admits to a comprehension gap. Tracking the lynx's mating habits is easy compared to solving the complexities of human behaviour.

"The Andalusians have an incredible history," he points out. "They were more Roman than the emperor, more Muslim than the caliph, more Catholic than the Catholic Kings, more republican than the president, more monarchist than the king. They feel themselves to be oppressed victims, yet this land is favoured in so many ways. They are reluctant to make an effort, but they produce philosophers and great intellects in abstract subjects such as mathematics. They have this affection for folklore and yet they are not more primitive than other Spaniards. On the contrary, they are more refined and polished."

Indeed, even the humblest *campo* worker, though he may be numbered among Andalusia's 10 per cent of illiterates, is capable of unusual courtesy and delicacy. He can be surprisingly patient with strangers and tolerant of their ignorance. He still calls *"¡Vaya con Dios!"* ("Go with God!") to passers-by, though he may never attend Mass, because that is women's business. He belongs to an agrarian society that largely disappeared elsewhere in Europe long ago. Nearly one-quarter of the region's two million workforce is in agriculture, and industry is still a minor force.

Tourism has boosted Málaga province. New techniques have yielded a fortune in early vegetables in Almería's desert. But, measured in spending power, much of the region lingers near the bottom of the national league. Yet, however poor an *andaluz* may be, he breathes pride and dignity. His attitude is best illustrated in a cartoon by the well-known humorist, Mingote. It showed a king haughtily tossing a few coins to a ragged beggar. But this beggar was surely an Andalusian one, for he too wore a monarch's crown.

The key to the Andalusian's refusal to accept inferiority merely because he is lower on the social or financial scale lies in what Seville anthropology professor Isidoro Moreno calls his "anthropocentric nature". And Moreno believes it is in this trait, in the intensity of personal relations, that the Andalusian's culture differs from others.

The Andalusian's sense of confidence and security is founded in the solidity of personal ties. From birth he is buffered against life's perils by concentric rings of defence. At the core of this matriarchal-machista society lies *la familia,* offering total, often stifling support. It is not uncommon to meet a graduate aged 30 or more who prefers to stay jobless rather than leave home, where he is subsidized and cosseted by parents. Naturally, there is a price to pay. When the parents are old and infirm, he or she will be expected to return the favour.

At the heart of the family is *la madre,* slave, queen and symbol of fertility. Traditionally, the Andalusian mother raises the children and her husband has little to do with them. She wildly indulges her sons and they depend on her to a level that sometimes seems to go beyond filial bounds. Motherhood is idealized to a point where human affection and religious belief intermix.

Such veneration goes alongside a deeply embedded machismo. More open-minded youngsters have changed their attitudes, but Women's Lib has made only superficial advances. Woman's place remains at home and no true macho would be seen helping with the washing up, unless he wanted to be called a *maricón,* literally, a queer.

"¡Ay, mi macho! ¡Que malo es! [My man! How naughty you are!]" I heard one mother cry admiringly, as her four-year-old son reduced his sister to tears by belabouring her head with a broomstick.

A Málaga career woman tells me: "My boyfriend is intensely jealous. He says that if I go with another man he'll kill me, and I believe him. It hardly seems fair when he has a wife and two other girlfriends. But there's no point in looking for another fellow — my previous boyfriends were just the same."

Such double standards give the Andalusian male enviable freedom. But living up to his virile image binds him in a straitjacket and poses obstacles to his progress, for inflated pride forbids a man admitting he is ignorant of any subject or that he has erred. Dialogue is a rare beast in such an environment.

Beyond the family, a man has his friends, with whom he probably spends a good deal more time, and these circles are harder to break into than one might imagine. The *andaluz* has a surface openness and friendliness, but Moreno maintains that this is deceptive. "Personalized relationships," he says, "create many small groups and it is difficult to penetrate them."

Then there is the community. This is more real to the Andalusian than regions or nations, for the solidarity of a particular *barrio* (quarter) or *pueblo* (village) is exceptional. When a neighbour's son died, the traditional wake took place in my village. All night long, villagers visited the grieving mother to present their condolences. Neighbours and relatives crowded the tiny living-room until the hour of the funeral, as in all village bereavements. The unusual aspect was that the dead man had died in Argentina, where he had emigrated 30 years before.

"Spain is a nation without being conscious of it," comments José Manuel Cabezas, language teacher in a Málaga school. "The frontiers that for centuries divided the region between Arabs and Christians established hostility towards the neighbour. Deep down, there is no cohesion or union. Inhabitants of one pueblo regard those of another as potential enemies, although admittedly many of these rivalries are disappearing."

With his facility for words, the *andaluz* mixes venom with humour when talking of his rivals. *"En Andújar, la que no es puta es bruja* [In Andújar, she who is not a whore is a witch]" goes one refrain. *"En Baeza, orgullo y pobreza* [Baeza, pride and poverty]" runs another. Travellers are warned: *"Si llevas dinero a Estepa, que ni el alcalde lo sepa* [If you take money to Estepa, don't even let the mayor know]." And *"A Huelva una vez y nunca vuelvas* [One trip to Huelva is enough]". Then there is, *"Granadino, ladrón fino* [Granada native, a sly thief]", the *"Cordobés, falso y cortés* [the Cordoban, false and courteous]" and *"Hijo de Sevilla, uno bueno por maravilla* [It's a miracle if you can find a good sevillano]".

Some natives will quote such calumnies about their birthplace, while accepting no criticism from a stranger, with the same gusto they would display if dubbed a *malo,* a bad guy. In Andalusia, it is not necessarily complimentary to be labelled a *bueno* or straight-up type. It suggests that you are a little simple. Far better to be known as *un listo,* a clever character.

Disparaging rivals boosts morale in communities so isolated from outside events that they resemble mini-states. Laws made in Madrid appear less relevant to a villager than what his neighbours are saying. After analysing Grazalema in the sierras of Cádiz, sociologist Julian Pitt-Rivers concluded that there was a tribal aspect to the pueblo, true authority residing in collective social values and sanction by public criticism. Television and wider travel are altering minds, but a frequent explanation for why something is done in a particular (apparently illogical) way remains: "It's the custom." Argument over.

While to the outsider, all Andalusians seem to share common characteristics, that is not how they see themselves. The region's dialect rolls more rhythmically off the tongue than stiff Castilian. It is easily recognizable by the dropping of "d" and sometimes "s" too, so that a word like *pescado* (fish) becomes *"pecao"*. But there are pronunciation differences within provinces and even cities. Because of their exaggerated lisp, *gaditanos* (from Cádiz) have to put up with jokes about *maricones* (homosexuals). Upper-class *sevillanos* tend to pronounce "c" as an "s", while more humble residents pronounce it "th".

Sevillanos and gaditanos have the reputation for being most witty and ready to sing and dance. Land-girt Jaén and Córdoba are regarded as more sober and restrained than coastal areas such as Málaga which vaunts its extrovert high spirits. Proud and serious, Granada inhabitants are the butt of jokes for their miserliness. They in turn mistrust the *malagueños* as lightweights.

One historical anecdote, related naturally by a Granada native, tells how in the 15th century a courtier reported to the Catholic Monarchs that a number of people were awaiting audience. They consisted of, he said: "Squires from Jaén, knights from Córdoba, mariners from Huelva, nobles from Seville, lords from Cádiz, gentlemen from Almería, and also some...er...characters from Málaga."

Not surprisingly, trying to create a sense of identity among Andalusians has been an uphill fight. In Catalonia, the chief architects of autonomy were the wealthy merchant class. In contrast, Andalusia's *burguesía* have looked to Madrid as the focus of their ambitions. They regarded a man like Blas Infante Pérez as a dangerous subversive.

Born in Casares (Málaga), Infante was a notary who used his spare time to preach self-rule. Schooldays in Archidona left an indelible impression: "Nailed in my conscience since infancy, I have the sombre image of the *jornalero* [seasonal worker]. I have seem him parade his hunger through the village streets."

Devoting his life to the Andalusian cause, Infante created a flag, an anthem, a dream. "We have to reconstruct a Zion," he declared. One of the first things the Nationalist rebels did on taking Seville in the Civil War was to execute Infante. His last words were, "Long live Free Andalusia!"

Years later, at least a part of his dream was realized when Andalusia achieved autonomous rule, although the cynics would say the strings are still pulled from Madrid. And a number of Andalusians believe autonomy is an unhealthy step backwards.

"It is a tendency towards isolation. We don't have a separate culture from the rest of the nation," claims writer Antonio Muñoz Molina. "Just when Spain is opening up to Europe and we are smashing the idea of Andalusia as the land of the bullfighter and all that, we are turning in on ourselves. Spain has not just entered the Common Market of potatoes and tomatoes but the Common Market of the mind, and we should be a part of it."

There has, however, been a resurgence of interest in all things Andalusian: its fiestas, its roots, its special character. Nobody can get near to understanding that character unless he digs just a little into history. Evidence of its richness is turned up almost daily, by a fisherman's trawl, a ploughman's blade, an archaeologist's trowel. Men were daubing the walls of La Pileta and Nerja caves around 15000 BC. When the Egyptians were raising the pyramids, other incredible feats of engineering were under way to build the megaliths of Antequera. Two thousand years before Christ, a community of at least 2,000 people prospered at Los Millares near Almería.

Andalusia's wealth was known in the days of Solomon. Tarshish (to the Hebrews) or Tartessos (to the Greeks) was a legendary place at the end of the world. The Old Testament tells us that "Every three years once came the ships of Tarshish, bringing gold and silver, ivory, and apes and peacocks." The Phoenicians established Gadir, site of modern Cádiz, 3,000 years ago. Waves of invaders followed: Phoenicians, Romans, Vandals, Visigoths, Moors, the Christian armies. They were seduced and absorbed.

According to the philosopher José Ortega y Gasset, Andalusia's tactic has always been to offer no resistance. "In this way," he wrote, "Andalusia always ended up intoxicating the invader's harsh impetus with its delights."

Ortega y Gasset's theory of Andalusia was that it was an agrarian culture which had elevated man's union with the earth into a spiritual relationship. Whereas Castilians regarded the land as a battlefield, he claimed, in Andalusia the warrior had always been scorned.

Unfortunately, misuse of Andalusia's wealth has long meant that only a small section of society enjoys its full fruits. The Romans invented the *latifundio* (big estate) and the Catholic Kings re-invented it when they parcelled out the region to their captains and courtiers after the defeat of the Moors and reunification of Spain in 1492. They dealt a few more hammer-blows. The ejection of the Jews removed a vital entrepreneurial class. After the Muslim Andalusians were chased out, valuable arable land became sheep runs.

Last century the privatizing of common land and the confiscation of church property only entrenched a new breed of proprietors, wealthy burghers who saw land was a good investment. The landless and the thousands of farmers with pocket-handkerchief plots on which they could barely survive looked on with frustration. Many owners never went near their properties and demonstrated a feudal indifference to the fate of the people there. In comparison, the paternalistic English country squire was benevolence itself.

Misery, anger and revolt went hand in hand. Anarchism took root and risings were put down with brutal ferocity. This was the era of *Andalucía trágica,* when the seeds of hate were being sown for the Civil War. After that conflict, hunger drove many Andalusians to emigrate. The army of more than two million homesick exiles has been called the region's "ninth province". Few could emulate the rags-to-riches story of bullfighter El Cordobés and end up shooting partridge with General Franco. Instead, they provided cheap labour for industry in Barcelona, Bilbao and Madrid, Northern Europe and further afield.

"Hombre, if I had a job offer, I would go home tomorrow," one tells me after 20 years in Melbourne, Australia.

And when somebody asks for the mayor of one echoing, empty Almería village, he is told: "He's in Barcelona, like everybody else."

Andalusia's bitterness is reflected in the anguish and grief of *cante jondo,* the deep, serious style of flamenco singing. The singers seem to tear at their own entrails, wrenching out a cry for deliverance that comes from the very soul of Andalusia. But deliverance for the region's 200,000 *jornaleros* appears unlikely, short of a revolution. The vast estates are still in the hands of relatively few. Two per cent of Andalusian proprietors own 50 per cent of the land and five great aristocratic families, Arcos, Infantado, Medinaceli, Medina Sidonia, and Osuna, dominate veritable kingdoms. Progress has meant not fewer absentee landlords but more professional farm managers. The estates are becoming more efficient and more productive but with less labour.

Jornaleros watch the new machines with loathing. To survive, they trap sparrows, collect snails and wild asparagus, sneak through the fences of the big estates to poach rabbits or search for olives missed in the harvest. Scoffing at mild attempts at land reform, some storm on to large farms to stage symbolic occupations, clashing with their traditional enemy the Civil Guard. In communities where Lenin's portrait hangs beside the bar, there is apocalyptic talk. Sons of the landless decamp daily to join the rootless in dismal suburbs that girdle the cities. Others become bricklayers, waiters and cleaners on the Costa del Sol, whose affluence is like a mocking beacon.

In contrast, thousands of farmers see a new prosperous era beginning, as Spain's membership of the European Community aids exports of everything from avocados to carnations.

Andalusia has never been subject to so much pressure to change. Conservative ideas are fragmenting. Growers of newfangled crops send their children to take computer courses. Unquestioned values and ancient customs crumble, and Hispanist Allen Josephs believes that "when the generation of rural Andalusians born before the Civil War... dies out, the unbroken chain of civilizations stretching back to the Tarshish of Solomon's time may well have ended."

But customs formed over millennia will not so quickly be swept away. Far from dying out, old rituals have been revived or have gained in popularity, as though the people cling to them for reaffirmation of their roots. Around a million people flock to the Rocío *romería,* many of them youngsters city-born and raised.

Materialist values do not yet rule every facet of existence. An American writer found that to his cost. After scoring a hit with a Broadway play, he tried in vain to settle on the Mediterranean. A *malagueño* shrugged his shoulders. "He made a big mistake," he said. "He thought by talking big bucks, he could get things done faster and the way he wanted. But he did not undertstand. That might work in the States, but here it can have the reverse effect."

On such cultural misunderstandings, however, many a misconception is based. One, which I have never understood, maintains that the Andalusian is lazy. Ortega y Gasset himself, born in Madrid, propagated this notion. He argued that people could live with minimum effort because of the climate and fertile soil, suggesting that doing little was the Andalusian ideal.

It is true that the climate is easier to bear than in some parts of Europe, although anybody passing through Ecija in midsummer or trudging the sierras in winter, would dispute that. Andalusians are not burdened with puritanical northern ideas. "We don't see work as something that redeems you," said one. And some are experts in surviving without obvious means of support. The *pícaro,* who lives on his wits, has been around since at least the time of Cervantes. Today's version adds to his income by picking up unemployment pay.

But to generalize about this subject is to do the Andalusian a gross injustice. The strutting *señorito,* the rich man's son who does little but put on airs, is becoming a figure of the past. Thousands of seasonal workers spend months away from home, picking grapes in France, asparagus in Navarre and doing other jobs for low pay. The hopelessness and inertia that grip many rural towns arises not from laziness, but from lack of business initiative and opportunity.

From my observation, few people have such a capacity for work. Anybody who toils along with a farmer digging up his sweet potatoes or with construction workers when the temperature is at 40 degrees centigrade swiftly learns how ridiculous are these stories of laziness. The long hours worked by many, particularly in service industries, continue to amaze me. And the idea of taking weekends off or going "on holiday" is still a novel one for many folk.

"How can I close the shop?" a barber asks me. "If I put a 'closed for vacation' sign up, the neighbours would think I was putting on airs. I would never live it down."

Andalusian pride and stoicism have been moulded on the anvil of a long history. An added dose of fatalism was injected by the 700-year presence of invaders from Africa and the Middle East. But his fascination with death and especially the ritual of the corrida (the bullfight) must stretch back into the dawn of man. Death has a strange fascination for all humans, but elsewhere it is pushed into the background. The *andaluz* has no such inhibitions.

"It's true that we make a joke of death," one tells me. "But that's because we believe in living."

Josephs comments: "The essential paradox that a culture of death is actually a culture of life fits the Andalusian character and Spanish character perfectly. The use of the word 'death', the mention or discussion of which borders on anathema in our own culture, reminds us to what an extent this historical culture of Andalusia has been un-Western, non-modern, anti-rational, non-violent and anti-materialist..."

The closeness of death is what sometimes seems to impel the *andaluz* to live life with a shocking frenzy, resisting sleep and commitments for the sake of the *juerga*. At annual fiestas, a year's savings may be blown in the flamboyant heat of the moment.

"We live close to the skin," say Andalusians, explaining their volatile emotions, the quick show of sentiment. Rub two together and you can spark a party. Put three in a bar, turn on the television, the sound system and the slot machines, and you have the makings of an all-night fiesta. An Andalusian needs commotion about him to confirm he is truly alive. His noisy exuberance and demonstrative gestures are not always understood, however, in other cultures. A migrant worker told me how, when he met an old friend in a Frankfurt street, they embraced and exchanged excited greetings. "The next thing, two policemen threatened to arrest us for disturbing the peace. What sort of a country is that?"

"The *andaluz* is attached more to the form than the depth of something," says one academic commentator, Antonio Miguel Bernal. "We lose ourselves in metaphors, in brilliance."

Love of fine words, a cavalier attitude towards time, and an intense belief in human contact are traits that betray the Arab heritage. Even though Andalusians are notorious for their lack of interest in books, businessmen, shop assistants and students have a common interest. They write poetry and, given the chance, declaim it. This genius for imagery won Nobel prizes for Vicente Aleixandre and Juan Ramón Jiménez and international esteem for Lorca, Alberti, Becquer, Cernuda and the Machado brothers.

Dreamers in a land trodden by Noah cannot be expected to enslave themselves to Greenwich Mean Time. As Granada poet José Heredia Maya explains to me: "We do not see virtue in doing things fast. Everything should be enjoyed slowly. Like a pass in a bullfight." He spreads an imaginary cloak for a charging bull. "You see, slowly. Much prettier."

Asked for a receipt, my local builder finally hands it to me with the pride of a job well done, two years later. At 4 a.m. in a convivial bar, a friend looks at me in amazement: "You are going home? But you are enjoying yourself. Don't throw this moment away. It will never come again."

Here is one reason Andalusians have to work so hard. Procrastination eventually provokes crises. That provides the chance to demonstrate their flair for improvisation, which often requires superhuman, last-minute effort.

When a Seville businessman failed to turn up for an important appointment, an American called him to ask what had happened.

"I had another meeting at that time," was the reply.

"But how is that possible, when you fixed to see me?"

"Don't you understand?" came the slightly exasperated reply. "I made another appointment *after* the one I made with you."

This sort of logic is irrefutable. In New York, or London for that matter, business is done fast, coldly and, possibly, efficiently between robots. In

Andalusia, robots have a hard time. Personal relationships are all. If you do not have an *enchufe* (a plug, meaning an influential connection), you must work to create mutual respect. Without it, in even routine transactions prepare for tears and frustration. But, once you are recognized as a fellow human, anything is possible.

On one occasion, trying to collect a package from a railway station, I was bluntly informed that this was out of the question. Firstly, it was a public holiday. Furthermore, I had not got the proper papers. And, in any case, the employee in charge of such matters was away. I was about to walk off, but stayed to indulge in idle conversation. After a few minutes, the receipt was plucked from my hand and the parcel handed over with a smile. Human relations had triumphed again.

And there lies the secret of Andalusia's appeal. Beguiling, infuriating, perplexing, intoxicating, it can be all of these. But it is also one of the most human places left in the Western World.

King of Rivers, River of Life

ON a glittering spring day, Bonanza lives up to its name. Salt-stained, heavy-bellied craft come rolling in from Cádiz Bay, from the Canaries, from Africa, to disgorge gleaming treasures — bonito, lobster, mullet, grouper, anchovies, ray, squid, swordfish. Sweating men joke and curse as they heave tray after tray across the quayside into the big, echoing auction shed.

Bawling through a megaphone, the auctioneer moves from catch to catch. Weary, unshaven fishermen crowd around, eager to know how much their share of the catch is worth. Afterwards they crowd a nearby bar, boisterously celebrating a successful trip.

"This is nothing," says the one-eyed barman above the racket of conversation, television and fruit machines. "Only about 80 boats have come in. You should see a good day. Then it's a real madhouse."

Bonanza stands near the mouth of the Guadalquivir, where the silt-laden river drifts to meet the Atlantic with the majestic calm of one who has experienced too much to see any point in hurrying. A few weeks earlier I had witnessed other men fishing in the same river, but these were casting for trout near the source, where the waters skip clear and clean in the first reckless flush of their beginning.

A journey along the 660-kilometre length of the Guadalquivir between those two spots — past Roman bridges, 20th-century hydroelectric plants, sprouting crops, mills built by the Moors — is a voyage through the history of southern Spain. For the story of the Guadalquivir, king of rivers, is the story of Andalusia itself.

Since early times it has been the life-blood of the region, watering its fertile basin, used both as a highway and a barrier against the march of invading armies.

To the Greeks, it was the Tartessos river, named after the fabled kingdom whose capital may have been close to the Guadalquivir's mouth. The Romans preferred Betis, a word of Celtic, Iberian or Ligurian origin. Later it was called Nahr Qurtuba, river of Córdoba, but around the 12th century it came to be known as Wadi al-Kabir, Great River, from which the present name derives.

Generations of wordsmiths, philosophers and poets have been inspired to recite the praises of the Guadalquivir. Not long after the birth of Christ, Marco Valerio Marcial quilled: "Oh Betis, your mane crowned with fertile olives, in the crystal of your waters you reflect the splendour of golden leaves..." In the 16th century, theologian Fray Luis de León was moved to write of "divine Betis". Luis de Góngora, poet of Spain's Golden Age, also waxed lyrical about this "abundant river, king of all others". This century, Mariano Palancar Penella pondered: "A thousand voices have sung to you/But who knows you,/Oh, Guadalquivir?"

This river has as many faces and as many moods as any female temptress. It bubbles, runs and idles past snow-tipped crags and steamy rice fields, olive groves and orange orchards, pinewoods and factories. Drought may reduce it to a trickle and a cloudburst can swell it to a rampaging torrent. Only recently has man begun to bring Spain's second largest river under some sort of control in order to avoid the more disastrous flooding and to draw electric power from its fitful flow.

The Guadalquivir is fed by more than 800 tributaries, draining a 22,000-square-mile (57,000 square kilometres) basin, which extends into all eight Andalusian provinces. Five provinces, Jaén, Córdoba, Seville, Huelva and Cádiz, are bathed by its waters.

The Guadalquivir's drainage area is one of Europe's richest and most varied areas of plant and animal life. Half of the continent's plant species, plus most of those of the North African subtropical zone, are represented. And Las Marismas, the marshlands on its estuary, form one of Europe's most important sanctuaries for bird and animal life.

Farmers, local authorities, ecologists, power companies, politicians, navigators, fishermen all have individual interests to defend in connection with the river. The Confederación Hidrográfica del Guadalquivir listens to them all, but balancing rival claims is a delicate business.

The Confederación, an autonomous body dependent on the Public Works Ministry and the Andalusian government, was formed in the 1930s to create water resources that would ensure a rational and efficient irrigation system to boost energy sources and to assure water supplies to communities in its area. Since then, dozens of dams have been constructed, the area of irrigated land has risen to around 400,000 hectares, and electricity production from 33 power stations averages 700 Gwh annually, although the figure can fluctuate dramatically depending on rainfall. The average annual precipitation in the basin is 600mm, but evaporation can swallow more than two-thirds of this.

Biologists, engineers and laboratory technicians are among the 1,500 employees of the Confederación, which has its headquarters in the echoing chambers of the Plaza de España building in Seville.

"Our biggest problem is that this is a river with a very irregular flow," explains technical director Vicente Aycart Benzo. "In the past, when there was little control, the flow could vary from thousands of cubic metres a second after heavy rain to as low as five or six cubic metres a second. Now, thanks to the dams we have built, we can regulate the flow better. We have to maintain a minimum level through Seville, for example, to prevent the tide bringing salt up the river.

"Rainfall is not dependable and evaporation is high so, with the water we've got, we cannot permit the luxury of thinking of new uses. I don't see much possibility of expanding the irrigated area."

Pollution, from villages pouring in untreated sewage and from industry, is a continuing problem. But some progress has been made. A commission checks water quality and can impose sanctions. Sugar factories have to purify water before expelling it and olive oil factories, among the most serious offenders, are obliged to channel waste liquid into collection ponds instead of pumping it straight into the river.

"The river has improved in Seville. Four treatment plants now clean up city waste and there are more fish than there were," says Vicente. "Would I swim in the Guadalquivir in the city?" He smiles. "Well, no, I don't think I would."

Where one *can* swim, amid pristine natural surroundings, is near the river's source in the sierra of Cazorla. It springs to life in a glen known as La Cañada de las Fuentes, 1,350 metres above sea-level. As the stream cascades north-east through mountains formed 200 million years ago, wild goats and deer slip like shadows through the pines to quench their thirst in its crystalline waters.

The river slows on entering El Tranco de Beas (one of the largest of the Guadalquivir basin's 30 reservoirs), designed to hold up to 500 million cubic metres of water and to generate 50 million kilowatt/hours of electricity annually. The 300-foot-high dam, completed in 1945, marks the point where the river makes a U-turn and heads west, soon to enter the kingdom of the olive.

Perceptibly slackening pace, the Guadalquivir skirts the historic towns of Ubeda and Baeza and the copper, lead and sulphur mines of Linares to the north, and bypasses the provincial capital of Jaén, 24 kilometres to the south. The Arabs knew Jaén as Geen, a way station for passing caravans, and built a magnificent fortress. It is still there, dominating the town from its hilltop, and still magnificent, though much restored. Known as Santa Catalina castle, it houses a parador which offers panoramic views. Under the Romans, Jaén was famous for its silver mines and was always an important crossroads between Castile and Andalusia.

Today, Jaén is heavily dependent on the production of the olive groves which roll up to the banks of the Guadalquivir. At Andújar, a pleasant, industrious town, the river slips under the 14 arches of a Roman bridge. Nearby is where the proudly independent town of Iliturgi once stood, until — fed up with its rebelliousness — Rome sent Scipio's forces to reduce buildings and inhabitants to dust.

To the north lie the twisted oaks, game preserves and bull ranches of the Sierra Morena. To the south, as the plain widens and the river meanders into Córdoba province, barley, wheat and rye mingle with olive trees marching to the horizon.

From Andújar, the river — averaging a flow of 70 cubic metres a second — is followed by the NIV, the main artery between Madrid and Seville. Traffic sweeps past the old towns, each with its tale of past bloodshed, triumph and tragedy, as though they were not there.

Ripe, Epora, and Cantara were some of the names attached to a typical settlement sprawling across five hills in a wide bend of the river, until — to the clash of swords — Alfonso VII of León and Castile dubbed it Montoro. The Phoenicians are said to have navigated up the river as far as Montoro and chronicler Rodrigo Méndez de Silva reported that in the Middle Ages it was "embellished by a strong castle and good bridge, most fertile in bread, wine and oil, cattle, fruit and vegetables, with 1,000 inhabitants, a parish church and 13 hermitages."

The solid stone bridge which traverses the river here was designed by Enrique Egas, of Brussels, architect of the Catholic Kings. It cost 220,000 ducats and took more than half a century to complete. The monarchs were suitably impressed by the townsfolk's effort and in 1501 they exempted Montoro from lodging and supplying their army.

Work of any sort would be welcome these days in this town (population, 10,000), which has a stagnant air. Men linger idly in the narrow streets or in the main plaza where the plateresque façades of the pink-stone San Bartolomé church and the town hall are mocking reminders of past glories.

"Last century, when the church land was confiscated and sold off to tenants, Montoro prospered. That's when some of the fine houses here were built," says Manuel Leon Canete, a former mayor, whose own home, with its many books, great studded doors and big patio, was built in 1851. "But now the wealth of the olive has been lost. Some trees around here are 200 years old, when best production is between seven and 60 years. There are no longer many big estates, because the land has been split between families. The trouble is, many of the smaller properties are hardly worth working."

"It's true that there's a lack of initiative in a place like this," notes Pepe, one of Manuel's seven children, as he tends the town's well-stocked library. "But things are changing. I would say that more than 50 per cent of the old people cannot read, but for the first time youngsters are interested in books and are widening their horizons. This library is quite an advance in itself, because until the early 1980s we had only a handful of books."

A little west of Montoro and 37 kilometres before Córdoba, drivers on the NIV blink unbelievingly at the sight of two slim minarets rising from a white building by the side of the highway. The Basharat Mosque at Pedro Abad is another indication of changing times. It illustrates the new religious freedom in post-Franco Spain and marks the return of Islam after an absence of nearly five centuries.

The imam greets visitors effusively. Abdul Sattar Khan is a short, bespectacled Pakistani who smiles a lot and offers visitors Pepsi-Cola in the mosque's comfortable reception room. It is lined with copies of the Koran in several languages and literature on the Ahmadiyya sect, founded in 1889 when a Punjabi named Mirza Ghulam Ahmad declared he was the Messiah. Though persecuted in some Muslim countries, notably Pakistan, the movement now has 10 million adherents, about 100 of them in Spain.

"We aren't many," admits the imam. "But it is better to have a few practising members who set an example. If God wills, one day the majority of Spaniards will accept Islam."

The 35 million pesetas needed to construct the mosque came from the Ahmadiyya community in Britain. When the sect's leader laid the foundation stone on October 9, 1980, it was the first mosque founded in Spain since Moorish times, although one at Marbella was the first to be completed. (In one of those quirks of history, a Christian army camped near Pedro Abad in 1234 when trying to wrest Córdoba from the Moors.)

At first, Pedro Abad villagers were puzzled by the new arrivals, and suspicious. But the sight of the imam's veiled wife doing her shopping is now taken for granted and his two daughters happily attend a school staffed by Catholic nuns.

In the green-carpeted prayer room, five orations are said every day, the first before dawn. Worshippers are few, but Islam is gaining a foothold and there are plans to build a mosque at Granada too.

"We are a pacific movement. We're known internationally for that," stresses the imam. "Our slogan is 'love for all and hate for nobody'. Our movement is a revival of the essence of Islam as set out in the Holy Koran."

The imam presses tea and pamphlets on his visitors, and smilingly bids them farewell: "The peace of God be with you."

Poplars and eucalyptuses offer shade along the banks as the Guadalquivir weaves steadily westwards, slowing here and there into a placid lake, before tumbling through the turbines blocking its path. One power station lies near El Carpio, a peaceful town dominated by a Gothic-Mudéjar tower. Pigeons perch atop the crumbling structure, their every flutter threatening to send the cornices crashing into the street. The tower dates from the 14th century and is built on land donated by King Ferdinand, saintly smiter of the Moors, to one of his warriors, Garci Mendez de Sotomayor.

Closer to Córdoba, a monument on the Alcolea bridge recalls a famous battle in 1868 when a victory by General Serrano's revolutionary troops led to the exile of Isabel II, an amorous lady whose marriage to an effeminate cousin prompted her comment, "What can I say of a man who on his wedding night wore more lace than I?"

More recently, the nearby village of Alcolea, renowned locally for having *mucha guasa* (leg-pulling), provoked national headlines when a clairvoyant announced treasure was buried there. The Civil Guard were sent into action to prevent gold-hungry villagers digging up a road.

Halfway along its journey to the sea, the Guadalquivir loops through Córdoba. Two millenniums of history unfold along the banks as the river runs mud-brown past modern anti-flood ramparts, past the Great Mosque, the Botanic Gardens where once a caliph's medicinal herbs grew and past the Catholic Kings' fortress. It tugs at the pillars of a bridge, restored many times since its construction in the days of the Emperor Augustus. The bridge still carries traffic and at its centre melted wax spills over the roadway from candles burning before a statue of San Rafael, Córdoba's patron saint.

According to the Greek historian Strabo in his Third Book of Geography, in ancient times the river was navigable above the city. But man's increasing exploitation of its waters created hazards for both boats and fish. As far back as 1398, Seville boatmen appealed to the king of Castile because the owners of waterwheels and weirs between Seville and Córdoba had "put obstacles along waterways where the boats carrying wheat and flour ply, causing us great damage. The boats sink and lose their cargoes."

Construction of dams in the past century has sealed off the middle reaches of the river. Just outside Córdoba fishermen used to eke out a living near one of Spain's first hydroelectric stations, built in 1895. But a massive new barrier downstream at Peñaflor blocked the passage of shad seeking spawning grounds and the industry died.

Anglers are comparatively few in these parts. Although the rivers harbour barbel and bass, the finicky complain about their muddy taste. Many communities along the Guadalquivir ignore its possibilities for sport and diversion and, above Seville, surprisingly few pleasure-craft use the river.

Twenty-five kilometres west of Córdoba, mighty battlements glower over the main railway line to Seville and the town of Almodóvar (on route C-341). Many a prisoner mouldered in Arab and medieval times in this castle's dungeons. One was Juana de Lara, daughter-in-law of Pedro I of Castile, who also stored his treasure here.

A feudal aspect lingers along the Guadalquivir in its stately progress towards the sea. Great estates stretch away to the horizons, but in the towns and villages landless labourers scrawl on street walls hopeless pleas for *pan y trabajo* (bread and work), while they rust in idleness for much of the year. Attempts at agrarian reform make slow progress. The land-owners argue that most properties are now efficiently farmed and splitting them up will produce few extra jobs.

In fact, job opportunities recede as more machines work the endless, unhedged fields of sugar-beet, sunflowers, asparagus and cereals. In autumn, the roadsides are dusted with snow-flakes, which prove to be cotton bolls blown from passing lorries. Seeing the tobacco and cotton plantations, were it not for the occasional ruined fortress and whitewashed settlement, a traveller might imagine he had strayed into America's Deep South.

West of Almodóvar, I notice two men wandering on a hillside, turning over stones in their quest for ants which they would use as bait in illegal bird-traps. Nearby, two stocky *jornaleros* (workers employed by the day) check whether the cotton is dry enough to pick after a heavy rainstorm.

"Let nobody say the *andaluz* doesn't know how to work," comments Miguel Ocaña, one of the *jornaleros*. "They should try breaking their backs picking cotton hour after hour, or humping sugar-beet. It's a killer when the temperature climbs towards 40 degrees." He pauses and looks over the acres of cotton. "You know we can grow the best-quality crops here, but we have no industry. Those with cash won't risk it. They prefer to rent out their land to people from Navarre and sit in the bar, like *señoritos*."

"That's the trouble," agrees Manolo Aguera, Miguel's friend. "Nobody will start a factory here. We grow asparagus but they take it to the north to can it. The olives go to Seville. The cotton goes to Barcelona. And we're left without work."

South of Almodóvar, towards Ecija, the flat, bleak country is dotted with small breeze-block huts. They house irrigation pumps. Small solar panels on the roofs provide power.

At La Carlota, on Highway NIV, a 1967 monument pays tribute to those who made it possible for "men of diverse nations of Europe, attracted by Andalusia's legendary fame, to transform these sterile and desert lands into industrious towns."

The inscription refers to a remarkable experiment initiated 200 years ago by Carlos III. The idea was to create a pure rural society, unencumbered by class or privilege. The king first thought of colonizing Texas, then decided to repopulate Andalusia, where half a million people had been wiped out in a plague around 1600. A Bavarian adventurer named Juan Gaspar de Thurriegol promised to bring 6,000 Germans and Flemish to Spain.

Thurriegol had no difficulty in luring settlers, although he did have to stretch the truth a little. They were told that "the Door of Happiness" and a "Rich Treasure Chest" awaited them. Each settler was promised 50 *fanegas* (80 acres) of crop-growing land, plus terrain for planting trees and vines, and two cows, five ewes, five goats, five hens, and a sow.

Some settlers went to the Sierra Morena. Others came to the zone south of the Guadalquivir. "Paradise" soon proved to have blemishes. The indigenous population resented the progressive new ideas. Some settlers were expelled when it was found they were Protestants. Others were scourged by epidemics. Assured they would "never feel rigours of cold and heat", the new arrivals found they were in an area known as *La Sarten de Andalucía* (Andalusia's Frying Pan) because of its brutal summer climate. Some took refuge from the hardships in drinking and gambling, allegedly encouraged by licentious soldiery. Families arriving at the new town of Fuente Palmera were forced to live in barracks because there were no houses.

Austere, heat-bludgeoned Fuente Palmera is still no paradise, although life now is more comfortable. Bundles of old documents in the town hall archives record the community's pioneer days. A clerk showed me the yellowed "Royal Certificate of His Majesty and Members of his Council", dated 1767, which decreed the statutes for the new town.

Local surnames like Piston, Herman and Hens hint at the area's unusual past, as do certain customs. Every year on December 28, Spain's Day of the Innocents, a group called *Los Locos* perform an unusual dance at neighbouring Fuente Carreteros which is said to have its origins in Northern Europe.

When winter rains have greened this fertile soil, the gently rolling landscape pleases the eye. But under the cloudless skies of high summer the area becomes a furnace. Ancient Ecija, called the City of the Towers for its many belfries, may well be Spain's hottest spot. It once registered 52 degrees centigrade.

Past Ecija's baroque churches and convents and Renaissance palaces flows the Genil river. Nourished by the snows of the Sierra Nevada, it snakes through burnt farmlands to join the Guadalquivir near Palma del Río.

Palma appears more prosperous and better cared-for than during the grim post-war years when Manuel Benítez was raised there. Then, few had a good word for the illiterate, barefoot youth, but now every second person in Palma

27

claims to be the cousin of the man better known as El Cordobés, the Beatle of the Bullring, who instead of dressing his family in mourning made millions from his reckless performances as a matador. To test his skill, El Cordobés used to sneak into the fields by night and play the bulls.

The fighting stock of the Morenos still roams local pastures and one of the family, Alonso Moreno de Silva, lives in a former Franciscan monastery dating back to 1500. Young and enthusiastic, Alonso and his wife, Carmen Martínez de Sola, used Roman columns, hand-painted tiles and massive beams in converting part of the rambling structure into a restaurant and small hotel. Moorish-style dishes first created seven centuries ago and now prepared by the Morenos' Basque chef, are served in what was once the monks' refectory.

"We named the hotel rooms after the mission stations in California," explains Alonso. "Fray Junípero Serra almost certainly visited this monastery when he travelled through Andalusia seeking monks to accompany him to the New World, where he founded those missions."

In a leafy patio, he indicates the orange trees. "Junípero Serra took fruit from Andalusia to plant in California and some probably came from these trees, which are at least 400 years old."

Alfonso and Carmen represent a new, progressive generation in a region which in the past was notorious for its absentee landlords. Partly educated in England, Alonso applies the latest techniques to this highly-mechanized, 1,000-hectare property. Carmen could handle a horse or a sherry perfectly in the Seville fair, but more usually reports on agriculture for a daily newspaper.

Below Palma, the Guadalquivir slips almost imperceptibly into Seville province. With the Genil's waters, it reaches an average flow of some 170 cubic metres (36,000 gallons) a second, but much is siphoned off to quench the thirst of orange and lemon orchards and fields of vegetables. To the north, the eroded hills of the Sierra Morena rise to nearly 3,000 feet, but the river basin is flat and monotonous.

South of Lora del Río, lean men ride out every day to check the cattle. They never approach them on foot, for this is the home of the respected Miura *toros de lidia* (fighting bulls), renowned for their size and lethal horns. Don Eduardo, the leathery septuagenarian patriarch of the Miura clan, sees changing times: "More and more land is being converted for arable purposes and the bull can no longer find the good grass he needs so much."

Curving southwards, the river wanders close to the ruins of once-thriving Italica, birthplace of the Roman emperors Trajan and Hadrian, before entering Seville where it played a vital part in the city's history, bringing both riches and occasional disaster.

Under Muslim rule, ferrymen were forbidden to carry passengers bearing containers across to Triana, the suburb on the north bank, in case they should buy wine from the Mozarabs (Christians) living there. To protect the port from attack, the Moors stretched an iron chain across its entrance between two towers, one of which — the Torre del Oro — still stands.

When a squadron led by Admiral Ramón Bonifaz smashed through the chain in 1248, it proved decisive in Seville's fall to Christian forces. Now scullers skim past the Torre del Oro, and the old quaysides, once the launching pad for the conquest of the New World, are left to pleasure-craft. Navigators like Magellan and Elcano began or ended epic voyages here, and excited crowds watched cargoes of Inca gold and Mexican silver being swung ashore.

After Seville lost its domination as home port for the Indies' trading ships, silt clogged the river and floods frequently converted the city into an island trapped behind its own walls. To avert disastrous inundations, this century the river was re-routed and the old course became a mere slack-water canal.

But, after years of cold-shouldering the Guadalquivir, Seville has re-awakened to the importance of this unique asset. Its waters were cleaned and its banks spruced up in time for Expo '92. The barrier known as the "Chapina bung" was removed, allowing the river to flow once again through the city, at a rate of some 200 cubic metres a second.

Galleons may no longer tie up at the quaysides, but Seville's modern port, even though it is 88 kilometres from the sea, handles more than three million tons of merchandise annually. Ambitious projects are under way to upgrade facilities.

"This is Europe's most southerly navigable river and has great commercial possibilities. But improvements are needed to accommodate today's bigger vessels," points out José María Vidal, director of the navigation division of Seville's Chamber of Commerce, Industry and Navigation. He spread out blueprints in the Chamber's offices, located in the Plaza de Contratación, where back in 1503 a "house of trade" was established to regulate commerce with the New World.

"One project the chamber considers urgent is the cutting of a canal and construction of a new lock 300 metres long, which would reduce sailing time to the sea by 40 minutes," says José, a former sea captain. "Born," he says, "with my feet in the river."

Out at the port entrance, veteran keeper Juan Parra controls the gates of a 200-metre lock. Well over a thousand merchantmen up to 16,000 tons pass through every year.

Local pride and ancient custom dictate that vessels must employ two pilots. They pick up the first from Sanlúcar at the river mouth, and drop him off 20 minutes later at Bonanza, to take a Seville pilot for the four-hour journey at a steady 10 knots up the well-buoyed channel to the port. Constant dredging maintains a 20-foot depth.

Passenger services are few, although summer pleasure-craft run down to Sanlúcar. Last century, one of Spain's first steamboats chugged along this route. El Betis, launched in Seville in 1817, had exclusive rights to navigate the river. An 1827 poster, displayed in the Torre del Oro maritime museum, advertises trips to Sanlúcar for 36 to 52 reales, while denying responsibility for armed robbery and shipwreck.

At Coria, where a ferry crosses the river, fishing boats spread nets like butterfly wings to dry over long booms. Eels, shrimp, dace and shad are among the harvest. Once there was caviare as well. The Catholic Kings ceded the right to prepare it to Carthusian monks. A factory operated in the 1930s too, but closed when the sturgeon catches kept dropping.

Big skies rim infinite horizons on the last stretch of the river. Beyond banks of reeds, the flat landscape bakes in summer and wallows in dank mists in winter. This is Las Marismas, the salt marshes bound on the Atlantic by shifting dunes, which support a rich wildlife and form a breeding ground for thousands of waterfowl, a way station for millions of migrating birds and a sanctuary for the rare imperial eagle and lynx. But man is crowding in on what is one of Europe's most important wildlife zones.

Giant harvesters roar and squelch across rice fields in a right bank area known as Isla Mayor. (Once the Guadalquivir marshes were a lake.) British agronomists first made tests here with rice around 1930, but the hungry years after the Civil War forced huge development. Now more than 30,000 hectares are sown with the grain.

"They sow by plane, you know that? Not like when I started, planting by hand, mud up to your knees," says Josempere Perejón, a grizzled worker driving a rake over rice drying near the hamlet of Alfonso XIII.

Harvesting as much as 250,000 tons of rice a year, Seville province far outstrips Valencia where rice-growing started much earlier. But there is a cost. Tons of chemicals are regularly sprayed over the fields. Poison is used to control the red crayfish which infests waterways. Inevitably, these chemicals take their toll on fish, animals and birds.

In addition, polluted water filters into the 76,000 hectares of Coto Doñana, Spain's biggest national park. Schemes to drain, cultivate and irrigate large areas adjacent to the park also threaten the delicate ecosystem. One survey warns that by the year 2005 serious depletion of the water-table could imperil the reserve, although growing awareness of the Coto's value may prevent the worst happening.

Nodding at empty tracts of ploughed land, Isidro Fernández, one of the Coto's experienced guardians, comments: "Drained at tremendous cost and now look at it — useless! Nothing grows and all the birds have left."

At the end of a track, a solitary house sits next to the *lucio* (lagoon) of Mari López, where flamingos, geese and other waterfowl paddle. It is the lonely home of Pepe "Clarita", another guardian.

"If you went out of the cabin where I was born, you stepped straight in the water," he recalls with a chuckle, as a sharp wind blows off the marshes. "It took a day riding my horse through water and mud to reach the nearest village. You couldn't get sick then. There was no way to call a doctor."

A handful of families still live in thatched homes whose style has not changed since the Bronze Age. According to Javier Castroviejo, some of their ancestors emigrated to the Americas where, expert at riding and handling cattle, they became the first *gauchos*.

"There are villages in Las Marismas that could be in the Wild West. This area is unique," says Javier, zoologist and indefatigable campaigner for the Coto. For some years he directed the Doñana Biological Station, which coordinates research under Spain's *Consejo Superior de Investigaciones Científicas* (Department of Scientific Investigation).

The station is centred on the old eucalyptus-shaded hunting lodge of

Doñana, the name reputedly coming from Doña Ana, wife of a Duke of Medina Sidonia. In the late 16th century, the duke built a fine two-storeyed building for her. Philip IV stayed there when he hunted boar and buck, for the Coto was a favourite royal hunting ground. In the 1920s Alfonso XIII came to enjoy the chase, until he himself was chased out of Spain. Photos on the palace walls show the king and his companions posing stiffly over vanquished game.

Steering a Land-Rover through the Coto, Javier pauses to indicate cork-oaks crowded with spoonbills.

"We now mark the birds with plastic rings with large numbers so that they can be easily identified through binoculars. It's proved an enormous help in studying their habits," he tells me.

Deep in the park, a naturalist listens intently through earphones. "This is how we check on the lynxes. Seven or eight have radio transmitters fitted around their necks. We can track them as each is on a different frequency and the tone changes when they move. When the batteries fail, we either retrieve the transmitters or they eventually fall off."

A wild boar, rooting in mud, glowers at us belligerently before scuttling away. A red-legged partridge struts importantly along the dusty track and a marsh harrier wheels low over bracken and scrub.

"Nobody goes too near them," says Javier, pointing to grazing cattle, among them a calf beside its impressively-horned mother, which eye us suspiciously. "Those are really wild — and dangerous."

Nobody gets too close either to the wild camels that roam the Coto. Introduced early this century, they appear now and then, like mirages amid the shimmering pools, the dunes and umbrella pines.

On the final run of its lengthy journey, where the Guadalquivir forms the boundary between Huelva and Cádiz provinces, salt-flats and sand dunes usher it towards the ocean. Just beyond the bustling fish wharves of Bonanza, Sanlúcar de Barrameda reclines at the river mouth.

This port enjoyed a golden age when treasure boats hove-to before ascending the river and the Medina Sidonia family held feudal sway. The ducal palace still exists, most recently occupied by a strong-minded woman misleadingly nicknamed The Red Duchess. But now Sanlúcar has the seedy demeanour of a colony in the tropics left behind by the Conquistadores.

Columbus upped anchor here for his third voyage to the Indies, after being forced to delay departure because his crew had joined the Pentecost pilgrimage to the Virgin of El Rocío, far off amid the marshes. These days the annual trek to render homage to the Queen of Las Marismas has grown so popular that landing-craft are called in to ferry pilgrims, horses and vehicles across the river.

Sanlúcar's salty breezes are said to give a special tang to the sherry wine maturing in its bodegas. Delightfully light and dry, *manzanilla* goes down well with a plate of fresh grilled prawns, taken on the waterfront as the Great River glides towards the Atlantic rollers and the setting sun.

Over at Chipiona, the lighthouse starts to blink, the first sign of home glimpsed by generations of mariners as creaking wooden hulls bore them back

from the edge of the world. And it marks the end of a journey that inspired
Seville's great poet Antonio Machado to pen:

¡Oh Guadalquivir!
Te vi en Cazorla nacer,
Hoy en Sanlúcar morir.
Un borbollón de agua clara,
Debajo de un pino verde
Eras tu, ¡Que bien sonabas!
Como yo, cerca del mar, río de barro salobre
¿Sueñas con tu manantial?

Oh Guadalquivir!
I saw you born in Cazorla
And today in Sanlúcar die.
A flash of clear water
Beneath a green pine
You were, and how happily you played.
Like me, close to the sea, river of brackish mud
Do you dream of your beginnings?

Facing page: *the Guadalquivir river*
starts its journey in the sierras of
Jaén as "a flash of clear water ".

Pilgrims on horseback make their way to El Rocio, a ghost village on the edge of Huelva's marshlands that for three days every spring becomes the spiritual capital of Andalusia.

Where The New World Begins

ORANGE blossom and marigolds frame the cool, whitewashed walls of the old monastery of La Rábida. Brown-robed Franciscan monks move along quiet cloisters, pausing to listen to a burst of birdsong or the sigh of Atlantic breezes through the palms and cypresses. La Rábida is still a place of sanctuary, 500 years after a weary traveller consumed by dreams and ambition knocked at the door seeking help — and history was changed.

It is such a pleasant, unpresumptuous spot that the visitor hesitates. Can this really be where it all began, where a stranger with a crazy dream received the backing he needed to launch him on one of man's greatest adventures?

The 1992 celebration of the fifth centenary of Christopher Columbus's landfall in the Americas has focused attention on this patch overlooking the Río Tinto and on what, for a long time, was one of Andalusia's most underestimated regions. Locked into a corner on the Portuguese border, overshadowed by Seville, Huelva — in the words of one native — "has never been on the road to anywhere."

Yet Huelva's mineral wealth was legendary in biblical times, when the fabled kingdom of Tartessos may have been located here. Phoenicians and Romans tapped its gold, copper and silver. Even so, only in the 1980s have newer harvests encouraged confidence that the Sleeping Beauty is finally rubbing her eyes.

If Columbus had travelled through modern Huelva, he might just have opted to stay. The temptations and opportunities are attractive enough, for within its boundaries it offers oyster farms and strawberry mountains, densely-forested sierras and unspoilt beaches stretching into the sunset.

A 118-foot-high monument dedicated to Cristóbal Colón (as the Spaniards know him and he preferred to be called) stands at the junction of the Odiel and Tinto rivers. Gertrude V. Whitney sculpted the statue which was donated by the United States in 1929. It gazes out to sea, close to the city of Huelva, resolutely ignoring the petrochemical plant which blights the adjacent coast. A modern bridge crosses the Tinto to La Rábida monastery where Columbus asked for bread and water for his son Diego. He was given traditional hospitality and an attentive hearing to his navigational theories by the friar-astronomer Antonio de Marchena and the prior, Juan Pérez. Their support proved vital in finally winning royal approval for his plan to reach Asia by sailing west.

"This is where Marchena and Columbus talked for many hours," says the Franciscan guide, indicating an austere little room. In the chapel he points to a battered, alabaster image, "Here, before the Virgin of the Miracles, Don Cristóbal prayed before making his famous voyage."

Just up the road lies Palos de la Frontera, the little port from where the *Niña,* the *Pinta* and *Santa María* set sail on August 3, 1492. The old quayside fell into decay long ago, leaving only a deserted waterfront and a polluted, heavily silted river. Outside San Jorge church, where Columbus and his crew gave thanks for their safe return, a white monument, raised in 1985, pays homage to the 35 voyagers from Palos. They included Columbus's partner, Martín Alonso Pinzón and his two brothers. Their family home still stands at number 38 on the main street of Palos. And below San Jorge restored brickwork marks a fountain, now dry, where the crews reputedly filled their watercasks for the journey to the edge of the known world.

Horizons are more limited for the pickers bending their backs in the fields between Palos and its neighbour, Moguer. They are part of the strawberry boom.

"A good worker can pick 100 kilos a day," says farmer José Luis Teller, checking the crates as they come in. "We put new plants in every November and the first fruit is ready by January or February. I replaced grape-vines with strawberries because they show more profit. But it's a costly affair. The soil is poor, so I had to spread a thick layer of earth, then fertilizer. Black plastic protects against frost and keeps the fruit clean."

José's strawberries, the largest, most luscious I have seen, are trundled off to a packing plant run by newcomers from Valencia, who are old hands in fruit exports. But the local giant is the Cooperativa Santa María de la Rábida at Palos, an unexpectedly sophisticated operation which hums with activity around the clock in April and May. Every day scores of refrigerated trucks, each carrying 10,000 kilos of *fresones,* rumble off to domestic and foreign markets.

"We're the biggest co-operative in Europe," claims director José Luis Gutiérrez. "Our representatives all over Europe are in touch daily by telex and we play the market. We listen eagerly to the weather forecasts, because we know that on a nice day in England housewives go out and buy strawberries. In three years we paid off the cost of our whole plant, 250 million pesetas."

Of the 80,000 tons of strawberries produced annually in Huelva, a quarter come from this co-operative. The revolution in local agriculture is due to a combination of ideal climate, American hybrid plants, clever marketing and old-fashioned labour.

"Our 230 members share everything, both the credit and the sweat," says José. "No other area has such a long season. When we replant the strawberries from our nursery in the cold north of Spain, they think it's spring, even in October."

Like many Andalusians, José has a taste for linguistic flourishes, as a piece of his colourful prose among the computer read-outs and telex messages on his desk testifies.

"We are poets and philosophers and sometimes you need them, as well as engineers," he reflects. "Just imagine if engineers had been in charge at the time of Columbus. The great adventure that started in Palos would never have been launched."

He believes the Huelva character is harder to identify than most — "You will not find a typical *onubense*." Residents of the provincial capital are known as *onubenses* because Onuba was the ancient name for the city. They are also called *choqueros,* thanks to their appetite for *chocos* (cuttlefish).

"Huelva folk are very upright," a *choquero* tells me. "Although they have been isolated from outside influences until recently, they are very welcoming to strangers. But they are suspicious of *sevillanos* because they think they take over everything."

One of the curiosities of Huelva, an undistinguished city, is the Barrio Reina Victoria. Built late last century by the British-owned Río Tinto mining company, it is a strangely exotic island of English suburbia girt by bustling traffic and lofty apartment blocks. Many of the residents, living amid neat fences, gable ends and quaint chimney-pots, are retired company employees, paying peppercorn rents. "The English bosses used to say we live better here than they did," recalls Elena Caro, a widow whose father worked for Río Tinto.

East and west of Huelva stretch some of Andalusia's finest beaches. With Cádiz province, they form part of the Costa de la Luz. Spared the worst excesses that uncontrolled growth inflicted on the Mediterranean, the coast will be developed, say the authorities, with proper respect for natural beauty. The policy came too late to halt Matalascañas, a high-rise tourism complex in the dunes uncomfortably close to the flamingos — and mosquitoes — of the Coto Doñana nature reserve.

Punta Umbría is Huelva's liveliest summer resort, but further west, sheltered by pine woods near the fishing village of El Rompido, phenomenal growth is under way. Millions of oysters and clams are bred in the Aguas del Pino marine research centre. Along with another hatchery at Puerto de Santa María, it is part of a billion-peseta drive by the Andalusian government to create a new aquaculture industry, a scheme which is forcing tougher measures to control serious coastal pollution by industry.

"A revolution in fishermen's attitudes is required, because they are having to change from hunters into farmers," says Ignacio López Cotelo, the biologist in charge of Aguas del Pino. "We are showing unemployed fishermen how to cultivate shellfish in reclaimed marshes. They are doubtful at first, but change their minds when they see that oysters do, in fact, grow."

The centre offers expert help to private firms and workers' co-operatives, guaranteeing a supply of baby shellfish to sow in the rapidly spreading fattening beds along the coast. Oysters reach commercial size within two years here, against three years in France, says Ignacio. "And they taste excellent!" he adds.

Oysters have a bizarre sex life, as young biologist María Paz Sánchez endeavours to explain to me with due solemnity when we visit the laboratory and breeding tanks. Three species are cultivated at the centre.

"The *Ostrea edulis* (European flat oyster) is both male and female, so that this year one will expel eggs to be fertilized by another and next year the roles will be reversed. Only 0.01 per cent of its million eggs may survive in the wild, but under controlled conditions as many as 10 per cent reach maturity."

María indicates some microscopic molluscs.

"Those are larvae. After 15 days they are big enough to fix themselves to plastic sheets. Since the oyster can only fix itself once in its life, when it has been carefully scraped off the sheet it cannot move again and is more manageable."

The footless oyster gathers strength on a plankton diet, then is switched to baskets or trays suspended in the sea. Measuring only one millimetre across at one month old, within a year an oyster will swell to 80 times that size.

Prawns are also on the Huelva menu. Over at Ayamonte, foreign and Spanish interests have created nurseries to breed a fast-growing Japanese species on a colossal scale. Such ventures are changing the face of Huelva's coast where to date isolated fishing communities have struggled for existence. Some are comparatively new, tossed up by the tides and with little interest in the land behind them.

Settlers from Almería established lonely, wind-scoured Punta del Moral, where your car bogs easily in the sandy, unpaved streets. Isla Canela, the peninsula on which it stands, has been proclaimed the site of a grandiose tourism development.

Just across the water, Isla Cristina, settled by Catalans, appears about to sink beneath the waves. Dig two feet into the earth here and water is likely to spout up. The large fishing fleet brings in splendid seafood and visitors flock to the beaches in summer. Carnival time in February, however, is when the Isla and border town of Ayamonte truly explode with high spirits. School-children hardly blink an eye if teacher turns up wearing fancy dress.

A ferry carries vehicles and passengers across the Guadiana river at Ayamonte to Vila Real de Santo Antonio in Portugal. Under cover of darkness many an illicit cargo, from butter to bullets, has slipped past the frontier guards, in one direction or the other. The *contrabandistas* can now try their luck on a four-lane highway leaping the river by way of a suspension bridge 660 metres long. Symbolizing a new era of international co-operation between two countries which have usually turned their backs on one another, the bridge brings Portugal's popular Algarve coast to within a few minutes' drive of the Costa de la Luz.

On the Ayamonte-Huelva highway (N-431) stands Lepe, long famous for its figs and melons. The *leperos* have become famous for the wrong reasons. They are the butt of the Spanish equivalent of Irish or Polish jokes, which annoys them intensely. Originally, the *leperos* were renowned for their astuteness: one is said to have outwitted King Henry VII when he was jester to the English court, and another, Rodrigo de Triana, was the look-out who first yelled "Land ho!" as Columbus neared America. Far from being stupid, the *leperos* are proud of their progressiveness and business acumen, and large areas near the town are planted with new crops such as asparagus and oranges, their growth aided by modern irrigation methods.

Heading further north, crops give way to trees, including the omnipresent eucalyptus. Ecologists have turned their wrath against massive planting of this thirsty, fast-growing stranger, on the grounds that it sucks the soil dry of water and nutrients and is highly inflammable.

Just beyond Alosno (44 miles from Huelva on route C-443), a village renowned for its fiestas and *fandanguillos* (flamenco music related to the *jota* of northern Spain), lie the pyrite mines of Tharsis. The name has a biblical ring and a 1961 find proved an intriguing clue to the Tartessos enigma. A small stone carving turned up in an old vein. Known as the Mask of Tharsis, possibly dating from 700 BC, it shows oriental influences, encouraging conjecture that it portrays Arganthonius, the Tartessian king.

In the northern part of Huelva province, at the western extremity of the Sierra Morena, lies one of Andalusia's greenest and most enchanting areas. The Sierra de Aracena is a rolling carpet of cork-oaks, holm-oaks, chestnut and walnut trees, broken here and there by the thrusting battlements of medieval fortresses. Around the villages of Galaroza and Fuenteheridos (on route N-433 from Seville to Portugal) apples, pears and cherries flourish.

Water bubbles from fountains at every turn in the narrow, cobbled streets and in Galaroza the villagers go wild every September 6 when crowds flock in for a water fiesta and they douse themselves and everybody in sight.

"It started out as a children's game," municipal policeman Juan Manuel Martín tells me. "Now it's not safe to go out in the street. What do I do?" Juan grins. "Keep out of the way!"

When he is not controlling traffic or delivering council bills, he attends to Galaroza cemetery. Otherwise he is working with his wife Francisca in their orchard.

"Taste this apple. Nothing like it," says Juan.

Luis Fernández agrees with him, and points out: "We have a perfect microclimate here for fruit. The same sort of apple tastes better here than in Asturias because we are 600 metres above sea-level and we have the sun of Andalusia. Nobody can match that."

Before retirement, Luis ran a fruit-canning factory. Now the building is used as a collecting centre for the mushrooms that thrive in these sierras. Two children arrive, bearing a basketful of rare-coloured fungi, quite unlike the pallid *champiñones* sold in markets. Mushrooms are being pickled in brine, while others are laid out to dry in the sun.

"This is a specialized business and you have to know what you're doing, as there are species which can kill in half an hour," says Marcel Olle, a Catalan like many of the buyers. "We have collecting points in village bars. Mostly we buy the *boletos edulis* variety which you find near oaks and chestnuts and we pay up to 1,000 pesetas a kilo, depending on quality. Yesterday a specimen weighing three and a half kilos turned up. It was a bit knocked about because it had been shown off in every bar around."

The mushrooms are dispatched to Barcelona for processing and export. But not all leave the Aracena district. In a bar I sample the *pinatel,* a fleshy, orange mushroom, prepared in a delicious, garlicky sauce. A steady stream of customers brings in mushrooms for weighing and payment.

"Try the ham. This is the real *pata negra,* the best serrano," suggests another customer, Juan Vázquez, a pig buyer in this region famed for its hams. "You can tell if it's the real thing, reared on acorns and allowed to root in the field. The fat melts in the hand and the meat melts in your mouth."

Black-footed, brown pigs snuffle about the forests of Huelva by the thousand, descendants of the wild Iberian species and very different from modern breeds. Gourmets swear that their flesh, enriched by natural diet and cured in brisk mountain air, has a special flavour.

Jabugo is the name identified across Spain with the hams of the Aracena district, but — predictably — neighbouring villages claim that their products are as good, or better. If you follow the railway line that snakes up from Huelva to Zafra, you reach Cumbres Mayores near the Extremadura border. Riding the heights more than 2,500 feet up, it boasts no fewer than 12 slaughterhouses and most of the inhabitants live from their output of hams, sausages and black puddings.

Off one of the streets stands the Navarro family's curing plant, where up to 10,000 hams may be hanging at one time. Plácido Navarro, in his eighties, is fiercely proud of his village product. He stresses, "We turn out better hams than Jabugo because we have a better climate, better acorns and a higher altitude."

Removed from animals butchered at 12 to 18 months when they weigh around 13 *arrobas* (150 kilos), the hams are packed in salt for 10 days or so. This reduces moisture. Then they are washed and hung in dry, fresh air. In summer the hams sweat, ensuring that the yellow fat mixes with the meat.

"See that batch?" José Galván, Plácido's accountant, points to rows of mould-blackened hams. "They've been ordered for Pamplona's San Fermín fiesta. They must have two years' curing and the more dirt they collect from the atmosphere the better."

While the benificent mould gathers on the hams in their dark sanctuaries, in the caves of Aracena, capital of the sierras, the stalactites and stalagmites grow too, at the rate of one centimetre every 35 years. Although the grotto's existence was known for centuries, most of it was flooded. Only when the water was drained and it was opened in 1914 was the magnificence of the Gruta de las Maravillas finally revealed.

Lofty chambers dripping with frozen cascades, marble pillars, pink organ pipes, and vivid colours amid dimpled rock formations are reflected from limpid pools. During the guided visit, covering more than one kilometre, you might sometimes feel a cake-maker has run riot with the icing. In the Sala de los Desnudos, Rubens has clearly been at work. Only he could have created these voluptuous curves.

On the hill above the caves sleep the ruins of a Moorish castle, once occupied by the Knights Templar. Their church still stands, with its beautiful main portal and Mudéjar tower. An open-air museum of contemporary art has been added to Aracena's attractions and potters sell their work to an increasing number of visitors. However, you have to explore the steep back streets of nearby Cortegana to find truly traditional pieces, turned out by Francisco Ramos, the last of a long line of artisans.

South of Aracena naked bodies of cork-oaks display their rusty beauty. Soon they give way to a tortured landscape, ripped and gouged, to expose raw multi-hued rock. Oxides bleed into a river and you see how it acquired the name Río Tinto (Coloured River). From Pozo Alfredo, a 2,000-foot-deep cut, comes copper; from the Colorado cut, copper, silver and gold; from a third, pyrites. Columbus roamed the Caribbean looking for "where gold is born", but he could more easily have found it here.

Soccer is said to have been introduced to Spain in Río Tinto and Nerva, next door, last century when Britons arrived to manage the mine. London banker Hugh Matheson headed an international consortium which acquired Río Tinto for £3.5 million. The original *colonia inglesa* mingled little with the "natives", but in paternalist style did introduce educational, medical and housing improvements that were envied in other parts of Spain.

The expatriates made themselves at home in Bella Vista. It still exists, a tranquil, leafy suburb of red-tiled villas with cream stucco walls. Within it, next to tennis courts and swimming pool, stands the old English club with its heavily-stuffed armchairs and Herring's hunting scenes on the walls. But these days, in the club, the accents are mostly Spanish, although British interests still have shares in the mine through Río Tinto Zinc.

On its journey to the sea, the Río Tinto winds past the walls of Niebla, on the Huelva-Seville highway. Four gates give entrance to the old town which is protected by walls more than 50 feet thick. In Moorish times Niebla was capital of a kingdom. It fell to Christian forces in 1257 after a nine-month siege in which gunpowder was employed for possibly the first time in the peninsula.

More than 12,000 hectares of this eastern part of the province are clothed in vines. The first wine drunk by the discoverers in the New World is said to have come from here, El Condado de Huelva. Sixty million litres are produced annually by 190 bodegas, but Augusto García Flores, secretary of the controlling board, tells me profound changes are under way.

"Where there's water, thousands of vines have been torn up to make way for strawberries," he says. "Our wine has always been made with the same grapes and methods as sherry and often sold as sherry abroad. Now we're upgrading the wine and starting to market the *finos* and *olorosos* under our own name. But the big innovation is a light, white table wine made from Zalema grapes. It is fermented under controlled temperature and bottled immediately. It is proving very popular."

At Bollullos del Condado, where *domingueros* (Sunday trippers) arrive in force to sample shellfish and wine from the barrel, a controversial sport also brings in a wide audience. Families tuck in to lunch at a restaurant whose centre-piece is a circular, sunken arena. Gamblers shout encouragement as fighting cocks duel. One winner of the national championship, worth half a million pesetas, chuckled: "There's nothing like breeding champions. Altogether I have a hundred of these cocks." He smiled at his voluptuous companion. "And I have three wives, too. Life is one long party!"

One Sunday afternoon I come across a more peaceful scene. Along a country road, past fields ablaze with spring flowers, four men, accompanied by women and children, carry an image of Christ. As they plod towards a hermitage near the village of Beas, an old man on his donkey pauses to doff his cap in simple respect to the lily-decked float. It is a striking contrast to the clamorous, frenzied ceremony that takes place every Pentecost amid Las Marismas, the marshlands near the Guadalquivir.

El Rocío, Andalusia's biggest fiesta, has its roots in the misty past. Legend holds that sometime in the 13th century, in the reign of Alfonso the Wise, a shepherd roaming the marshes with his flock came upon a beautifully carved image of the Virgin in the hollow of a tree. He started carrying it to the village of Almonte, but en route stopped to rest. When he awoke, the Virgin had disappeared. He found her back in the tree.

A hermitage was built on the spot and it became a place of pilgrimage. Today, a simple country fiesta which celebrated the event has grown into a colossal jamboree in which the sacred and the profane are bewilderingly mixed. Seventy brotherhoods thread their way on horseback, foot and wheeled vehicles over dunes, rivers and forest tracks, camping, singing, dancing, drinking, praying, to keep their annual appointment with the Virgin, adored as the Queen of the Marshes.

Drum and flute music accompanies the *rocieros* as, weary and dusty, they converge on El Rocío. More than 50,000 people travel with the brotherhoods. But by the time the celebrations reach their peak as many as one million people have crowded into El Rocío, a ghost village the rest of the year. Hucksters, roisterers, politicians and celebrities join the simply curious and the truly devout in this date with the *Blanca Paloma.*

One year I joined the vast caravan of pilgrims threading their way across the sandhills and marshlands of the Coto Doñana for the annual date with the Virgin. Each brotherhood brought is *simpecado,* a portrait of the *Blanca Paloma* mounted in an elaborate, flower-festooned float. For two nights we slept in the open.

Campfires flared in the darkness and the *tamborileros,* musicians who cheer the pilgrims on their way, drummed and blew and sang as men and women spun and swayed to the lively rhythm of the *sevillanas rocieras* (a variation of the usual *sevillana* flamenco music). Macho posturing and feminine flirtation are an integral part of the *romería* (pilgrimage). Traditionally, Rocío is where boy meets girl, when the barriers come down out there in the dewy nights of Las Marismas.

On the third day I was invited to a sumptuous paella, prepared in a sun-dappled glade of eucalyptuses. My hosts, a mixed bunch, including a bank manager, a leather-worker, a butcher and a farmer, had spared no expense to make the trip.

Lázaro, joker-philosopher of the group, reflected, "Some people spend all their lives making money, when all that's important is making friends."

A few hours later the sanctuary itself appeared, a dazzling white monument soaring above the marshes. For most of the year the orderly lines of houses near it are deserted, but now the hamlet of Rocío was buzzing with activity as pilgrims poured in. Carriages, horses and pedestrians thronged the dirt streets as the bells of the sanctuary clanged out a welcome.

After three days in the wilderness, we found ourselves in an instant city. The odour of barbecued chicken, drifted over passing crowds. Plastic snakes and gaudy images of the *Blanca Paloma,* hot dogs and colour photos of the Virgin were selling fast. A little gypsy girl peddling carnations took time off to perform a barefoot flamenco.

"Hey!" called a swarthy huckster. "Are you Portuguese? You wanna buy valuable Mexican coins, all silver? Feel the weight!"

The fortunate find beds or floor space in the *casetas* (lodges) where the wine and food flow freely. Most sleep in their cars, in tents, or never go to bed at all. Day and night rockets soar into the air, the *rocieros* visit friends' *casetas* and *tamborileros* beat out the unceasing rhythm of the *sevillanas.*

Miguel Suárez, a 32-year-old *tamborilero* from Aznalcóllar near Seville, told me: "I've been coming to the Rocío for 15 years. I live it. There's no other feeling like it."

And he broke into one of his songs: *"Madre de Dios, Puerta del Cielo, Paloma de la Gracia, La Virgen del Rocío ya está en mi casa."* (Mother of God, Door of Heaven, Dove of Grace, the Virgin of Rocío is already in my house.)

Around midnight I walked through the sanctuary. Behind an iron railing, the tiny image of the Virgin arrayed in splendid robes gazed down on the faithful. They gazed back at her in awe, crossing themselves, praying, or just staring at the *Blanca Paloma,* some with tears spilling down their cheeks.

Beneath her robes and six petticoats, the Virgin may only be a couple of pieces of timber, but she is capable of whipping up extreme emotions; emotions that are claimed to go back to the ancient worship of an earth-mother.

"Some come here out of curiosity and to amuse themselves, but at any moment they are likely to feel the impact of this event and enter into the Rocío spirit," declared José María Pérez López, a 60-year-old farmer who was *hermano mayor* (chief brother) of Seville's Triana Hermandad.

"We of the brotherhood live our devotion all year around. For our 3,500 members the *romería* is a serious business. On the track we awake at 4.30 a.m., attend Mass at 5 a.m., and start walking with our 28 ox-carts at six. I've been coming for 35 years and one member flies over from Canada every year to attend."

The entry of the Triana procession on the Saturday morning, when each brotherhood pays its respects to the Virgin, is one of the most spectacular. But it has to take its turn. Ritual is everything at the Rocío and the brotherhoods pass by the sanctuary according to their seniority. The senior brotherhood is that of Almonte, the nearest village to Rocío, which controls the hermitage, souvenir sales and film and television rights, and zealously guards the Virgin as its own.

After each brotherhood has paid homage, the national anthem crashes out, rockets fly and the bells ring. All day the ceremony continues, while the drinking and dancing go on unabaited.

One bleary barman who had been working six days with hardly any sleep

41

told me: "There are some pretty girls here. But to catch one you need the right gear and you must rent a horse, which costs 60,000 pesetas and more. Just hiring a bed for a week can cost 30,000 pesetas. And for a house, well, people pay as much as 100,000 a day. Yet working folk will save all year to play the *señorito* here."

Sunday passed in a blur as the annual spring ritual moved to a climax. By midnight thousands were squeezing into the plaza outside the temple. Tension grew. A fireworks display lit up the excited faces. Then, just before 3 a.m., a cry went up: "They've jumped the fence!" Impatient members of the Almonte brotherhood could wait no longer and had swarmed over the protective railings to seize the Virgin. She was borne out of the sanctuary on their shoulders, rocking wildly as though on a stormy sea as the youngsters struggled violently for the right to carry her.

"¡Viva la Blanca Paloma! ¡Guapa, guapa y guapa!"

The atmosphere was ecstatic. Spectators hurled flowers towards the Virgin. Others struggled to break through her escort in a bid to touch the float. A man pushed his four-year-old child over the heads of the *almonteños.* The little girl, in her gypsy dress, wept with fear. But she reached the float. Beaming proudly, her father carried her away.

For yards around the Virgin, the sweating, fighting bodies raised the temperature to an uncomfortable level. Dressed in khaki, the muscular young *almonteños* resembled a commando squad. As one group tired, another barged in, violently pushing anybody from their path. They were possessed. In their exalted state, after days of drinking and little sleep, they were in another dimension. They saw only the Virgin, *their* Virgin.

"I touched her! I touched her!" yelled a woman, tears trickling down her bruised cheeks.

"¡Guapa, guapa y guapa! ¡Bonita, bonita y bonita!" roared the multitude, as the Virgin zigzagged into a purple dawn. One by one, the Queen of the Marshes visited the brotherhoods outside where the *simpecados* were drawn up. Hoisted shoulder-high, the chaplain of each *hermandad* launched an impassioned torrent of praise for the Virgin. Amid swooning faithful, the Virgin swayed on, finally returning to her temple in early afternoon.

One cleric has described the Rocío as "the meeting of Love with the Mother". According to anthropologist Isidoro Moreno, the seizure of the Virgin is a symbolic act of rebellion by the common people, who briefly assume power. Almonte's president Angel Díaz sees it differently: "Where the Rocío begins, politics end. Andalusia is the land of incomprehension and this is a mystery, not a social phenomenon. Only an *andaluz* can understand it."

Most Andalusians, of course, don't try to understand it. They simply live it. But this bizarre mosaic of flamboyant fiesta and simple faith can bemuse a stranger. It is possible to feel very alien at El Rocío.

As a wide-eyed girl from Algeciras patiently explained: "This is part of our history and our culture. It's part of us."

It happens every spring, in Huelva.

Every Street A Stage

HERE may be punks in the suburbs and traffic jams in the city centre, but the 20th century hardly appears to touch the Seville Fair. Rich man, poor man, beggarman... all splash out feverishly at the annual display of relentless exuberance. It is an annual spring rite where anybody going to bed before dawn is regarded as a party-pooper.

Those with *enchufes* (the right contacts) have access to one of the hundreds of *casetas,* or entertainment booths set up in a park near the Guadalquivir. Chance brought me an invitation one year to the tennis club *caseta.* Dodging a cavalcade of gleaming carriages, elegant horsefolk and castanet-clicking girls, I reached the entrance, only to be blocked by a stern guardian. Only after dropping the name of a well-known member was I waved through.

Inside, a crowd was engrossed in eating, drinking and occasionally casting an eye at the passing parade. In one corner, some young beauties swirled a rainbow of flounced dresses to flamenco rhythms. There was not a tennis racket in sight.

Gaining access to the private world of the *casetas* is not as difficult as it once was. They are no longer the sole domain of the rich and privileged. A variety of clubs, associations and unions — even the *revistas del corazón* (magazines devoted to celebrities) — have their stands. But the stranger should not fool himself. He is only there on sufferance.

Manuel Machado, the poet, commented that "the *caseta* is home itself, conjugal, paternal, fraternal". It is for offering and receiving hospitality, for gossiping, flirting and dancing, with the added spice that the excluded public is watching it all. It is an extension of the animated, non-stop show staged in the capital of Andalusia.

For Seville is one big *caseta.* Few cities flaunt their attractions so boldly, yet remain so impenetrable. The visitor is dazzled by the grand opera, but cannot help wondering what — if anything — lies behind it.

The surface charm alone can be enough to persuade travellers to put down roots here. American photographer Robert Vavra arrived in the city in 1959, was smitten by the people's *gracia* (pronounce it "grassia"), a special mixture of grace, wit and charm, and their sense of tragedy, and stayed to create a number of books.

"The city is the same in many ways as when Merimée wrote Carmen," believes Vavra. "Superficial things have changed. But matadors still get dressed in dark hotel rooms, gypsies still tell fortunes on the street, you can still meet smugglers, and knife fights still break out over affairs of passion. And those faces one sees on the streets — they all look like Fellini characters."

Sevillanos do not believe in being modest about themselves or their city, which — though history has passed it by since its golden age in the 16th century — they know is the centre of the world.

"We're open and full of gaiety, gregarious and hospitable," one told me. "That's because we have a special philosophy of life — the most important thing is to live."

There's no denying the *gracia* of the *sevillanos*. Ask somebody the way and he will quite likely take you by the arm and lead you there, relating an anecdote en route. Have a drink with him and he will be quoting poetry about his city; few places can have had so much euphoric verse and flowery prose written about them. At the clink of a sherry glass, somebody will launch into heart-wrenching song and half the people in the bar will spin into flamenco.

Even so, first impressions can be deceptive. Basque thinker Miguel de Unamuno found the people *"fino y frío",* (cold and courteous). No doubt he was referring to the higher echelons of society; Seville is where many of Andalusia's aristocrats and wealthiest land-owners have palatial houses. But writer and journalist Antonio Burgos has similar views. And he was born here.

"The *sevillanos* have many acquaintances, but few friends. They greet many people in the street, but receive few at home. They speak to everybody, but converse with few," Burgos has written.

He warns visitors to distrust the local who smiles at you, tells a joke, or asks you about yourself, because he will most likely be indulging in a favourite pastime, pulling your leg.

Possibly, he overstates the case. But Seville does tend to carry things to extremes. It offers a stereotype of Andalusia, a film-maker's overblown, multicoloured, all-singing, all-dancing version of reality. *Sevillanos* have a taste for living legends, particularly if there is a dash of tragedy. Singer Isabel Pantoja's sob-in-the-voice style was popular enough, but the fatal goring of her husband, Paquirri, rocketed *"La Pantoja"* into another dimension. Matador Curro Romero hovers between farce and near-tragedy in his failures and obvious fear in the ring, but his devotees forgive him because of his rare moments of brilliance.

In Seville, everything is *"exagerao"* (exaggerated), as an Andalusian would say. Such as the climate. Heat strikes like a hammer in summer; dampness chills the bones in winter, making a mockery of the open-plan houses built around patios. Even the regional virtues of unpunctuality and putting pleasure before business reach epic levels.

Trying to contact somebody at work is not recommended. If you should miraculously succeed, you deserve a testy greeting, for your accomplishment has come close to an intrusion into personal privacy.

One day I called Burgos at his office. It was midday.

"He's not in yet," said the operator. "Try later."

At 1.30 I called again.

"He's gone for lunch. Call after five."

I called at 5.30. This time the operator informed me my man was on the phone. So I rang back 10 minutes later. By this time the voice at the other end was growing slightly impatient.

"Don Antonio isn't coming in. He's on holiday for two days."

No, the secret is to beard your quarry where *real* business is done — in his favourite café. Popping out for a coffee or an *aperitivo* has been raised to a fine art here. And few rituals are more important than *el tapeo.* No city can cater so well to this infinitely civilized Spanish custom. It takes four to *"tapear"* to perfection, say aficionados, and seven is the ideal number of *tapas* to try, unless one plans to miss lunch or supper.

Triana above all is the quarter where the tapa trail is richest, from the upmarket elegance of Bodega La Albariza, where shrimp tortilla is the speciality, to the antique seediness of back-street bars, where the clients munch *pringas,* tasty bits of pig's parts wrapped in toast.

Triana prides itself on being the heart of it all. In the darkly mysterious Sol y Sombra bar, papered with original bullfight posters, a veteran carpenter proudly claimed: "Seville is in the province of Triana. Here, in this *barrio,* is where you find the roots of Andalusia, of its traditions."

Most of the old *corrales,* where dozens of families lived in stifling proximity around central courtyards, have been torn down and their inhabitants have moved to modern suburbs. But Triana retains its magic. From a street-corner studio floats guitar music. Mario Escudero, a greying maestro who has performed everywhere from New York to Moscow, tries patiently to teach young students the basics: "Do you want to learn the proper technique or just any old way? You can't do just what you want in flamenco, you know. One has to follow the rules. Rhythm alone is not enough. There must be a balance of harmony and rhythm."

Down an adjacent street, not far from the Alley of the Inquisition, Japanese, Swedish and American students are earnestly flicking fingers and stamping feet at a flamenco school.

In Holy Week, when all Seville is a thunder of drums, Triana does its utmost to outdo the other districts with the splendour of its processions and the fervour of its support. Visitors to Seville that week, northern Spaniards included, are often astonished at the pagan aspects of the Easter processions and the unembarrassed release of emotion. They would be equally surprised if they knew that those spontaneous outbursts of songs known as *saetas,* which punctuate the processions, were planned and paid for by city hall.

Semana Santa's medieval mixture of solemnity and revelry is symptomatic of a city that lives its past. Other rituals play a similar role. Twice a year, for example, military drums beat out in the great cathedral, when a silver urn is opened. It contains the uncorrupted remains of San Fernando, the king who threw out the Moors in 1248. And on the morning of Corpus Christi, before the cathedral altar, 10 young boys known as *Los Seises,* in doublet and hose and plumed hats, dance a strangely graceful dance half-way between a minuet and a *seguidilla.* Once, members of *Los Seises* were castrated to preserve their treble voices.

Like so many other things in Seville, the cathedral is *exagerao.* At one corner stands the city symbol, the Giralda tower, the soaring minaret built in the 12th century by the Almohades as part of a mosque. When the mosque was being demolished in 1401, the ecclesiastical authorities declared, "Let us build a cathedral so immense that, on beholding it, everybody will think us madmen." No expense was spared in the construction, which lasted more than a hundred years. At the end, Seville had the largest Gothic cathedral, after St. Peter's in Rome and St. Paul's in London. The cavernous vault, whose interior extends more than 400 feet, is adorned with the works of an army of craftsmen and artists.

The Archbishop of Seville, one of Spain's most august prelates, could be forgiven for swelling with pride when he views this monument. But he cannot ignore a constant irritation: the presence in Seville of an upstart rival who has his own cathedral and claims to outrank him. Pope Gregorio XVII is blind and chubby, with a taste for scandal and good living. Otherwise known as Clemente Domínguez, he founded the ultra-reactionary order of the Carmelites of the Santa Faz after the Virgin Mary appeared to him and stigmata erupted on his body. Followers in Europe and North and South America financed the construction of a grandiose basilica, enclosed by a massive wall, at El Palmar de Troya (48 kilometres from Seville, near Utrera), the scene of numerous visions. There, the faithful pay homage at services conducted in Latin to two of their saints, General Franco and José Antonio, founder of the Falange party. Female worshippers are only admitted if they cover arms and heads and wear respectable underwear. Unworried by his excommunication by the pontiff in Rome, Gregorio affirms he is the true Pope. He and his cardinals and bishops are often to be seen in Seville, robes flying as they hurry religiously from bar to bar.

Bizarre though Pope Gregorio may seem, he looks less out of place in Seville than he would in some cities. The picturesque and the picaresque have always flourished here. Rogues, mountebanks and divers adventurers rubbed shoulders in its taverns and on its quaysides in the time of Cervantes, when precious metals, spices and pearls poured in from the New World, and Seville was dubbed the "Great Babylon of Spain". When the city lost its monopoly of trade with the Indies, decline set in and it was left with little more than inflated ideas and fine buildings.

Anybody observing only the city centre and "tourist Seville", may surmise that the city is frozen in time, but they see only the façade. True, scholars still sift through the Archives of the Indies. But these days they can call up the 1505 letter from Columbus to his son Diego, or Cortes's report to the king of Spain on an expedition from Havana to Mexico by merely tapping a key, as the files which hold millions of documents are being stored on computers. Crowds still flock to the Maestranza bullring, but more *sevillanos* go to watch the city's two soccer teams. Old men still gaze out through the windows of the Circulo Mercantil e Industrial club on Sierpes, the shopping street at the city's heart, but the modern fashions on view may cause them to choke over their sherries. Troubadours still strum guitars in the labyrinth of Santa Cruz, the old Jewish quarter, but rock and jazz mix with the rhythms of the light-hearted *sevillanas.* Today's Carmens demonstrate their emancipation by puffing cigarettes and sporting punk hair-styles. Gays and transvestites enjoy new-found freedom.

Unfortunately, not all the changes are so harmless. Behind the old romantic image lies another Seville, with serious social problems. One-fifth of the 700,000 inhabitants can barely read or write. Many of these people live in the ugly, high-rise suburbs thrown up to rehouse city dwellers and thousands of poverty-stricken refugees from the countryside.

A third of the population is under 16 and many youngsters' chances of finding work are remote. Aimless, irresponsible, often hooked on drugs, a new breed of delinquent has earned Seville an unenviable reputation in recent years. The city has always been notorious for harbouring *picaros* (rogues) who could pick your pockets or swindle you out of your life savings with a certain *gracia.* But there is little that is *gracioso* about a hold-up at knifepoint or a *tirón* (bag snatch), or the *semaforazo,* in which thieves smash the windows of out-of-town cars at traffic lights, grab anything in sight, then escape on motor-cycles. Even crime is *exagerao* in Seville, unfortunately at a time when national and foreign attention has focused on the city.

Significant events are dragging Seville out of its provincial obscurity. In 1982, despite protests from jealous competitors also hungry for the prestige, patronage and cash likely to be generated, Seville became capital of the new autonomous region of Andalusia and seat of the Andalusian parliament.

Far greater was the impact created by the 1992 world exhibition, marking the 500th anniversary of Christopher Columbus's voyage of discovery and devoted to discovery in every field of human activity. More than 100 nations were represented at Expo '92, which attracted millions of visitors to its site on the city outskirts at the Isla de Cartuja. It was an appropriate spot, for Columbus was familiar with Expo's focal point, the Carthusian monastery of Santa María de las Cuevas (the name came from the caves dug in the clay by potters, in one of which a wooden image of the Virgin was found). He used the monastery as a refuge and lodging place and formed a close relationship there with Gaspar de Gorricio. He exchanged many letters with this cultured, Italian-born friar, who acted as his intermediary before the Pope and later was the executor of his will.

Columbus was first buried in the Santa Ana chapel crypt at La Cartuja, but controversy continues about his final resting place. Four figures, symbolizing the kings of Aragón, Castile, León and Navarre, shoulder the Discoverer's coffin in the sepulchral gloom of Seville cathedral. However, there are serious doubts about what lies inside this impressive tomb. Scientific tests have indicated that Columbus really rests across the Atlantic in Santo Domingo, capital of the Dominican Republic. The Admiral's remains were transferred to Santo Domingo cathedral in 1544 and the bones and ashes returned to Spain in 1898 may be those of his son, Diego.

Within La Cartuja's grounds stands a marmalade, or umbra, tree, indigenous to South America. According to tradition, the tree was planted by Fernando Columbus, younger son of the Admiral of the Ocean Sea. A more incongruous sight next to the monastery's dome and tiled roofs are the bottle-shaped furnaces built there last century, when Charles Pickman, a practical-minded English entrepreneur, bought the buildings and converted them into a factory producing quality ceramics. Fifty-six expert potters were brought over from Staffordshire, Pickman eventually became the Marqués de Pickman, and the firm still turns out fine porcelain, though no longer at La Cartuja.

Having survived disastrous floods, war and the Industrial Revolution, La Cartuja has been restored to former grandeur at immense cost. An even greater transformation was worked by Expo on Seville itself. Two railway stations were swept away and a new one built to accommodate a new high-speed train that can whisk passengers from Madrid within three hours, seven new bridges thrown across the Guadalquivir, river promenades opened up, historic buildings renovated, and much-needed bypasses constructed. At last Seville has its own opera house, La Maestranza, where works set in the city, such as Bizet's *Carmen,* Mozart's *Don Juan* and Rossini's *The Barber of Seville,* can be staged.

Naturally, some *sevillanos* were sceptical about all these developments. They recalled the Iberoamericano Exhibition of 1929 which incurred such a huge debt that the citizens were still paying it off 40 years later. The Expo organizers said they had done their sums to the last peseta and this time the budget would balance. They referred only to the exhibition itself, not to the works on a Babylonian scale associated with the great event. Nobody could count the ultimate cost of the infrastructure, including the high-speed train and 1,000 kilometres of new highway, designed to integrate Andalusia into Europe physically and mentally — although it is not clear whether the Andalusians were consulted about this latter possibility.

More optimistic citizens welcomed Expo's impact on their city. After centuries of admiring its reflection in the turbid waters of the Guadalquivir, Seville had appeared in thrall to its frozen rituals and rigid social attitudes. "Seville society is like a pyramid, but with the middle sections missing," commented one Catalan executive posted to the Andalusian capital. Gaining access to an exclusive *caseta* at the annual fair is unlikely to be any easier in future. But, after 1992's cash flood and the influx of skilled professionals from other regions and abroad, Seville's highly-stratified society could surely never be quite the same again.

More pilgrims ride beside the Guadalquivir river on their way to El Rocio.

Clockwise from above: *villagers wend their way through a field of wild flowers to a small springtime religious fiesta in Huelva; yachts cruise past orange groves towards the sea at Sanlucar; mantillas catch the eye at Seville's famous spring fair, and wagons carry pilgrims through the Coto Doñana park to the shrine at El Rocio.*

Hunters from all over Europe converge on the Sierra Morena eager to bag trophies such as these (above) *adorning the walls and ceiling of a lodge near Hornachuelos.*

The Frontier Land

A NOTHER fiesta. In honour of another Virgin.
It had hailed the night before.
The rain had lashed down all day. But the pilgrims were not deterred. On horseback and by car, in carts and in buses, they trekked up narrow, winding roads to the mountain shrine. As night fell, they still came.

They tackled the last stretch on foot, running the gauntlet of hucksters and beggars' outstretched palms. Some, enduring exquisite pain to satisfy personal vows, climbed the steep stone steps on bare knees. The priest's amplified tones goaded them on, booming out from the bleak sanctuary on its rocky buttress.

Flames snaked upwards from a huge torch, fed by the faithful's discarded candles. As black-toothed storm-clouds swallowed an angry, dying sun, the smoke drifted up from hundreds of fires sprawled over the meadows below the shrine.

Cloaked and mud-spattered horsemen spurred their mounts up to the church doors, striking sparks from the cobble-stones. Doffing their flat-brimmed Cordoban hats, they uttered hoarse cries:

"¡Viva! ¡Viva la Virgen!"

They had come to see *their* Virgin, *La Morenita* (the little dark one), the *Virgen de la Cabeza.* They hail her as Queen of the Sierra Morena. And in its way the annual *romería* to the lonely sanctuary 33 kilometres north of Andújar (Jaén) is appropriate for Andalusia's frontier territory.

Miners, hunters and herdsmen inhabit the Sierra Morena. Austere, sparsely populated, the range forms a formidable physical and cultural barrier between southern Spain and the tablelands of Castile and Extremadura. Running 300 kilometres through Jaén, Córdoba, Seville and Huelva provinces, its endless slopes and valleys clothed in scrub, oaks and pines bar easy access to the lands beyond. The sierra has shaped the people. They are hardy, unpretentious, less given to the flamboyance of the soft-living lowlanders around the Guadalquivir.

Illustrious personalities are thin on the ground among the more than 200,000 people who flock on the last weekend in April to acclaim the Virgin

49

of La Cabeza (the name comes from the rock on which the sanctuary stands). The ritual has neither the fame nor glamour associated with Huelva's El Rocío pilgrimage. It is fervent, raw and rustic.

Sipping a glass of dry Montilla wine, young farmer Manuel de la Torre admitted: "I've almost lost my voice from shouting *Vivas* and my behind is sore as hell after riding eight hours in the rain to get here. But it's worth it when you have a special feeling for *La Morenita.*"

As youngsters gyrated to flamenco music in the religious brotherhoods' lodges, scores of stalls peddled plaster and plastic souvenirs, chocolate and *churros*. A legless man pleaded for alms. Black-eyed gypsies sold pictures of the Virgin.

She herself proved to be a small, brown image in a gold-braided red robe. Visitors queued to kiss one of her ribbons. Tradition claims that St. Peter dispatched this image to Andújar. It was hidden on the invasion of the Moors. Then, in 1227, it appeared before a one-armed shepherd from Granada. In return for assuring that a temple would be built on the spot, his arm was restored and centuries of *romerías* and miraculous happenings were under way.

The original image and the previous building were destroyed in the Civil War when the historic siege of the sanctuary held all Spain's fascinated attention. Two hundred and thirty Civil Guards under Captain Santiago Cortés took refuge here and on a neighbouring strongpoint, declaring their support for the Nationalist rebellion.

After nine months of tank and artillery bombardment, the attacking Republican forces had swollen to 20,000 including the International Brigade. Still the defenders held out. But on May 1, 1937, the sanctuary went up in flames. Captured defenders were surprised — they expected the "Reds" besieging them to speak Russian. Cortés, acclaimed a hero, died of his wounds.

"Do you want to meet the oldest survivor of the siege?" I was asked.

One of those who was there, Patricio García Camacho, a solemn-faced man from La Mancha, proudly introduced a frail woman in her late seventies, his mother Dolores. Every year she and her family make a pilgrimage back to the shrine where, among the 1,200 trapped, were 870 women, children and old people.

"It was a grim experience. We expected relief from the Nationalist troops, but none came," said Patricio, whose father was a Civil Guard. "We were so short of food that people ate what they could — a whole family of six died from eating poisonous herbs. Supplies were dropped from the air. They nicknamed the Junkers that brought the bread *El Panadero*. See, the supplies usually landed just over there."

Just after midday on Sunday, to a torrent of noise from the excited thousands, the sanctuary bells and the loudspeakers, the image finally emerges into the sunshine.

"*¡Guapa, guapa, guapa!*" chants the priest, his voice rising to a crescendo.

"*¡Viva la Virgen de la Cabeza!*" yell the crowds ecstatically, as she makes a turbulent progress through the sea of bodies and outstretched arms.

Two white-robed acolytes sit alongside the image, tossing carnations to the crowd. Babies and articles of clothing are passed up to be blessed.

"¡Guapa, guapa, guapa!" thunder the amplifiers repeatedly, hypnotically.

Only that evening does tranquillity return. The crowds depart, leaving a trail of rubbish as a reminder of their visit. Thyme and rosemary regain ascendancy over the aroma of incense, fried chicken and hamburger. The Sierra Morena breathes again...

The wildness of these mountains, although the highest point is little more than 4,000 feet, long made them a lawless zone, haunted by footpads, highwaymen and fugitives. (Wolves too were common and a few pairs still roam free, now protected by law.) Indeed, the *bandolerismo* rampant in the sierras last century contributed to the founding of the Civil Guard.

No bandit was more notorious than José María, *"El Tempranillo"*. Born in 1800, at Jauja, near Lucena (Córdoba), by the time he was 22 he could make the oft-quoted claim: "The king may reign in Spain, but in the Sierra I do." He demanded an ounce of gold for each vehicle that crossed his domain.

Unlike his cut-throat competitors, the king of the Sierra Morena had a gallant streak, which boosted his legend. Short but well-built, blond and charming, he allegedly never swore and was always courteous, particularly to women. Even as he stripped a lady of her jewellery, he would kiss her hand and murmur, "Such a pretty hand needs no adornment." It hardly seems fair that later, pardoned and working on the side of the law, he was treacherously murdered by an old comrade.

A number of towns in the Sierra Morena owe their existence to the threat posed by banditry. Silver from the Indies arriving at Seville and Cádiz was a juicy target for outlaws as Madrid-bound bullion wagons threaded their way slowly up the mountains and through Despeñaperros Pass, the spectacular gorge which is the strategic gateway between this part of Andalusia and the north. To improve security on a new highway and develop industry and agriculture, Carlos III — one of Spain's more enlightened monarchs — approved an ambitious colonization scheme.

Six thousand settlers from Germany and Flanders were lured to the sierras and other areas of Andalusia with promises of land and livestock. La Carolina (on route NIV just south of Despeñaperros) was founded in 1767 and used as headquarters for some years by Pablo de Olavide, a Spaniard born in Peru who directed the project. His palace is one of the sights.

You will find little trace of the Germans who toiled in sulphur, lead and copper mines and watched over the mountain tracks, but a string of "new" towns guards the approaches to Despeñaperros.

This pass always formed a major obstacle for invading armies and one of Spain's most significant battles occurred in the area on July 16, 1212. A shepherd guided the Christian armies of Castile, Aragón, Navarre and León along an unprotected route so that they could surprise the Almohad forces of Caliph Muhammad an-Nasir. At Las Navas de Tolosa, near La Carolina, Alfonso VIII scored a crushing victory, opening the way for the Reconquest of Andalusia.

Moorish fortresses fell one by one, including Baños de la Encina

(11 kilometres from Bailén). The 15 towers and lofty walls of this majestic, thousand-year-old stronghold dominate the village of Baños and surrounding olive groves. A worn plaque in Arab script at the entrance records that the Caliph Al-Hakam II ordered the structure to be built in the year 357 of the hegira (AD 967).

As the sierras run west into Córdoba province, they enfold a plateau which looks as though it has strayed in from Extremadura. One scenic approach route winds steeply north from Montoro on the Guadalquivir, past olive trees that gradually give way to holm-oaks and pastureland. The road levels out at the village of Cardeña, with its rose-lined main street, to enter the Valley of Los Pedroches.

Magpies flutter away from the motorist's wheels as he follows the arrow-straight C-420 over undulating country, past granite walls, fields of barley, herds of pigs and flocks of sheep and goats. And past endless oak trees. The modern traveller can easily see why the Arabs called this region the Plain of Acorns.

Covering 3,500 square kilometres, a quarter of the province, Los Pedroches is an isolated zone of sober folk, big skies and cuckoos calling across broad acres. Every church and castle tower has its stork's nest. Granite is the most popular building material. Variations on the *jota,* rather than flamenco, are the popular folk music. Holy Week is celebrated in solemn Castilian style rather than in the extrovert Andalusian manner.

North of the sleeping village of Pedroche, on the road to El Guijo, Miguel, an ageing guardian, watches over his black hens and pigs and the white sanctuary of Nuestra Señora de Piedrasantas. "The priest says we're not to touch the storks," he mutters, shaking his head and indicating the sprawling nest atop the tower where swallows have established squatters' rights. "It looks such a mess."

The sanctuary is a focal point of the seven towns which, until last century, administered the valley's lands. Instead of being monopolized by the aristocracy as in much of Andalusia, the land was public property. Councillors from seven valleys met at the sanctuary to pay homage to the Virgin and renew their allegiance to Pedroche, the old capital of the area.

Pedroche's most striking feature is a 180-foot-high church tower. The base is square, with an eight-sided section above. Alarming cracks fissure the granite blocks, which were recycled from the castle ordered demolished by the Catholic Kings in a bid to control the rebellious nobility.

Inside El Salvador parish church, a sign announces the fees for special services: 1,500 pesetas for "normal" marriages; 2,000 for a burial; 500 for a baptism. Outside, a plaque indicates the heavy price a country pays when it fails to find just solutions to its social problems.

It lists 97 men who "fell for God and for Spain" on July 26, 1936. A black-draped woman passing by remarks: "The Reds took those people out of the houses and shot them. The widows and the children paid for the plaque to be erected. I was only 11 at the time, but I know about it. My father and my father-in-law were two of those who died."

Death and drama never seem to be far away in Andalusia and Pozoblanco, regarded as the modern capital of Los Pedroches, found its own sombre niche in Spaniards' memories on September 26, 1984. It was the annual fair. Francisco Rivera, or Paquirri as all Spain knew the matador, was the big attraction at the main corrida.

A lean black bull named Avispado (Wide Awake), with no special qualities, ripped into his right thigh and some hours later, in the ambulance rushing him down the tortuous road to Córdoba 85 kilometres away, Paquirri succumbed to shock and loss of blood. He might have survived if he had been taken to Pozoblanco's new hospital. But the hospital only opened, after years of delay, after his death.

"There were no facilities for a major operation. At least we have our own hospital now," says bullfight aficionado and local historian Andrés Muñoz Calero.

A retired lawyer, Don Andrés lives in a book-lined residence opposite Santa Catalina church, where Juan Ginés de Sepulveda, has his tomb. Chronicler of Philip II, Sepulveda is one of Pozoblanco's most famous sons, although his views on Indians' and women's "inferiority" would hardly make him a hero today.

At 2,100 feet above sea-level, with a population of 14,000, Pozoblanco has an industrious air.

"There's a great vitality here," notes Don Andrés. "The Pedroches valley has always been isolated. We've been passed by, militarily, politically and administratively. The climate is harder here and the soil cannot be compared to that south of the Guadalquivir. People have had to make the best of their own resources. And this has been an advantage because people know what hard work and endeavour mean."

Pozoblanco's industrious spirit pervades the workshop of José Salamanca Calero. With his sons Eusebio and Sebastián and daughter Inés, he produces furniture and also finely-wrought carving.

"There are few carvers left," José comments, as he puts the finishing touches to a lion etched out of chestnut. "You must have a love for the work or you'll never make a good craftsman."

While the months of April and May appear to be one long *romería* in the villages of Los Pedroches, the community of Añora, a short distance to the north-west of Pozoblanco, has particular fame for its preservation of old customs and traditional dress. The *jota* rings out loudest of all on the first Saturday in May when the villagers set up crosses outside their doors and greet visitors with cakes and refreshment.

In the far corner of Córdoba province, the sweep of cornfields is interrupted by the glowering bulk of Belalcázar *(bello alcázar)* castle. Rebuilt 400 years ago, the Tower of Homage, magnificent in its ugliness, throws out a stony challenge to the surrounding countryside, to be answered only by the drone of a tractor or the clang of cow-bells.

In Arab times, Belalcázar was known as Gafig and one of its sons became Emir of Córdoba. Also born here was one of the Conquistadores, Sebastián de Belalcázar, who helped Pizarro crush the native people of Nicaragua and Peru.

Just out of town, the storks swoop over the decaying roof of the Santa Clara de la Columna monastery. Visits are only by special arrangement, but a steady stream of customers crosses the courtyard to order the sticky-sweet cakes made by the nuns.

After pushing a bell, they wait for a return jangle, signalling that they must open a small brown door set in the monastery wall. A revolving hatch is revealed and a voice asks what you require. When I expressed doubt as to what I might like to buy, I was told to wait. Soon a small, round-faced nun with a friendly aspect and a blue habit appeared in the main doorway and showed off an ornate cake of icing sugar and marzipan. My order of a quarter of a kilo was greeted with surprise at its miserliness.

Near Belalcázar stands Hinojosa del Duque, with a pleasant square and the "cathedral of the sierra", the vast John the Baptist church dating from the 15th century.

South of Hinojosa and away from Los Pedroches, the true sierra reasserts itself in forested hills and large estates dotted with oak trees. The Guadiato river valley cuts through the range and alongside the N-432, which runs from Córdoba to Extremadura; a series of communities mine for coal and lead.

Peñarroya Pueblonuevo is the largest. In the past it was two towns, one called Pueblo del Terrible; not because of some dastardly event but because a hunting dog named Terrible sniffed out coal deposits there around 1870. Bélmez, another mining town nearby, once controlled passage along the valley from its castle atop a fist of rock.

Fuente Obejuna boasts some interesting monuments. But its name is best known through the title of a Lope de Vega play which was based on the inhabitants' 15th-century rebellion against a tyrannical local ruler.

From Fuente Obejuna, the C-421 zigzags through the mountains into Seville province and to several towns with traces of Iberian and Roman occupation. The name Guadalcanal may have a familiar ring. One of its adventurous sons discovered the Solomons' island which was the scene of the bitter World War II Pacific battle. A plaque on the town hall commemorates Pedro Ortega's achievement.

Cork-oaks and chestnut trees carpet the area around Cazalla (its Arab name meant "strong city"), a dazzling white enclave amid the sierras, known now for its production of firewater — aguardiente and anís — and in the past for its iron foundries.

Pozos de la Nieve, on the way to Constantina, marks a spot where once the winter snows were stored so that they could be shipped out and sold in sweltering Seville during the summer. Today the *sevillanos* cool off by fleeing the 87 kilometres to Constantina, a community of about 10,000 people. It owes its name to a son of Constantine the Great, and in his era the citizens of Rome enjoyed nothing more than drinking the noted *"cocolubis"* wine, imported from the far-off Andalusian town.

Throughout the Sierra Morena, hunting is a favourite local pastime and an attraction that draws many visitors. Rabbit, hare and partridge abound. So, too, do deer and wild boar. In Córdoba province alone, hunters, many of whom fly in from abroad, annually bag 6,000 stag and 2,000 boar.

On a damp December day, I attended a typical *montería,* a Spanish-style hunt, in one of the wilder areas of Córdoba province, near its border with Seville. Turning off a narrow road running between Hornachuelos and Constantina, I bumped over a dirt track to La Loma, a 1,200-hectare *dehesa* (range). Deer peered at me curiously through the mist, then scampered off into the holm-oaks.

It was a raw dawn and in the gamekeeper's quarters a hardy bunch of helpers warmed themselves before a blazing fire and gulped slugs of anís. One helped gamekeeper Antonio Jiménez into his tight green jacket and leather chaps and handed him his cockaded hat. A large bowl of *migas* stood on a table outside and everybody tucked in.

Inside the *cortijo* dining-room, it was a different story. The hunters were tucking into fried eggs, cakes, coffee, brandy and whisky. They had arrived in gleaming four-wheel-drives and luxurious, imported saloons, and wore expensive, fur-lined cloaks and immaculate hand-tooled boots and chaps. Each had paid 200,000 pesetas for the chance to bag an impressive trophy without having to suffer that tedious, uncomfortable business of actually stalking the prey.

On the veranda, the owner of the property, Manuel Rodríguez, organized the draw to allocate two persons to each of 27 shooting posts. Only three trophies were allowed per blind and each was controlled by a "secretary", one of the cheerful *migas*-eaters whose task was to make sure only appropriate animals were shot and to verify who had killed what.

Rain swept down and the mist thickened, making it difficult and dangerous to shoot. The hunters sipped drinks impatiently in the comfortable cortijo, the ceilings of which were covered with hundreds of horns from animals shot by the owner and his wife, and glanced through the farm's history, contained in a silver-bound volume.

Once, the book tells, these lands were owned by a religious order which had occupied the nearby San Calixto monastery. The monastery was destroyed by Napoleon's forces. In the 1940s, a previous owner was killed by the outlaws who roamed the sierra. After buying the property, Rodríguez set about restocking it with game and encircling his land with a seven-kilometre-long, six-foot-high fence. Photos of *monterías* since 1972 show proud hunters with scores of carcasses.

"This is a fantastic area for the sport," commented one local land-owner. "Last year I attended a *montería* where in two days with 30 guns we shot 200 deer. Where else in the world can you do that? I know some people are against hunting. But without the hunters there would be no animals. Nobody would invest so much in stocking and looking after the deer."

Finally, after midday, the hunt got under way. The hunters were spared any walking. Vehicles dropped them off at their posts which were strung out along the hillsides. Then, six packs of dogs were released to flush out the game.

With Antonio Lozano, a sturdy *perrero* from Hornachuelos, I struggled up a boulder-strewn hillside as his 20 hounds raced excitedly about seeking a scent. I soon understood the need for leather leggings. Antonio's were worn black from the spiky scrub that tore at flesh and clothing. Directing his voice by cupping one hand to his mouth, he bellowed ear-splitting commands to his dogs, occasionally rallying them with a blast from a conch horn.

Suddenly a buck and a doe broke cover below us, running for their lives, smashing through the scrub as though it did not exist. We lost sight of them, but a few seconds later a shot rang out from a blind.

"Don't get in the way of one of those beasts when we scare 'em out," warned Antonio. "They go like hell and run right over you."

He lit another cigarette. Although in his sixties and always puffing black tobacco, he never seemed out of breath as we climbed up and down the slopes through wet brush that was often head-high.

"I'm not so good. I felt bad yesterday," admitted Antonio in his sandpaper-and-aguardiente voice. He gestured. "See those dogs go! I haven't fed them today, so they're really eager. They're a mixture, Andalusian *podencos* and some smaller breeds."

Tough, independent types, the dog-handlers do a gruelling but essential job. Traditionally, they have the right to receive payment of bread, tobacco and one pound of gunpowder, but today they work for hard cash. Sometimes they must risk their lives. If a boar menaces their dogs, it is their responsibility to go in with a knife to save them. It is safer to be a hunter, though a little more costly.

After about three hours, the hunt was over. The visitors, as impeccably turned out as ever, drove back to the cortijo to sip sherry and discuss their luck. Some were smiling complacently. Others tried to hide their disappointment; 200,000 pesetas is a lot to pay if you have nothing to hang on the wall afterwards.

"Love of hunting is a worm inside you, like smoking. You do it because it is part of you," reflected José Cabello, an amiable Córdoba gunsmith who admits he is an addict. "But you have to start young. That lad over there, for example. He killed his first deer at seven."

Although in his seventies, non-smoking and non-drinking José will rise at 4 a.m. to go striding over the sierras after partridge. His equally enthusiastic son, José María, records *monterías* on video for sale to hunters around Europe.

As the day's bag — 55 stags already gutted and tagged by the secretaries — was brought in by tractor, José remarked: "You're seeing a *montería* with a lot of style. Things are done properly here. Guests have the run of the cortijo. The trophies are properly laid out at the end. You get people with education, not like at some *monterías,* where people just grab their trophies and go."

The hunters drifted outside to examine the trophies arranged in rows in the courtyard, each with its head neatly turned the same way. That was for the photographs. The organizer climbed a ladder to obtain a better angle. Then he posed with his wife and the game-keeper amid the fallen deer. Then the paying clients posed and posed again with their trophies. They would keep the head and horns to take home. But there would be no venison on their tables. The meat was already sold and would soon be en route to Germany in refrigerated vans. No matter. The cameras went on clicking.

On the twilight trip back to Hornachuelos, my headlights picked out a trio of young deer. They paused, sniffed the air, and eyed me calmly. Then daintily, without hurry, they crossed the road and were swallowed up by the soft darkness of the Sierra Morena.

City of Caliphs

M ORE than 750 years after the Moors were expelled from their golden
metropolis on the banks of the Guadalquivir, a robed descendant of the
desert invaders was invited back to Córdoba for a solemn ceremony at city
hall.

It was a curious affair. Córdoba had twinned itself with Smara, a small
community in the western Sahara which is dominated by the kingdom of
Morocco. The female ambassador who signed the genial accord, however,
represented guerrilla forces which for years have fought against Moroccan
sovereignty.

The twinning, in April 1987, was significant in several ways. It illustrated
a new awareness of Islam and the Arab world on the part of an Andalusian
city profoundly marked by its Moorish past. At the same time, it was a piece
of political cheek by Córdoba's left-wing council, since the Madrid government was not on speaking terms with the guerrillas.

It was a quixotic act of independence, but an understandable one from a
city that once outshone all Europe and now is reduced to a mere provincial
capital. When Julius Caesar could take the trouble to sack you, when a whole
empire trembled at your edicts, when Christendom once paid you court, it is
not easy to accept that history has passed you by.

So rich was Córdoba that fountains once ran with quicksilver and millionaires jostled one another in its streets. So cultured was it that philosophers, scholars and poets of diverse races and beliefs thronged its seats of
learning.

Today, nearly 300,000 people lend an air of bustle to this city, sitting
comfortably between sierras and fertile plains. But modern Córdoba is the
most provincial of Andalusian capitals, except possibly for Jaén. Other cities
have become more cosmopolitan and outward-looking. Landlocked Córdoba
clings to its quiet rituals.

"You can recognize a true *cordobés,*" says one regular, as he sips a dry
Montilla wine in the Taberna de San Miguel, a traditional spot near the city
centre. "His routine never varies. Every day at the same time, he goes to the
same bar and orders the same drink. He wants the glass always filled to

exactly the same level. He talks to the same group of friends and at the same time every day, he leaves."

"One thing the *cordobeses* do have is class," believes Rafi, a young professional born in the city. "But it's very difficult to get them moving if you want to start a new project. They won't risk a penny unless the results are guaranteed. To be honest, I like going to Málaga, because there's more happening there. People here keep more to themselves."

The *cordobeses,* cautious and conservative, are often said to be "senecaesque", meaning that they have much in common with Lucius Annaeus Seneca, the witty, cynical philosopher born in Córdoba about 4 BC, when this was the capital of the Roman province of Baetica.

Seneca went to Rome, became tutor to the infant Nero, and later one of the most influential men in the tyrant's court. He was a statesman, orator and stylist — and no mean businessman. His stoicism, intoxication with language, sense of honour and courage are qualities Spaniards respect and aspire to themselves.

"If you know how to use it," said Seneca, "life is long enough." It is the sort of view that appeals to the fatalism of Andalusians and matches the tragic sense of destiny of a city in which one of the most-visited monuments commemorates Manolete. "Anyone may take life from man, but no one death: a thousand gates stand open to it," wrote Seneca. The gate swung open for Córdoba's maestro of the ring when he was impaled on a horn. Seneca's moment came when the crazed Nero ordered him to commit suicide. He did so — calmly and with fortitude.

Córdoba has produced more than its share of illustrious citizens. Long after Seneca, when it was the centre of the Moorish caliphate of Al Andalus, it gave birth to two whose brilliance shines down the centuries.

Abu al-Walid Muhammad Ibn Ahmad Ibn Muhammad Ibn Rushd — or Averroës, as Latin scholars called him — was an astrologer, a mathematician, and one of Islam's greatest thinkers. From Islamic traditions and Greek philosophy, he created his own system of thought.

While Averroës applied his penetrating mind to explaining Aristotle, and even as the Almohads, fanatical invaders from the Atlas mountains, shook the city, another 12th-century *cordobés* was studying at the Talmudic school, which was ranked among the most outstanding centres of Hebrew scholarship. After religious persecution forced Moses Maimonides to leave Córdoba, he went to Egypt to become physician to the Sultan Saladin. Amazingly advanced in his ideas and with prodigious energy, Maimonides' writings had far-reaching impact on Judaism, philosophy and medicine.

Córdoba's glorious era had reached a peak earlier, in the 10th century, when Abd ar-Rahman III proclaimed himself Caliph of the West with influence stretching from North Africa to Portugal, the Balearics and Northern Spain.

Córdoba became the trend-setter, Europe's largest and most sophisticated city, a centre of civilization and learning. Arab historians claimed it had a million inhabitants, 80,000 shops, and 300 mosques. From Córdoba issued romantic poetry, the latest in Andalusian music, the finest silk materials, intricate leatherwork, religious literature, tales of legendary splendour.

An idea of the Caliph's style can be found on a hillside just west of Córdoba where a team of archaeologists is painstakingly reconstructing Abd ar-Rahman's dream palace, built, it is said, for a favourite with the wealth of one of his concubines.

Piecing together the jigsaw puzzle of Medina Azahara is a task for a lifetime. The city-palace was a wonderland of marble, ivory, jasper, carved stone, mosaics and roofs of silver and gold. Ingenious fountains and water-channels played a symphony of 60 distinct sounds amid lush gardens; just to feed the fish in those waters legend tells that 800 loaves had to be baked daily. Thousands of eunuchs, dancing girls and serfs attended to the potentate's every whim.

It is a hard act to follow. Centuries later, Córdoba — a community which had already seen everything when Madrid was still an obscure settlement — knows it can never put all those broken pieces together again.

"People here let things pass them by. Instead of taking a stand on anything, they go off to the sierras," says Carmen López Mateos, a lively professor of humanities. "You only have to see what happens in elections. This is a very conservative place, but the conservatives don't bother to vote."

The workers, living in the stark apartment blocks that have ringed Córdoba since the 1960s, do vote, however. Their support gave the city the first Communist mayor elected in a Spanish provincial capital. Julio Anguita was sometimes compared with Seneca because of his keen intellect, agility with words and ability to spark a controversy. Swiftly he was dubbed the Red Caliph.

Dig anywhere into Córdoba's soil and the chances are you will stumble across a Phoenician pot or a Roman tomb. When Mayor Anguita's council tried to construct an underground carpark, excavations revealed valuable archaeological remains. Anguita wanted to push ahead anyway, but the Red Caliph did not have the power of his predecessors and the project was blocked. Unperturbed, he was soon battling with the local Catholic hierarchy over arrangements for 1200th anniversary celebrations of the Great Mosque's founding.

That year, 1985, coincided with the 850th anniversary of the birth of Maimonides, and the mosque became a rallying point for religious tolerance and understanding. Jewish, Christian and Muslim dignitaries marked the occasion by meeting in Córdoba.

To this day, the mosque is Córdoba's most representative feature, a source of local pride and the single most important reason tourists flock to the city. And it can still arouse fierce passions.

First a pagan temple stood on the site, then a church, then the mosque, the heart of which was torn out by Christian conquerors to build a cathedral. Many think that was an error, but few go as far as prominent national newspaper columnist Francisco Umbral. On the occasion of the anniversary, he dared to suggest that it was time for "an artistic, religious and historic reconversion of the mosque, ridding it of Catholic and imperial adhesions."

Demolishing a cathedral in Catholic Spain is an unlikely event, and the truth is that the mosque is of such breath-taking proportions, its 850 marble columns and double-tiered arches fading into distant shadows, that it is possible to be unaware of the Gothic-Renaissance monument at its core.

Even George Borrow, the opinionated eccentric who propagated the bible across Spain last century and declared Córdoba "a mean, dark, gloomy place", could not help but be impressed by the work of the Moors. "A mosque," he maintained, "is, in externals at least, such as a house of God should be — four walls, a fountain, and the eternal firmament above."

French writer Théophile Gautier thought Córdoba was "a white and calcined skeleton" when he visited 150 years ago. That would be a mistaken judgement today, but the African quality he noticed is still there.

Just as the mosque hides its interior beauty behind dull, unadorned walls, many of the old quarter's cramped, crooked streets present an inscrutable face, reminiscent of Fez. Córdoba hugs its privacy behind walls that would stop a cannon-ball, studded wooden doors that would resist an Inquisitor's battering ram, and iron grilles that would blunt the enthusiasm of any scimitar-wielding marauders.

There are schools behind those walls, and nunneries and restaurants and cottage industries, printers setting type, scholars scouring parchments, sewing machines whirring, tired old men collapsed before televisions, mothers berating, teenagers romancing.

Córdoba is not non-stop theatre like Seville. True, its patios, ablaze with astonishing colour and greenery, are for public admiration, particularly during the May patios fiesta when the streets ring with music and high spirits. But, usually, between patio and street lies the *cancela,* a solid wrought-iron gate.

If the *caseta* symbolizes Seville, allowing public exhibition of frivolity, the *cancela* stands for Córdoba. It allows visitors to be inspected before admittance. Only then will a hidden lever be pulled, the barrier swing open and the stranger allowed entry to the inner sanctum in the most private of Andalusia's cities.

The Heart of Andalusia

HERE is no shade in the vineyard of Antonio Tejada Jurado. At 5.30 on a late summer afternoon, heat muffles the countryside in a stifling embrace. On the skyline, Montilla shimmers like a mirage. Heat bounces from its roof-tops and ripples about the old tower of Santiago church.

They are preparing for a fiesta in Montilla. The town will echo to the ritual exuberance of an Andalusian holiday, as gaily-decked carts parade through the streets, the grapes are ceremonially crushed and the first must of the harvest is offered to the Virgin of the Vines. Drinking and dancing will tire the night out.

But that is tomorrow. Today, under a pitiless sun, Antonio, his wife Aurora, and their two children, Francisco and Rafi, toil in the vineyard, bending and bending again to clip the bunches of fat grapes.

"It's a family affair because that's the only way for small farmers like myself," says Antonio, when he pauses to quench his thirst from a *botijo* (an earthenware water container). "The small man can't afford to employ anybody even in a good season, not with the price the co-operative pays for grapes."

He looks around proudly. "But at least this is mine: two and a half hectares of vines, all Pedro Ximenez grapes. You won't find better wine than Montilla. Drink as much as you like and you won't get a hangover."

He bends again, and the rhythmic snick-snick that began at 8 a.m. continues. It will go on until after sundown. Francisco loads the grapes on to a cart which a placid grey mare hauls to the road. The tarmac is stained with juice and the air heavy with the odours of the *vendimia*.

At harvest time the Montilla-Moriles wine lands have a mellow, satisfied air. Their product is esteemed by those who know it, but it has yet to win wide international recognition. And the same goes for the other offerings of the whole triangle of Córdoba province bounded by Montilla, Lucena and Priego.

In many ways, this is the heart of Andalusia, a mixture of sierras and fine agricultural land, ancient settlements and idyllic pastoral scenes, strong local pride and deep-rooted respect for tradition.

Yet tourists whistle past, intent on reaching Granada, Córdoba or Málaga.

Towns like Priego de Córdoba, in the zone's eastern corner, do not even rate a mention in their guidebooks. Priego — one of the jewels of Andalusia!

It is just as well. Montilla-Priego is no place for the spoon-fed. It is somewhere to wander through at leisure, unhustled by tour guides and souvenir-sellers, a place where the inhabitants cast a curious eye over visitors, then politely carry on with their own lives. It is the Andalusia you read about but which has long vanished from the coasts.

Spring or autumn are the seasons to enjoy this region. In summer the heat is intense. Not too surprisingly, La Campiña and the neighbouring part of Seville province are known as "the frying-pan of Andalusia".

La Campiña (open country) is the name given to the area south of the Guadalquivir basin, an undulating carpet of cornfields, olive groves and vineyards extending to the mountains of Cabra, Rute and Priego. Castles frown over bleached villages, as they have done since the days of the *Reconquista,* when Moorish and Christian armies stained these rich clay soils in a bloody tug of war.

East of route 331, the mighty towers of Espejo castle can be glimpsed towering over the surrounding vineyards well before the whitewashed dwellings humbly clustering at its feet creep into view. The fortress is the property of one of the great aristocratic families of Andalusia, the Dukes of Osuna. Two hundred years ago the Osunas, the Albas and the Medinacelis were said to own most of Andalusia.

Castro del Río, the next town, boasts a Roman bridge and some significant events in its past. Pompey's troops may have camped here before fighting the Battle of Monda nearby. And in a room of the town hall Cervantes was once imprisoned for about seven days. In September 1592, after the future creator of *Don Quixote* had pledged to write six of "the best plays ever presented in Spain", he was tossed into jail, accused of illegally seizing some wheat during his work as a tax collector. He could not have loved Castro del Río. After an earlier trip there, he had been excommunicated for daring to order the detention of a sacristan unwilling to pay his dues.

Even in Cervantes' time, Baena, south of Castro along route N-432, was noted for the quality of the olive oil produced by the trees which grow in its baked, chalky soil. The golden oil of Baena is recognized as one of Spain's finest. It is strictly quality-controlled, bearing an official *denominación de origen* label.

From a distance, at least, Baena hardly appears changed since Cervantes was squeezing the populace on behalf of his greedy masters. Narrow streets run precipitously up to old walls within which Gothic churches, Renaissance palaces and Moorish battlements struggle for space with the huddle of dwellings.

Outside the Dominican convent of Madre de Dios, children skip over a long length of elastic, chanting in time.

"The nuns live here," they confide. "You never see them because they're always praying. They sell lovely *madalenas* (cakes). You should try them."

The 20th century has barely penetrated here. Within the 400-year-old convent, one of 900 such closed institutions in Spain, the nuns pray, meditate and bake. Even when the drums boom out deafeningly during the Holy Week processions in Baena, they stay enclosed in their cells. (Or do the more curious seek some secret vantage point to sneak a glimpse of the world outside?)

A river runs past Baena and on its banks, just south of the town, stands Marbella. But there is no danger of confusing it with any coastal resort. Marbella is a hamlet on an unmade road that leads to the fortress of Zuheros and the nearby Cave of the Bats.

In another dusty pueblo, Doña Mencia, with its attendant ruined castle, the youngsters escape the heat by plunging into a magnificent municipal pool set amid green lawns. It is a true oasis here in the dozing, desiccated Andalusian countryside, and a luxury that the children's parents could never have dreamed of.

Swinging west towards Montilla, the vines take over. In the sierras of Montilla, where the finest grapes come from, the harvest is getting under way. Tons of grapes are arriving at the crushing plants, most of them the type known as Pedro Ximenez.

Legend says that this grape originated in the Rhine Valley and was brought to Andalusia in the 16th century (or was it the 17th?) by a soldier named Pedro Ximenez (or possibly Peter Siemens). It does not matter. From the region of Montilla-Moriles (a village to the south where, naturally, they claim their product has the edge in quality) flows excellent dry white wine with an alcoholic strength of 14 to 16 per cent, as well as a variety of sweeter blends.

Many people cannot distinguish Montilla from sherry. In fact, the very name for pale, dry sherry, *amontillado,* is derived from Montilla.

This rankles a little in Montilla but, as far as market share goes, it is no contest. The wines of Jerez have a long-standing international reputation whereas Montilla is only just making itself known in Spain and abroad.

"Nobody can match Jerez's *olorosos,* but when it comes to *fino* (dry white), it's just a question of taste," reflects Juan Bosco de Alvear y Zubiria as he watches the grapes being unloaded at a plant owned by his family. Alvear is the largest bodega in Montilla and, founded in 1729, claims to be the oldest in Spain.

Juan points out, "Our wine differs from sherry in that we add nothing to it whereas sherry is fortified with alcohol." He adds that as well as their traditional wines the area now produces light, white wine to suit modern tastes. "Our zone has a great future," he says enthusiastically. "It's just a matter of work, work, work and quality, quality, quality."

Picturesque old ways of production are out. Juan checks the performance of a new 13-million-peseta German press with a technician from Frankfurt.

"This is the latest," explains the technician. "An internal rubber balloon inflates, pressing the grapes against the tank's epoxy-coated steel walls. The pressure is only two kilos per square centimetre — just as it used to be when our fathers used their feet."

These days fermentation takes place in huge temperature-controlled, stainless steel vats before passing first to cement containers known as *tinajas* and then to oak barrels where the company matures its wine through the *solera* system of blending, which is also practised in Jerez.

During the last weekend in April every year, they arrive on horseback and foot to pay homage to the Virgen de la Cabeza in the Sierra Morena, a religious fiesta that attracts more than 200,000 pilgrims, yet is little known to tourists.

Clockwise from left: *Miguel, the guardian of the Piedrasantas sanctuary in Los Pedroches; aficionados gathered for tapas and gossip in one of Cordoba's most traditional bars; Pozoblanca wood-carver José Salamanca hard at work; Belmez castle, which played a strategic part during the long struggle between Christians and Moors.*

Above: *rank upon rank of 'tinajas' (earthenware vessels) hold the newly-fermented Montilla wine.* Right: *grape-picker Francisco Tejada refreshes himself from a 'botijo' during the autumn harvest.*

Alvear alone has 21,000 of these casks, or *botas,* stored in the hushed twilight of its bodegas, but business for those practising the ancient art of barrel-making is bad.

"They call this the Valley of the Fallen," explains Miguel Rodríguez. "That's because so many bodegas over-expanded in the '70s and got into such financial trouble that they closed. And that came on top of the trend to use plastic, steel or concrete containers. But the truth is you can't beat a barrel of oak — it's the only material that adds to a wine's bouquet."

Miguel speaks with the pain of somebody witnessing the fading of an ancient craft. His father, Manuel, approaching 80, his brother and his teenage son all work in the trade. They have won national prizes for their skill.

In the cluttered Rodríguez workshop in a Montilla back street, a worker is *batiendo el barril,* using fire to bend the barrel staves so that he can hammer the iron hoops into place.

"That's what finished me," comments Miguel. "Both my father and I have to wear corsets now after so many years of killing work. When you get to 40, your waist won't take any more, not when you work 14 hours a day as we used to. It needs a hell of a lot of strength and stamina. I tell you, a *tonelero* would win any arm-wrestling contest."

The family now turns out small barrels with carved lids and fancy stands for sale as gifts, but Miguel's pride rests with the big league, including a cone-shaped monster capable of holding 17,500 litres.

He shows off some of the products at an exhibition to mark the annual wine festival in the first week of September. All Montilla crowds into a hangar-like bodega to see Miss Puente Genil, Miss Espejo, Miss Nueva Carteya and their counterparts receive their sashes as princesses of the *vendimia.* They are all groomed to the nines, their shining country faces betraying a mixture of embarrassment and pride. Except for the queen of them all, Miss Córdoba, who has clearly seen it all before.

The Cellarman of Honour is there too, a respected wine-maker who received his title for the year in a ceremony at the Casa del Inca, a solid mansion near the Montilla market.

Garcilaso de la Vega, of Spanish-Inca descent, lived in the Casa del Inca for 30 years in the 16th century, translating and writing about the Inca empire. Today, part of the building houses Montilla's library.

Montilla's most famous son, however, was Gonzalo Fernández de Córdoba, better known as El Gran Capitán. Born in the local castle in 1453, he went to the Castilian court at 13, conducted negotiations for the Moors' surrender of Granada, and distinguished himself as a military leader in Italy. His war-weary bones finally came to rest in San Jerónimo church in Granada.

On the road south from Montilla, another historic town has its quota of the baroque and the bizarre.

Aguilar de la Frontera — Ipagro to its Greek founders — offers splendid views over the countryside, an interesting eight-sided plaza, sleeping streets and a clock-tower soaring in solitary splendour.

In contrast, Lucena (further down N-331) has a bustling air, thanks to its variety of small industries which include furniture-making and the production of brass and copper ornaments. In the Middle Ages it was an independent Jewish republic within the caliphate of Córdoba and an important trading centre. An academy of Talmudic studies was founded there, but 12th-century persecution persuaded the town's Jews to take refuge in Toledo. Few obvious traces of Jewish heritage remain, although Santiago church is said to occupy the site of a synagogue.

But the Arab Tower of Moral still stands, a reminder that Boabdil, the last sultan of Granada, was once imprisoned here. Boabdil's attempt to crush the Christians at Lucena in 1483 is related in an old Moorish ballad, which after dwelling on the splendour of his army's departure from Granada reports his mother's farewell: "May Allah protect you, my son, and let Muhammad watch over you,/And return you from Lucena, safe, sound and with profit."

No wonder Boabdil was labelled *alzogoybi* (the poor devil) by his subjects. His troops were routed and he was captured by the Count of Cabra.

Arab, Jewish and even Roman influences live on here, as Isidoro Granados pointed out to me in the family pottery in a Lucena side-street.

Hefting a lustrous green, fat-bellied jar with a narrow neck, he told me: "This is a Roman design. You see, there have always been potters around here. And many of the terms we use come from the Arabs and Jews. *Sakifa,* for example. That's Jewish, meaning the entrance to the oven."

While his brother Luis was busy at the wheel, father Rafael, in his sixties, sweated at the task of feeding wood into an oven furnace. The process would have to continue for eight hours, and then a further eight hours for the second baking of pots sealed in the oven.

As he shoehorned vase upon vase, bowl upon bowl into a customer's sagging car, Isidoro calmed the owner: "Don't worry. You'll make it home. If it doesn't all fit, we can take the back seat out and send it on to you by train. We've done that before."

If you buy too much of a neighbouring town's speciality, they may have to send your liver on by train. Rute, a small town on the edge of the sierras, lies along a scenic road to the south. It has nearly 20 establishments producing that most lethal of spirits, *anís.*

"The industry started in Rute because we have magnificent water from the sierras," explained Francisco Molina, one of the owners of Anís La Zagala, as he showed me the distilling plant.

"There are no special secrets about the process. We fill this copper cauldron with 600 litres of water, some alcohol and anise seeds. Then for seven to eight hours we keep an olive wood fire going beneath it. The vapour passes through that coiled pipe, cools and ends up in the earthenware collector.

"We throw away the head and tail, as we call it, of the condensed liquid because it has a bad taste. But the rest is the cream: 144 litres of 96 per cent pure alcohol, the most natural product you can have. Then you adjust the alcoholic content by adding water. Here, try some."

I sipped some *anís dulce.* Syrup with a kick in it.

"Thirty-five per cent alcohol," said Francisco. "Now try our *anís seco.*"

It was crystal clear, dry, and produced instant results. I clutched a wall for support.

"Fifty-five per cent. The best," said Francisco. "Of course, it's poison. But in our society it's part of life."

After trying this firewater, a plunge into the refreshing emerald expanse of the Iznajar reservoir is a good antidote. It lies a few kilometres to the south of Rute. Half-way along the lake, the town of Iznajar boldly crowns an escarpment.

The bleat of goats and the whirr of cicadas are all that break the tranquillity here, but on June 28, 1861, one of the most significant events in recent Andalusian history occurred at Iznajar.

The streets rang to cries of *"Long live the Republic!"* and *"Death to the Queen!"* signalling the start of a rebellion planned to sweep the region. Thousands of landless peasants joined the revolt, the first of its kind against the rich Andalusian landowners. But the authorities acted swiftly, thanks to another sort of revolution — in communications. Warned by telegraph, they crushed the rising.

We are close to the province of Granada here, in mountainous terrain. Sinuous roads lead to Priego de Córdoba, nestling at the foot of Córdoba province's highest peak, 5,100-foot-high Tinosa, dusted with snow in winter, shimmering with heat in summer. Without a railway, off main routes, this community of 14,000 surrounded by 24 tiny hamlets presents an idyllic aspect of quiet contentment.

"Priego is like a slice of north-west Spain dropped in the heart of Andalusia, with its long, narrow river valley cut into the mountains, in each of whose folds or slopes springs a stream or rises a hamlet."

Thus was the area described by Niceto Alcalá Zamora, who spent the first 20 years of his life in Priego. Qualified as a lawyer by the age of 17, a brilliant orator, he became the first president of Spain's Second Republic, only to be forced out of office just before the country dissolved into civil war. He ended his days in exile, in Buenos Aires.

A plaque marks the house where he was born in Priego. Number 33 Calle Río is empty but retains the noble air of the mansions that line this street, home in the past of silk merchants, landed gentry and titled families.

Elegant ironwork and imposing front doors gleaming with polished brass line Calle Río in its serpentine approach to one of the most remarkable fountains I have seen. Adorned with statuary, the Fuente del Rey has three pools and no fewer than 139 gushing spouts. At least 136 were functioning at the last count.

A frontier town in Moorish times, Priego was badly battered in siege after siege. Its golden age came in the 18th century, when silk manufacture produced large profits and a blossoming of baroque architecture. But the industry collapsed when the English and Catalans began manufacturing cheap cotton.

Although another slump hit the local textile industry in the 1950s and '60s, causing many workers to emigrate, today the town jogs along comfortably, apparently untouched by social turmoil. Its factories turn out trousers and shirts, its small farmers produce olives, cereals and excellent apples.

In the old quarter where the streets are so narrow a broad-shouldered person needs to walk sidways, an old woman waters dozens of flowers glow-ing against the whitewash. We chat and she tells me: "I've known people cry when their job takes them away from Priego. This is a friendly place and a trusting one. We aren't afraid to leave our doors open here."

Nearby, I penetrate into the cool shade of the church of La Asunción and gaze in wonder at the amazing décor. In the octagonal sacristy chapel, the light plays softly over a cornucopia of intricate plasterwork, scrolls and cornices, saints and apostles. Like the main altar, the chapel is considered a national monument.

Masters of the art of baroque shaped the chapel two centuries ago when Priego's wealth attracted the finest sculptors, carvers and gilders. The tradition lingers, for at least a dozen skilled woodworkers and gilders are based in the town.

The veteran maestro of the craft, Francisco Tejero, has taught scores of carvers their art. Born in Baena more than 70 years ago, he himself learned the craft when living in Cuba. He followed his teacher back to Granada, came to Priego to do a job in 1932 and never left.

Showing me around his spacious house full of skilfully worked sculptures and scenes in bas-relief, Francisco notes: "I always use walnut or mahogany. You have a plan of what you are going to carve, but you may see something else in the wood and change your idea as you go along. It's a matter of taking away the unnecessary wood. When it's all gone, the work is finished."

It sounds easy enough, just as Francisco makes gilding seem child's play as he delicately lays wafer thin leaves of gold on a new carving, using a badger-hair brush. It requires a butterfly touch.

José Mateo Aguilera is also a carver, but I find him giving musical instruction to some youngsters in the Aurora church, another dazzling example of baroque architecture. José is preparing to lead fellow members of the Brotherhood of Nuestra Señora de la Aurora on to the streets. Rain, hail or snow, every Saturday midnight they sally forth to sing the praises of the Virgin to their fellow citizens and collect alms for the church. The tradition dates from the 16th century.

"In winter, our numbers may drop to only eight or so, but we never miss," José asserts. "We do carry a bottle of spirit and wear long cloaks to keep ourselves warm."

Sure enough, just after midnight the brothers begin their religious serenade. One man bangs a tambourine, another plays an accordion, others pluck guitars, and the words echo from the walls of Priego as they sing of "La Aurora divine, overflowing with the moon, dressed by the sun." They never run short of words since there are 400 *coplas,* handed down from the distant past.

The streets are crowded because it is one of the *Domingos de Mayo,* when Priego celebrates its preservation from the plague in the 17th century.

At San Francisco church, the brothers troop inside to pay homage to Jesus of Nazareth, whose robed image stands at the altar behind a phalanx of flowers. Their voices ring out lustily and at the end, faces shining with fervour, they bellow *"¡Viva el Nazareno!"* Then the group disappears into the side-streets, and the sound of the *coplas* gradually fades into the night.

A deafening welcome greets Christ's image when it finally emerges from the church on the Sunday evening, swaying on the shoulders of a team of white-shirted faithful. A roar flies up from the townsfolk crowding the plaza, as the bells of San Francisco peal out and rockets light the sky.

Scores of women in black mantillas join the procession wending its way around town, while a master of ceremonies continues auctioning off donations for church funds. His amplified voice blares out across the plaza, successfully drowning competition from a group of folk dancers performing on a second stage. Sitting at trestle-tables laden with refreshments, the spectators gaily outbid one another.

"Here we have a plate of fine cured ham. What will you give me? Sold for 3,000 pesetas! And this beautiful bouquet of red roses? Yes, 10,000, 12, 15, gone for 18,000..."

Good-humoured in their Sunday best, the citizens laugh and gossip. The wine flows. The prices soar. Somebody presses on me a full bottle of dry Montilla. Instead of the usual label, it bears a picture depicting Jesus crowned with thorns. El Nazareno, the image for which Priego reserves its greatest emotion.

It's Sunday in Priego, a time of piety and revelry. And Monday is a long way off.

Subterranean Citizens

TWO partridges blink from their cages in a corner of José Antonio Sola's living-room. Photos of stiffly-posing relatives adorn the impeccably white-washed walls. A mighty television set dominates the room and a new washing machine has been installed in the adjacent bathroom.

Although he has the worn features of a man who toiled for years collecting esparto grass, José rarely stops smiling.

"Hombre," he says, pressing wine and home-made sausage on visitors. "My children will have a better life than I. They're learning to read and write, which I never did. And my sons have sent money home and helped us to make this place more comfortable. All the same, I wouldn't mind a house, although a lot of people will tell you how beautiful it is to live in a cave."

José is one of Andalusia's troglodytes. About half the dwellings in his village of Dehesas de Guadix are caves. Dehesas sprawls over a bare, dusty hillside, far from any tourist route. Corn-cobs dry in the sun and mules browse next to chimney-pots and television aerials which sprout from the earth. Around here, the low hills have been chipped by man and scoured by the elements until they resemble a cross between a moonscape and a Gruyère cheese.

About 35,000 people live underground in southern Spain, the majority in Almería and Granada provinces. In some communities in the area around the towns of Guadix, Baza and Huescar, more people live in caves than in concrete or brick structures.

Contrary to popular belief, most cave-dwellers are not gypsies and they do not yearn to move. Nor is there any social stigma about being part of this subterranean society. Accepting this, the Andalusian government is helping to upgrade cave amenities, ensuring that there is proper sanitation, access and street lighting.

"Agricultural workers have no use for an apartment," points out a Guadix Town Hall official. "They need somewhere to keep their animals and tools. Also," he added, "caves never leak, they don't collapse and you can't hear noisy neighbours!"

More than a third of Guadix's 21,000 inhabitants live underground, although not every residence is as grand as the 11-room labyrinth belonging to the Hidalgo family. All 22 children of the patriarch, Pedro, who died at 94, were born in the cave. One of his sons, Jesús carries on the family business, making rustic pine chairs with woven rush seats.

"The nice thing about cave life," says his wife, Carmen, "is that the temperature is always about 18 degrees centigrade even at the height of summer. And in winter, when it is freezing in Guadix, one fire is enough to keep the place warm."

Walking through Guadix's Ermita Nueva — also called Santiago — quarter, it is difficult to avoid stepping on somebody's rooftop. Drying peppers and pots of geraniums glow brightly against the white cave entrances. In the gypsy zone, the baying of an army of hounds greets the approach of any stranger. A jukebox blares in a bar gouged from the hillside and the devout pray in a nearby chapel that once was a cave dwelling itself.

No doubt, some people lived in caves here in ancient times because of the relative ease of excavation. The strangely-shaped hills are of an unusual hard, compacted clay, known as the Guadix-Baza post-pliocene deposit. But large-scale occupation apparently dates from the reign of Philip II in the 16th century, when persecuted Moriscos took refuge underground.

In the village of Purullena, six kilometres from Guadix, lives a man who has chipped out more homes than he cares to remember.

"If we started counting now, we wouldn't finish today, nor maybe tomorrow either," claims Torcuato Clares Mendoza, an amiable veteran who is as rough-hewn as the materials he works with. "When somebody has official permission, I get to work with my pick. With somebody to clear away the rubble, I can cut a room five metres by three in four days, depending how hard the rock is. The ceilings are always curved, like a half-moon. It's back-breaking work, but cave-digging is cheaper than building a normal house because you don't need bricklayers and cement."

Caves have title deeds like other property and sale prices have risen sharply, partly because Purullena has demonstrated more dynamism than neighbouring communities and set up several industries. Upwardly mobile young troglodytes now tend fancy gardens and park their cars in cave-garages.

Another indication of changing times can be found just back from the main Granada highway as it swings through Purullena. A two-storey maze of rooms honeycombs a knoll. For centuries the cave was a country inn, offering primitive shelter to muleteers and itinerant salesmen. Then, in the mid-1970s, owner Antonio Salazar had a bright idea. He converted it into the El Tempranillo disco, naming it after a 19th century utlaw. Now it is a nightly meeting place for local teenagers and a venue for wedding receptions and banquets.

Purullena folk boast that the area produces the world's tastiest peaches. Passers-by, however, see little of caves or peaches. They often imagine the village has a thriving ceramics industry, because of the number of stalls selling pottery along the highway. In fact, almost all the pots come from elsewhere. But first-class pieces in traditional style are turned out in a Purullena workshop by brothers Torcuato and Antonio Ubeda, who set up their own firm after returning from a 29-year stay in Valencia.

To the south of Purullena secluded villages like Lugros and Policar nestle beneath the misty, snow-clad fortress of the Sierra Nevada. South of Guadix extends the Marquesado del Zenete, which at 4,000 feet, is one of the highest plateaux in Spain. From the open-cast iron mines of Alquife, long lines of rail wagons rumble across the plain en route to the port of Almería, their passage guarded by an outstanding example of feudal architecture.

La Calahorra castle has frowned down in solitary splendour from its hillock since the Marquis of Zenete, bastard son of Cardinal Mendoza, ordered its construction between the years 1509 and 1512. On a visit to Italy, he had been so impressed by the Renaissance style that he brought an Italian architect back with him. Within the castle's austere walls with their rounded towers, the Italian created for Zenete a delicate wonder of marble balustrades, halls and staircases. The castle commands approaches to the Ragua Pass which climbs over the Sierra Nevada to the Alpujarras region. This lonely road, once haunted by outlaws, can be blocked by snow in winter.

North of the barley fields of the Marquesado plateau squats Guadix, one of those apparently unchanging Andalusian towns numbed by the weight of history. Two thousand years ago it was known for its silver, iron and copper mines. Imilce, a local princess with more silver than she knew what to do with, attracted the interest of the Carthaginian general Hannibal and he took her as his concubine.

The Emperor Augustus founded a colony here, strategically placed to command the Roman road network. Its name, Acci, possibly of Iberian origin, accounts for the term *accitanos* used to identify Guadix natives today. Later, as Wadi Ash (River of Life), it was a way station between the Caliph's court in Córdoba and Almería.

Quite a few *accitanos* owe their name to St. Torcuato, credited with establishing in Guadix Spain's first Christian bishopric. According to legend, St. Paul sent him with six apostles to evangelize the country. Torcuato died a martyr, a fate that also befell the Bishop of Guadix during the Civil War.

Relics of St. Torcuato can be seen in the museum of the cathedral, a monumental example of Gothic architecture running into baroque, which like many of Andalusia's churches is built on the site of a mosque. Diego de Siloe, the great Renaissance architect who left his mark on many fine buildings including Granada and Málaga cathedrals, created the apse and belfry.

Among Guadix notables buried in the cathedral is Antonio Mira de Amescua, a 17th-century dramatist. A quarrelsome priest, he created a scandal on one occasion by boxing the ears of a schoolmistress on the cathedral steps. Another Guadix writer enjoys reflected glory from the adaptation of one of his works. Pedro Antonio Alarcón's short story *The Three-Cornered Hat* was produced as a ballet to the music of Manuel de Falla. The piece has become a popular Spanish classic.

Guadix bred at least one conquistador too, in the person of Pedro de Mendoza. He was sent by the Holy Roman Emperor Charles V to colonize the Río de la Plata area of South America. There, in 1536, he established a fort and named it Nuestra Señora Santa María del Buen Aire. Mendoza died from syphilis on the voyage home, but the settlement lives on, as Buenos Aires.

From Guadix to Baza, the N-342 highway runs through steppe-like scenery, an undulating brown plain bordered by ochre mountains. The spectacular Gor river ravine slices across it and, here and there, fruit and vegetables flourish in oases of green.

Only 48 kilometres separate the two towns, but they might as well be on opposite sides of the country. Rivalry spilled into the open in 1986 when *accitanos* staged angry demonstrations over the decision to centre medical care in a new hospital at Baza. Some said they preferred to travel the difficult route to Granada rather than consult a doctor in the rival town.

Baza, with a thousand more inhabitants than Guadix, is the commercial centre for a large area and has important cattle markets. It too can boast a long history, the most outstanding evidence of which is La Dama de Baza, a life-size, painted stone sculpture of a seated funerary goddess. The 800-kilo lady, estimated to be 2,400 years old, was found in an Iberian necropolis near Baza in 1971.

Known as *bastetanos,* the local folk regard *accitanos* as an introverted lot living in the past. One resident comments: "We're different. We are very open people. Baza is a paradise for the stranger because he'll find nowhere more welcoming."

They *are* a friendly lot in this small, intimate town. But one visitor gets a welcome that is too warm for comfort. Yet he comes back, every year. The annual fiesta of the *Casacamorras* revives the age-old rivalry between Guadix and Baza. It dates from a time just after the Catholic Monarchs ousted the Moors from Baza, in 1489.

A Guadix mason, allegedly named Juan Pedernal, was working on a new church when a desperate voice calling for pity issued from a cavity. It came from an image of the Virgin and Child. Joyfully he tried to carry it off in a cart to his home town. But the oxen would not budge. There was no way he could get it to Guadix. Despite bitter dispute, Baza kept the Virgin.

But Guadix has not given up. Every year on September 6, it sends El Cascamorras (origins of this name are obscure) to try to steal back the Virgin. To succeed he must reach the Virgin without a spot on him. But there is little chance of that. A welcome committee, composed of hundreds of Baza teenagers, awaits him on a scarred hillside rising above the town. They prepare by pouring used engine oil over themselves.

"*Cascamorras... Cascamorras... ¡Olee! ¡Olah! ¡Olay!*" yells this pitch-black tribe. When El Cascamorras himself arrives, a short, inoffensive figure carrying a flag, they seize him and bathe him in oil too. Then the whole mob begins running the three kilometres into Baza.

A rocket announces that El Cascamorras has entered town and the church bells peal out, as thousands of well-dressed citizens dodge for cover. El Cascamorras belabours his hooting, whooping ebony escort with a buffoon's sceptre, a stick with a bundle of rags on the end. He is dipped in a fountain, then presented to the civic dignitaries who are safely lodged on a town hall balcony.

The trail of greasy footsteps and black hand-prints ends at the church and

Franciscan convent of La Merced, resting place of the Virgin. Thwarted in his quest, El Cascamorras is allowed to escape to bathe and take refreshment.

Since 1975, El Cascamorras has been José Villalba Pérez, a Guadix farm-worker. Although he is paid for his annual ordeal, it is the celebrity status he really enjoys.

"Everybody knows me and greets me like an old friend," says José who, perhaps because of his annual ordeal, has a melancholy air.

The day after the run, resplendent in a red, yellow and green uniform, he marches through Baza, twirling his flag over the children's heads and collecting offerings for the Virgin's brotherhood.

A high point for Baza's annual fair and for El Cascamorras comes on September 8, when Guadix officials and their brotherhood are allowed to take part, with Baza's officials, in a procession in homage to the Virgin. El Cascamorras steps proudly along in the place of honour — although next day when he returns to Guadix his failure earns him catcalls and a hail of rotten tomatoes.

"Cervantes used a similar figure to the Cascamorras in one episode of Don Quixote," points out Baza historian Antonio García-Paredes Muñoz. "It is very likely that it was based on what he saw when he visited this area collecting taxes in September 1594."

Another traditional rite takes place near Baza every year on the last Sunday in April. Pilgrims take the precipitous track to the top of Jabalcón, an isolated, 4,800-foot-high rock, to pay homage to another Virgin, La Cabeza.

Near Jabalcón the rising waters of the Negratin reservoir are slowly engulfing Baños de Zújar, a decaying spa. Before the spot is finally flooded, it is still possible to see the marble steps leading to private rooms where generations of old and infirm have sought relief. And, in the shadow of swaying gum and palm trees, to relax in baths of hot sulphurous waters where the legions of Hannibal must once have rested tired limbs.

Many armies have tramped across this corner of Spain. One conflict lasted 172 years. In 1981, scholars in Huéscar, 47 kilometres from Baza, at the foot of the sierra of La Sagra in Granada's extreme north-east, stumbled across the fact that since 1809 it had been at war with Denmark. Nobody had bothered to annul the declaration, made in the heat of the struggle against Napoleon's forces.

After considerable debate, the municipal authorities decided to negotiate with the enemy. The Danish ambassador to Madrid expressed himself willing to talk. And, finally, peace broke out in Huéscar.

ALMERIA

The Plastic Desert

IN the middle of a desert, Manuel Errasti was picking runner beans. He trod carefully to avoid crushing a row of swelling water-melons. Between them and the next line of bean-stalks, hundreds of plump cabbages were reaching maturity.

"After the melons we'll be putting in peppers, then maybe aubergines," said Manuel, a cheerful Basque. "You never stop planting and picking here. The work goes on all year round." He wiped the sweat from his brow. "If you think this is hot, come back at midday."

Beneath a roof of plastic, the heat and humidity were overwhelming. Crops grow at a phenomenal rate in this hothouse. And thousands like it cover 12,000 hectares of what was once a useless wilderness in Spain's most arid and God-forsaken corner. This "green revolution", which employs new agricultural techniques, has brought prosperity to a section of Almería, which until recently was the country's poorest province.

A glittering sea of *"plasticultura"* floods up to the unlovely boom town of El Ejido, whose previous claim to fame was that it spawned Manolo *(Viva España)* Escobar, a jaunty pop singer beloved by Spanish housewives. In one of his songs Manolo lauded his native province as a "paradise of love". Perhaps so, but the rest of the world neglected Almería. It was considered all right for making "spaghetti westerns" and growing esparto grass and luscious eating grapes, but little else.

Until recently, a curse seemed to lie on Almería and it is hardly surprising that some natives sought help from the Indalo. The earliest known representation of this stick figure holding aloft an arc was found scratched in ochre on the wall of Los Letreros cave, near the town of Vélez Blanco. It is thought to depict a prehistoric deity and popular belief credits it with the power to ward off disease, lightning bolts and other disasters.

Reflecting the isolation they have often felt, an *almeriense* commented drily: "The rest of Spain has always turned its back on us, as though we didn't exist, so we've become more outward-looking, true Mediterranean people, travellers. Even when it rains over the whole country, not a drop falls here. It's as if we're not a part of Spain, but somewhere else."

Almería is, indeed, a land apart. It is austere, stripped-down, spectacular and cruel. Dazzling light, flat-roofed dwellings, naked sierras, palm tree oases amid ochre wilderness, all speak of another continent, of Africa. Only 400,000 inhabitants are scattered across the province's 8,700 square kilometres.

Roquetas de Mar, once a simple fishing port, has great ambitions as a tourist resort and Mojácar makes a bid for up-market visitors. But you will seldom hear more than a goatherd's lament on lonely, cliff-hemmed beaches near the Cabo de Gata. Recently, 26,000 hectares of this largely virgin zone have been declared a natural park.

Considering that it is Spain's sunniest province, Almería is understand-ably put out by Málaga's appropriation of the title Costa del Sol. Did not most medieval references call the coast near the Sierra de Gador the "Sahal del Sol"? And did not a local hotelier produce a brochure in 1928 labelling the strip from Motril, in Granada province, to Cabo de Gata the "Costa del Sol"?

The unending sunshine is a valuable resource, as long as water is avail-able. Those farming under plastic, in so-called *invernaderos,* pump water from wells as deep as 100 metres. Thus, when snow covers northern Europe, tomatoes and strawberries flow from the once-barren fields around El Ejido, and thousands of freshly-cut roses, carnations and gladioli are shipped out daily to Spanish and foreign markets.

Pepe Fernández, one of the farmers riding the crest of the boom which began in the early Seventies, explained how it is done.

"A piece of desert here sells for millions of pesetas per hectare, but you can recoup your investment in two or three years — if you know what you're doing. First, you remove all the rocks, then analyse the soil to see what it lacks. Spread 70 tons of organic manure per hectare, plus maybe 4,000 kilos of fertilizer. Truck in 700 cubic metres of sand and spread it 15 centimetres deep. That retains heat and moisture in the soil. Pipe in water and cover the lot with plastic sheeting.

"Then, start planting, putting in another crop as one matures. It's simple. Of course, you have to work like a slave twelve months of the year."

Peasant farmers who could hardly rub two burros together now live well off one hectare of land and expect fresh impetus from Spain's membership of the European Community. Of course, problems do exist. Sudden wealth has provoked grave social stress and El Ejido has an alarming number of suicides and alcoholics. Experts have also warned that unrestrained tapping of the water table will cause salination problems.

Farmers without any water or the cash to invest in *plasticultura* have other concerns. Sadly surveying withered crops, one said: "They say all these *invernaderos* are stopping the rain falling. Or perhaps it's that solar energy station that's doing it."

A guaranteed average of 320 days' sunshine a year can be a curse, but if it can be harnessed on a commercial basis, it could transform Almería. One day solar energy could solve the water crisis by powering massive desalina-tion plants. One day...

They are working on the problem at a 100-hectare research centre near the town of Tabernas, a half-hour drive from the provincial capital. Arrayed over torrid scrubland, hundreds of heliostats follow the sun's path, like computer-guided sunflowers, bouncing their rays into receptors. The heat generated is enough to power turbines, thus creating current that is fed into the national grid.

Nine member-countries of the International Energy Agency started investigating the possibilities of producing electricity from solar radiation here in 1981. Two years later, Spain's Energy ministry began an additional 1,200-kilowatt project using all-Spanish technology.

"Costs are growing closer to those for conventional energy sources," said a researcher at Tabernas. "Don't ask me when solar power will be commercially viable. That's the 64,000-dollar question. Here we are testing prototypes and we don't know how much these components would cost if produced on a mass scale."

Apart from its dramatically-situated ruined fortress crowning a hill, nearby Tabernas is a nondescript town on national highway N-340. But it had its moments of glory in the 1960s when as many as nine films were being made in the vicinity at the same time. Clear skies and a lunar landscape reminiscent of the Arizona badlands, plus — at that time — low labour costs, brought the film-makers.

Clint Eastwood, Raquel Welch, Charles Bronson, Brigitte Bardot and a host of others sweated in the dust and heat of Almería. Epic "spaghetti westerns" like *The Good, the Bad and the Ugly* and *A Fistful of Dollars* were directed here by Sergio Leone. A torrent of cash flowed into Almería. But then the caravan moved on, and thousands of extras and stuntmen, specialists in playing Cheyenne Indians, Mexican bandits and US cavalrymen, were left with their dreams.

At Mini Hollywood, a replica of a Wild West settlement, they made more than 100 films. Lee Van Cleef once walked its dusty streets. These days you may come across another gunslinger, Pepe "El Habichuela".

A shrivelled figure in Western dress, Pepe will tilt back his stetson and tell you he had speaking parts in dozens of Westerns. Usually he died, violently.

"I got my nickname *'Habichuela'* (the Bean) from the time when I worked in transport for farm produce," he recalls. "Then I went into films and became famous. I'm known the world over. I don't need to call the directors. They know my number. 'Hey, Pepe,' they say, 'we need you.' "

They still make some films and a few television commercials in Almería, using the spectacular terrain, a ruined Mexican pueblo or the replica fort as backdrops. But Mini Hollywood relies mainly on tourists. You can have your photo taken on the town scaffold, head inside a noose, as a souvenir. And at weekends a bunch of desperados, headed by ex-amateur boxer Alberto Aleman Castillo, stage hold-ups and shoot-outs for visitors.

Between shows, Alberto and his stuntmen lounge in the Stela Saloon, gambling to see who should pay for the next round of Coca-Colas. Stubble-bearded Alberto, sporting a sheriff's badge, said: "We do everything — fights, falls from roofs and horses, you name it. We're true aficionados of the West. It still lives for us."

One of the same conditions that attracted film-makers, unpolluted, crystalline air, was an important factor in the installation by West Germany's Max Plank Astronomy Institute of a battery of telescopes in the Sierra de Filabres, north of Tabernas. At Calar Alto, more than 7,000 feet above sea-level, astronomers can study the heavens 200 nights a year, four times the number in Germany.

Below Calar Alto sits the typical town of Gérgal dominated by a squat medieval castle. The refurbished castle belongs to a local boy who studied pharmacology, went off to Cádiz to make his fortune, and returned to buy the most impressive residence in town.

Amid the bleak ranges of the Filabres, the village of Lijar straddles a ridge. It is about as remote a spot as you can find, but Lijar stirred international interest when it came to light that its 650 inhabitants were at war with France. (Andalusia's fiercely independent municipalities are not afraid to declare war on entire nations, see also Huéscar, Chapter 8.) Angered by an alleged insult to King Alfonso XII when he was passing through Paris in 1883, the Lijar mayor at that time — a Don Quixote character known as the Terror of the Sierra de Filabres — formally declared war. He was confident of the result since he estimated that each inhabitant was worth 10,000 Frenchmen.

News of the bloodless 100-year war provoked top-level diplomatic action. The French consul in Málaga travelled the winding road to Lijar to sign a peace treaty on October 30, 1983. A plaque commemorates the event on the school wall in the village square.

But Antonio, a waiter in a nearby bar, told me: "About 90 per cent of the people would have preferred not to sign the peace treaty. They thought the war should go on because, at the time, France had been acting in an unfriendly manner to Spain."

Even so, the main square is now called the Plaza de la Paz. It is paved in marble, a substance in abundant supply in this district. Nearby, explosives tear at a whole mountain of marble, and in the Olula del Río area (to the north in the Almanzora valley) more than 200 companies work with the beautifully distinctive material which comes in white, veined grey and green.

"Our marble is superior in quality to that of Carrara. Theirs is easier to work because it is softer, but ours lasts longer. They used it in the Alhambra in Granada, and that dates back to the 13th century," boasted Antonio Sabiote, who with brothers Diego and José runs one of the best-known firms in Macael, the industry's centre.

In the workshop, craftsmen cut and polish marble for chessboards and fireplaces and dining-tables. The monument to the 1978 democratic Constitution was made here. Now it stands on Madrid's Castellana avenue.

A number of Almería's poor, bleached pueblos shelter individualistic craftsmen. At Sorbas, an unlikely conglomeration of cubist architecture teetering on the edge of a chasm on the Almería-Murcia highway, José García, one of three brothers who are potters, demonstrates a particularly whimsical touch. Comic pigs and cross-eyed owls are among his creations.

South of Sorbas, a road twists over the arid heights of the Sierra Alhamilla to Níjar, also long-famed for its pottery. Set above an oasis of palm and orange trees, the village is also known for its production of *jarapas*, colourful blankets woven from odd ends of cloth. But many Spaniards associate Níjar with a dramatic saga of passion and fury played out in 1928.

Francisca was about to marry Casimiro, at a *cortijo* (farm) near Níjar. The marriage was hardly made in heaven. The young bride was lame and unprepossessing, but her father had settled land on her and a dowry. A sister is said to have encouraged the marriage, for which Francisca had no enthusiasm. A few hours before the ceremony, she eloped with her cousin, Francisco. They had only travelled a short distance when Francisco was shot down and Francisca only escaped by feigning death.

The sister and her husband were later tried and convicted. Casimiro, the groom, felt so humiliated that ever afterwards he refused even to look at a photograph of Francisca. She never married and lived as a recluse until her death in 1978, never speaking of her day of shame. The incident became famous because it inspired Federico García Lorca, who never visited Níjar, to write his play *Blood Wedding (Bodas de Sangre)*.

Bleached mountains and dry river-beds are a feature of Almería, but in some areas the vegetation provides a vivid contrast. North of the provincial capital, groves of orange trees flourish. West towards Canjayar irrigated grapevines raised on stilts smother the steep terraces in a green carpet.

Those Almerian eating grapes will make any mouth water. They used to be shipped out by the ton from Almería, packed in casks in sawdust or powdered cork. Now they are more likely to travel by refrigerated, juggernaut lorries.

With the closing of old iron mines, Almería's port has lost much of its bustle. But ferries still ply regularly to and from Melilla, the Spanish enclave on the African coast, bearing uniformed legionnaires and robed Moroccans. Another link with Africa can be found below the massive brown walls of the *alcazaba,* the impressive fortress towering over the capital. High-stepping antelope, timid desert foxes, and vicious-fanged jackals have found sanctuary in the Centro de Rescate de la Fauna Sahariana.

It was a close thing. Hungry tribesmen, oil prospectors, and finally a bitter guerrilla war in the Western Sahara all took their toll of desert species. Many came close to being wiped out. Set up in 1971 with support from the World Wildlife Fund, the rescue centre brought surviving animals, birds and reptiles to the European spot most closely matching the Saharan climate, Almería.

Dedicated sanctuary worker Mar Cano, a blonde, pony-tailed biologist, paused from the task of injecting a hyena to say: "We have brought back several breeds from the edge of extinction. Zoos in the United States and Germany have been supplied with animals and now we are starting to return animals to Africa, provided their safety is guaranteed."

From the ramparts of the *alcazaba* one can glimpse dozens of antelope and gazelle munching spiny titbits. The fortress too has found peace after centuries of being knocked about by earthquakes and cannon- balls. Much of it was constructed 1,000 years ago by Abd ar-Rahman III, Caliph of Córdoba. The greatest years for the city, known to the Moors as "Mirror of the Sea", came later when it ruled a kingdom covering a large chunk of Andalusia and Murcia. It was both a noted cultural centre and major exporter of fine silk. Twenty thousand men could shelter within the castle's triple girdle of walls. Today, much restored, the walls enclose pleasant gardens dotted with oleander, cacti and flowers.

No doubt the scent of jasmine filtered up to the *Ventana de la Odalisca* (the "Concubine's Window") when long ago the Moorish ruler's favourite stood there for the last time. She had tried to run off with a Christian prisoner with whom she had fallen in love. They were caught and her lover was hurled to his death from the window. A few days later, the grief-stricken concubine threw herself into the chasm too, or so runs the legend.

In Christian times, a bell in the Torre de la Vela used to toll the hours for those controlling irrigation in the adjacent countryside. It also sounded a warning when Barbary pirates were sighted. The devastation caused along the coast by the pirates eventually influenced the design of Almería's cathedral. When it was built in 1524 to replace the mosque, which had been pulverized by an earth tremor, it was given a heavy, fortress-like aspect.

Modern Almería, sprouting antennas and concrete blocks, has lost some of its elegance but also some of the colourful squalor that characterized the gypsy quarter of La Chanca. Faceless banks and office buildings have replaced the old mansions of the main thoroughfare, the Paseo de Almería. But the shady promenade retains its easy, provincial pace.

The pace is even more relaxed along the coast north of Cabo de Gata.

At La Isleta, a weather-scoured hamlet, I watched fishing boats rocking on an azure sea and at a small bar ordered fresh mullet. The helpings were big and the beer was cold and an old woman sang as she laundered at the communal wash-house.

Further north, beyond the gold mines of Rodalquilar, beyond the lonely headlands that plunge into translucent waters inhabited by sea anemone, octopuses and spear-fishermen, beyond the fishing community of Carboneras, they are busy fabricating the "new" tourist Spain. Mojácar was tumbling into ruin on its hilltop two kilometres from the sea until doctors, diplomats and artists moved in. Swiftly it became an Andalusian Chelsea, chic, then trendy, then, as package-deal tourism arrived, merely pretentious.

Mojácar is tasteful compared to most coastal developments, but the quaintness can be overpowering. With its boutiques and smooth bars, it does not really fit into Almería, the land of true grit. It looks as though it has been trucked in from somewhere else.

Totally unreal. Not at all like Mini Hollywood. There, when *"High Noon"* is sounding over the loudspeakers, desert dust is swirling about Boot Hill, and the stakes are high in the Stela Saloon, a man feels at home.

Cave chimneys sprout from a moonscape at Guadix with the cathedral and Moorish castle in the background. Thousands still live underground in the area but many, like José Antonio Sola pictured, left, in his Dehesa de Guadix living-room, enjoys all modern conveniences.

A "cowboy" bites the dust at a western film set in Almería while, below: villagers raise water from a well near San José.

Manuel Errasti picks beans in one of Almería's countless plastic-covered hothouses. Below: an oily fiesta at Baza.

*A young shepherd, with cigarette in hand, tends his flock
near the village of Portugos.*

South From Granada

IN winter, snow-chilled winds gust down from the Sierra Nevada, tugging at the television aerials and rattling the windows of the highest village in Spain. Families huddle around the circular living-room tables toasting their feet before the hot coals of the *braseros* (braziers).

Though the air is glacial and their breath steams, the hardy folk of Trevélez, in Granada province, don't complain. They know that, while the Alpine weather raises human goose pimples, it is working its magic on a regiment of pigs' buttocks.

It is one of history's ironies that the Alpujarras region, a last redoubt of Muslim settlement in Spain, should today be renowned for its sierra-cured hams. Yet slotted into a tight valley which climbs to Spain's rooftop, the towering bulk of Mulhacén, Trevélez — at 4,840 feet above sea-level — bulges with succulent hams. Few of them, however, orginate there. Instead, they are trucked in from other parts of Spain to mature in the frosty air and to acquire the seal that assures they have been mountain-cured.

"They bring them here because we have ideal conditions, 60 to 70 degrees humidity and a winter temperature of two to eight degrees," explains Joaquín González, who has more than a thousand hams hanging in his bar.

"The process is strictly controlled. See, this ham has been rejected." He taps one, indicating the hollow response. "For the first eight days the hams soak in a salt bath, then they are washed and hung. After five months we rub them with lard to stop them drying out, then hang them up for another seven months."

Joaquín, an energetic man in his forties, never went to school. He learned to read and write from his mother, roamed the country selling goods from his lorry, then returned to serve a term as mayor of his village. He has a taste for Mozart and Beethoven, and for speaking out.

"There are a lot of under-educated people around here," he declares. "If they own a dog, they think they're cattle-ranchers, and if they have a window-box, they reckon themselves landowners."

Not such a far-fetched statement. In the perpendicular landscape of Las

Alpujarras, wealth is a grove of almond trees or a herd of goats. That is the way it has been for centuries in one of Andalusia's most spectacular regions, a 75-kilometre-long piece of rumpled parchment cast down in Granada and Almería provinces between the Sierra Nevada and the Mediterranean.

Appropriately enough, considering the formidable terrain, the name Las Alpujarras, or La Alpujarra (either version is correct), may be derived from the Arabic *"abuxarra"*, meaning "the untameable". But that is only one of a number of theories. It could stem from *"al-busarrat"*, meaning "sierra of pastures", or from a warrior called Ibrahim Abuxarra. Another theory maintains that "alp" is an ancient European word meaning "white" and that Alpujarras evolved from *"alba sierra"*.

Echoes of Africa and old customs linger in the remote, flat-roofed villages of this region and for centuries it remained a truly hidden world because of its inaccessibility. When a young Englishman named Gerald Brenan arrived in the Alpujarras in 1920, intending to educate himself with his 2,000 books, and rented a house in Yegen for 120 pesetas a year, only mule tracks linked most communities. As recently as the 1950s, Swiss writer Jean-Christian Spahni recorded how children fled crying at his approach, believing he was the dreaded *sacamantecas* (a bogeyman who feeds on infant flesh). And one woman confessed she had thought his pack contained the heads of travellers he had killed.

Much has changed since then. Paved roads have reduced the isolation. Schooling and medical care are available for all. Newcomers — dubbed *los peludos* (the hairy ones) by the locals — have come seeking tranquillity and more adventurous tourists are penetrating the hidden valleys.

But much remains the same. The Alpujarras retains its distinctive character. It is as dizzying as ever to gaze out from the heights of Capileira, or Soportújar, or Mecina Bombarón, and marvel at the clarity of the air and the stillness, broken only by the music of goats' bells and tumbling water. In the terraced fields carved out by sheer determination amid angry crags and dark ravines, the *alpujarreños* hoe and plough with ancient tools, irrigating with a system devised by the Moors.

"There's no water like ours. Taste it. And no better fruit and vegetables. Try them," an *alpujarreño* urged.

In the shadow of 11,400-feet-high Mulhacén (named after Muley Hacén, 15th-century king of Granada), gushing snow-fed springs allow crops to flourish and groves of chestnut trees, oak, walnut and poplar to spread their shade. This landscape is very different from the raw mass, across the Guadalfeo valley, of the Contraviesa range, which is better known for its pink and hearty wine than for its water. Albondón, occupying a grandstand view of the Mediterranean, is the production centre for Contraviesa wine, often sold as *"vino de la costa"*.

Lanjarón, in contrast, lives from its waters. Like many spa centres, it has a certain melancholy air, but that does not worry the thousands of visitors, many old and infirm, who flock to the peaceful little town 46 kilometres from Granada and on the threshold of the Alpujarras. They relax tired limbs in bubble baths, enjoy underwater massage, take courses of inhalation and respiration, and sip the waters. Lanjarón promises relief from everything, whether sinusitis or arthritis, obesity or lumbago, bronchitis or nervous tension.

What is so special about the water? It is rich in a number of minerals which are good for the system and also, since the springs are fed by the snows of the Sierra Nevada, there is plenty of it. The company which sells the magical product over much of Spain has access to no fewer than 42 springs, from which bubbles water with a variety of contents and qualities. It undergoes a strict purifying process, being filtered again and again as it passes through gleaming stainless steel tanks. It is bottled at the rate of 400,000 litres a day.

Miguel Cuesta, the company's technical manager, indicates the germ-free bottling area, which spotlessly-overalled staff enter or leave via air-locks. "You see, we have tight controls. It's not simply a case of taking water out of the ground and selling it at a profit," he says, leading me to his laboratory. "This is where we check samples daily. Do I drink the water? Naturally. It's good for you!"

Water is so important to Lanjarón that a fiesta has been created around it. Just after midnight on the day of San Juan (June 24), a rocket fizzes skywards to announce the start of a water battle. Nobody who ventures into the street is likely to escape a dousing as the townsfolk lightheartedly splash their most abundant commodity around.

East of Lanjarón, Route C-333 winds down past olive groves and orange trees to Orgiva, capital of this end of the Alpujarras, a pleasant town which explodes into deafening life on the day of its patron saint, two weeks before Good Friday. Following a tradition of the zone's iron miners, the night is rent by a relentless succession of detonations: fireworks, shotguns, rockets and blasting charges.

An unusual building, just out of town, is a reminder that during the Civil War more dangerous explosions disturbed the peace of Orgiva. With its crenellated ramparts, the Castillo de Helios appears to be steeped in history. In fact, it was built in 1932. The owner obviously expected trouble since it features bullet-proof shutters and slits for defenders to fire through.

"When the Nationalist army confronted the Republicans in this valley, the castle became General Franco's local headquarters and radio station. You can still see bullet holes in the walls caused by attackers," points out Dutch-born photographer Karel Kramer, who, with his wife, bought the castle in 1977.

The Kramers are among new settlers attracted to the region. Some came to retire, others to work and raise a family, like Alberto Recio, from Aranjuez near Madrid.

"The winds brought me here," says Alberto of his decision to buy a bramble-covered plot of land with no road, water or electricity. A rough track leads to his secluded home, a two-storey dwelling in a wooded cleft near Pitres. Solar panels furnish electricity and a well provides enough water for bumper crops of strawberries and a swimming pool.

"An old fellow came from Granada with a divining rod and, sure enough, he found water just eight feet down," says Alberto, whose skill in making finely-crafted pottery earns an income for himself, wife Mabel and three young children.

A number of wanderers have heeded the message in blue and white tiles at the entrance of Pampaneira: "Traveller, stay and live with us." This community is the lowest of three pretty villages, Pampaneira, Bubión and Capileira, which mark, like steps in a ladder, the different levels of the Poqueira valley, one of the region's most picturesque — and most visited — corners. Some of the travellers who have stayed live far above the valley, at an altitude of 5,000 feet, in as isolated and bleak a spot as you could hope to find. A bumpy track, which swiftly becomes impassable after rainstorms, struggles up to a group of stone cabins clinging to the rocky hillside. On the steep paths connecting them signs request "Silence, please". Every morning, just before seven, a gong rings out to signal that another day has started in O-Sel-Ling, the Place of Clear Light.

This meditation centre received its name from the Dalai Lama, when he visited in 1982, and it is not unusual to glimpse a shaven-headed disciple of Buddha walking the paths, his saffron robe fluttering in the breeze. In 1987, the centre received considerable media attention when a 20-month-old Spanish boy was acclaimed by the international Buddhist community as a reincarnated Tibetan lama. His parents, bricklayer Francisco Hita and his wife María, who helped found the retreat, had no doubt that chubby little Osel was indeed the reincarnation of a Tibetan spiritual teacher, who died in 1984. "He passed all the tests," they said. "We feel privileged that he was chosen."

The family left the Alpujarras and moved to Nepal, where Osel received special tuition in a monastery. The centre, however, remains, attracting persons of all faiths, or no faith at all, who feel the wish to retire from the world for a time. In the words of François Camus, a Frenchman who once spent two months in one of the cabins without contact with another human: "Meditation and examining one's interior space is like travelling through the Amazon jungle. It's an adventure."

François lives in Bubión, one of the Poqueira valley villages which typify the unique Alpujarras architecture. This is closer to that of the Berbers than of other Spanish regions, reflecting the era when mosques, not church towers, dotted the hills. Narrow, cobbled streets often pass under the terraces or rooms of houses which are so piled on one another that if the wrong domino were removed, one can imagine the whole pyramid collapsing into the *barranco*.

In the past, the thick stone walls were not whitewashed. Embedded in them are beams of chestnut over which are laid slate tiles. This roof is topped off with earth and pebbles and then grey slate rubble. What look like stunted, flat-headed snowmen standing on the flat roofs prove, on closer inspection, to be chimney-pots.

When sultans ruled in Granada, great fortunes were made by silk merchants who traded the colourful blankets and carpets of the Alpujarras. Many artisan skills died with the eviction of the Moors and later competition from factory-made textiles, but efforts are being made to revive them. Near Pampaneira's church square I found a room ringing with the clack of a flying shuttle.

Francisco Tovar Lopes and Mercedes Carrascosa Martín, both in their twenties, create new designs in their workshop as well as following traditional styles. "I started weaving because no work was available, but now there is growing interest in these old skills," says Mercedes. And, indeed, schemes are under way to train local youngsters in handicrafts and even to bring back silk-weaving.

From Pampaneira the road wriggles up the valley to Bubión and Capileira, offering views of terraced fields, timber-clad slopes, precipices and distant peaks which are snow-capped for much of the year. Even though these villages are within yodelling distance of one another, rivalry has always been fierce between them. Until the last decade or so, a local youth needed considerable courage to court a girl from the next village. If he was caught out by his rivals, he risked being tossed into the fountain, or worse.

Greater mobility and acceptance of outside influences are changing the valley's customs and sweeping away taboos. Yet old ways die hard, as I found when I was drinking in a golden sunset from one of Capileira's lofty terraces and encountered Josefa. She was as wrinkled as a dried fig and had only two teeth left, but she still had apple cheeks and a chirpy manner. We chatted and, as I left, I offered my hand. She drew back sharply, declaring proudly: "I don't take the hand of any man. I never have, except that of my husband."

Close to Josefa's home stands Capileira's museum, displaying the region's typical crafts, tools and house furnishings. One of the odder items is a frying pan. It was used during his African adventures by Pedro Antonio de Alarcón, after whom the museum is named. His book, *La Alpujarra, Sixty Leagues on Horseback,* detailing his 1872 journey, is still worth reading.

Alarcón did not reach Capileira, but the beauty of its position and the clarity of its air make it a magnet for today's travellers.

Recent visitors include Felipe González (before he became the country's prime minister) and poet Rafael Alberti. Their photographs are in the celebrity line-up in the little restaurant run by lively Granada native Antonia Cobos. Her children, Eduardo and Montserrat, cook the typical Alpujarras fare.

Throughout the region, country food is served in quantities, with a friendliness and at a price you will find in few other parts. A *plato pampaneira,* for example, is a glutton's delight of ham, pork fillet, sausage and blood sausage. One of my most memorable meals consisted of grilled lamb chops, with fresh bread and an earthenware jug of Contraviesa wine, served before an inn's log fire as the snow-flakes danced outside.

Snow blocks the track beyond Capileira most of the year. But in midsummer cars can traverse this lonely route, at 10,000 feet up, the highest in Europe, as far as the Veleta peak before swooping down on a paved road past the Sierra Nevada ski station to Granada.

A turn-off before the Veleta takes motorists bumping seven kilometres along a track which ends just before the summit of Mulhacén. Apart from offering magnificent views, this is a place of pilgrimage. On the morning of August 5, villagers from the Alpujarras trek up Mulhacén to attend a mass in honour of the Virgin of the Snows. Once Trevélez folk used to walk or ride mules up overnight; now four-wheel-drives are favoured.

Cattle, sheep and goats roam these Alpine pastures in summer, watched over by taciturn veterans or youngsters like Juan, a cheerful 15-year-old with an adult's bearing. "Sometimes we truck the animals to the coast in winter. And in summer we walk them up to the heights," he said, puffing a cigarette. "Am I bored with this job? Never. It's fun. And better than going to school!"

But for those who stay home, life can be lonely. The deserted dwellings of Castaras, a hamlet riding a spur amid a jumble of crags and chasms, tell part of the story. Migration has halved the population this century, as young people moved away to seek better jobs and a more comfortable life in the cities or abroad. Perhaps they still dream of Castaras, south of Trevélez, at the end of a road to nowhere, but these days it is inhabited mainly by old folk.

Near the church lives Encarnación Garaluz, an erect, middle-aged widow. She wanders through the whitewashed coolness of her rambling, empty house and sighs: "The young go away because there is so little here. I've three daughters in Barcelona, a daughter in Cadiar, and a son in Orgiva. But in August [she brightens], they all come home. Sometimes I have 18 in the house... in August..."

Castaras has no resident priest, but it does boast a teacher, a doctor, a *practicante*... and a *curandero* (healer).

The Alpujarras has always had its share of curers with apparently mystic powers, and the one currently most celebrated lives close by, at Almegijar. Bus-loads of patients from the distant coast regularly endure the tortuous journey to consult "Pepe the Saint". Many claim miraculous improvements after his treatment, a mixture of prayer, massage, and natural remedies, employing herbs, lard or alcohol.

Pepe Saez's consulting room is in his modern house, the walls of which are lined with thank-you gifts, religious objects and cast-off crutches from his patients. He has no fixed charges. "Pay what you can," he tells his visitors. Their gratitude has been so overwhelming that, according to local gossip, the *curandero* is the wealthiest man in the village. Pepe prefers to make no comment.

On his only day off, Sunday, he takes a drink in the Bar Coca. He is well-built, in his thirties, with thick black hair and brows. There is nothing unusual about him, except perhaps the intensity of his gaze and a quiet assurance. Is it true that he can correctly diagnose an ailment merely by looking at a patient?

Pepe draws finger and thumb across his lips like a zip and says: "I don't want to talk about my work or explain anything. I do my own thing."

He says the same to all. The mystery remains intact and the sick and the lame continue arriving in hundreds.

Across the river-bed from Almegijar, route C-332 winds east to Cadiar, which comes alive twice a month on market days. About 20 mules may be tethered on the edge of the village while their owners chat together, waiting for buyers. If none turn up, it is of no great concern. They sling up a few purchases and ride back into the hills.

In the central square, near a fountain that spouts wine during the October fiesta, stallholders shout their wares. A copper-skinned gypsy woman squats by her roughly-woven baskets and farmers haggle over the price of pack-saddles, painstakingly built of esparto and rushes on a wooden frame.

At the February 3 market, there is extra animation as a band parades through the streets. Cadiar's patron, San Blas, is being honoured and the countryfolk flock in buying vividly-coloured ribbons outside the church before attending mass.

"We hang ribbons around our necks because everybody knows San Blas protects you from throat trouble," explains a veteran worshipper in a black trilby, speaking in a hoarse whisper. "I can't speak louder. My voice has gone after last night's fiesta."

Christianity has ruled in the Alpujarras for 400 years, but the last of the Moors did not go without a fight. It was at Cadiar, in December 1568, that a bloody, desperate war was sparked with the crowning under an olive tree of Aben Humeya, king of the Moriscos.

Inhabitants of the Alpujarras had long been regarded as warlike and independent. Christian attitudes after the Moorish kingdom of Granada fell in 1492 did not encourage them to change. Heavy pressure was exerted to persuade them to change religion, converts to Christianity being known as Moriscos. The last straw came in 1567 with an edict that banned the use of Arabic, Arab names, traditional dress, customs and music. Women were even forbidden to use henna as an adornment.

Raiding bands of outlaws, known as the *monfies,* had already posed a challenge to the Castilian rulers. With the crowning of Aben Humeya, a savage war erupted. The Moriscos sacked churches, and burned and slaughtered while the Christian soldiers plundered the land, seizing Moriscos as slaves. When Morisco families took refuge in caves, bonfires were set at the entrances. In a cave at Mecina Bombarón 260 Moriscos were captured, but another 120 were suffocated by smoke.

Finally, the Moriscos were crushed and the history of the Alpujarras took a new course. The Moriscos, an estimated 48,000, were expelled and scattered about other regions. In their place arrived settlers from Galicia, Extremadura and Castile. But crops, cattle and treasures of the Moriscos had vanished as booty and, initially, many of the new arrivals lived in misery.

The Alpujarras had been won for Christianity but ruined in the process. And poor Aben Humeya, an immature youngster with large, dark eyes, a small beard and a taste for female company, was killed by treacherous followers at Laujar in Almería province after a reign of barely 10 months. Surprised in bed, he was wrenched from his two lovers and strangled. (He is said to have hidden his treasure, known as "the golden fleece of the Alpujarra", in a cave near Trevélez.)

But Aben Humeya is reborn every year in his native village of Valor (east from Cadiar on C-332) when the battle of the Moors and Christians is replayed. It takes place in mid-September during the fiesta of the *Cristo de la Yedra,* whose image miraculously escaped the vengeance of the Moriscos.

Battle begins in the church square in the midday heat, before the rapt gaze of hundreds of villagers and visitors. Arrayed in splendid costumes, the mounted leaders of the two factions — aided these days by microphones —

hurl threats at one another as their armies of about 50 villagers, toting shot-guns, stand by.

"The words are not written down. It's all in our heads, passed from person to person," farmer Francisco Cobo, the director, told me. He plays the leader of the Christians with the authority that nearly 30 years' experience has given him.

Only once in living memory have the villagers failed to keep their annual appointment. It was during the Civil War when the costumes were burned. The play dates from the early 17th century and is based on a faded document in the town hall archives; it is said to be the oldest of its kind in Andalusia.

"A Granada writer noted down details of the script but the text is not complete. I've spent two years trying to trace it in the National Library in Madrid, but without success," says philology student Paco Escudero.

Paco is Aben Humeya. His team includes two spies and six horsemen. Rockets soar as they and their white-robed Morisco followers storm into the square and capture the wooden fort amid a fusillade of exploding blanks. The diminutive Christian governor, in doublet and hose, is ejected, head first, from the battlements. Then it's time for lunch.

Between liquid refreshments, the *moros* and *cristianos* cheerfully con-tinue blasting away with their shotguns, two barrels at a time for maximum effect, until the walls tremble and the air is thick with fumes and the smell of gunpowder. In the evening, the Christian soldiers — by now flushed and a touch emotional — return for a shattering climax, retaking the fort and restoring the portrait of Christ to its rightful place. Amid the swirling gunsmoke, Paco recognizes his mistake and promises to be a good Christian.

Valor is proud of its history. The village *discoteca* carries the name of Aben Humeya. So does a musical group which has won prizes in Alpujarran competitions held to stimulate the revival of traditional songs and dances, a haunting blend of Arab and Spanish culture.

"Although many Galicians settled here, we recently discovered that 40 families, a priest and a sacristan came to Valor from Ibro in Jaén province. The *libro de apeo,* the old record, shows this," local bank manager and civic leader Juan Manuel Martés Escudero informed me. "Settlers were given a piece of land, one cow, one mule and some tools. Today the average size of a farm is one hectare and we're no millionaires. But people are not as poor as they may appear."

Maize, beans, peppers flourish around Valor, and in high summer, the circular wheat-threshing platforms are scenes of dusty industry. Apricot trees cast pleasant shade at Yegen, Valor's humbler neighbour, brilliantly evoked in Gerald Brenan's book *South from Granada.* A plaque marks the one-time home of the English writer, who contributed so much to an understanding of Spain and its people.

"One or two folk were offended by the book," admit a group of teenagers in a sleepy Yegen square where the women come to fill their pails. "But that was only because they objected to certain references to their families. And some did not even read it. We think it's a fine work."

In *South from Granada,* Brenan recalls the excitement of the October fair at Ugijar, a crossroads in the more open country of the eastern Alpujarras. The fair still attracts large crowds. It honours the patron of the whole region, the Virgen del Martirio. During the Morisco rebellion she was ripped from her temple, dragged through the streets, burned and used as a foot-bridge. But Virgins are resilient souls. Her image was rescued by Christians and hidden. In 1606, when a well was being cleaned, she was found. "I am called Martyr," declared the Virgin, and ever since the well-water has been said to possess miraculous qualities.

From Ugijar, C-332 swings over the Alcolea river into the Almería section of the Alpujarras. The country grows steadily more desiccated, very different in character from the western Alpujarras. Eroded and treeless, the Sierra de Gador sprawls like a whale between the green valley of the Rio Andarax and the sea. But Laujar, near the river's source, is an idyllic spot. Even when no rain falls, greenery is guaranteed by the water seeping down from the snow of the high sierras.

It's easy to slip into the village atmosphere, dozing over heat-hazy views of irrigated fields from a mirador. Nearby, tiles crumble on the sign for the Biblioteca Villaespesa. Born in Laujar in 1877, poet and dramatist Francisco Villaespesa, a contemporary of Ruben Dario and Pio Baroja, achieved considerable popularity in Spain and Latin America.

Trellised vines patrol the slopes around the Andarax valley, whose villages — Padules, Ohanes, Canjayar — are justly renowned for delicious eating grapes. Laujar itself produces a characterful wine. But Villaespesa found his inspiration in the village water.

"Six fountains has my pueblo," he recorded. "And he who drinks their waters/Will never forget them,/So heavenly is their taste."

The lines are inscribed next to one of the fountains, in the centre of Laujar. But they could easily apply to any of the villages in the secret world of the Alpujarras.

This Place of Dreams

ON a crisp day in January the famous victory is celebrated with due pomp. It is a time of drums and bugles, when the golden crown of Queen Isabel and the sword of King Ferdinand are reverently lifted from their resting places in the cathedral and borne through the streets, solemnly attended by stern-faced military, graciously nodding clerics and swelling civic dignitaries.

From the city hall balcony, a top-hatted councillor cries three times: "Granada!" and three times the crowd roars back: "*¿Qué?*"

"Granada for the illustrious Kings of Spain, Don Fernando the Fifth of Aragón and Doña Isabel the First of Castile!" rings out the voice from the balcony. "*¡Viva España! ¡Viva el Rey! ¡Viva Andalucía! ¡Viva Granada!*"

Three times the royal standard is waved, and the national anthem booms out. Thus, Granada annually celebrates *La Toma,* "The Taking" of the city from the Moors, the culmination of the Christian Reconquest. It is a colourful, cheerful occasion. Afterwards, the crowd disperses, halting to buy hot chestnuts roasted on street-corner braziers, or to enjoy tapas, warmth and conversation in the bars.

Quite a few girls ascend giggling to the Torre de la Vela, the watchtower in the Alhambra, to ring the great, 12-ton bell. In days gone by, the bell was rung to regulate the opening and shutting of irrigation channels in the Vega (the fertile plain at Granada's feet). But on this one day in the year the *manolas,* as the girls are called, hope its peals will attract a boyfriend. Those who follow the tradition are supposed to find a husband within the year.

Not everybody, however, thinks the *Día de la Toma,* is one for rejoicing. Many Andalusians believe the events of 1492 should be mourned because they crushed a unique culture, which was more civilized and tolerant than the one that succeeded it. Indeed, before they went to their lead tombs in the depths of Granada cathedral, the Catholic Monarchs laid a shroud of repression and obscurantism over Spain — a legacy from which the country is still recovering.

Granada has never recovered the brilliance it enjoyed under the Nazarid dynasty, and some say this still rankles in its residents' subconscious. Jews and Muslims were drummed out of the once-thriving capital of the last Moorish kingdom. Warriors, feudal nobles and the zealots of the Inquisition imposed their will and Granada tumbled into steep decline.

At the beginning of this century, Baedeker noted that it was a hungry town. "The side-streets are full of filth and decay, and some of the more remote are not even lighted at night. The local aristocracy prefers to spend its rents in Madrid. A large proportion of the population subsists by begging alone."

With its bustling air of prosperity, modern Granada presents a very different scene. High-rise buildings have invaded the Vega. The clear mountain air is smudged brown by belching exhausts. Visitors negotiating the chaotic Camino de Ronda, lined with examples of urban madness, are tempted to forget the Alhambra and drive on. A bypass has chipped away more of the once-verdant, unpolluted plain.

Even so, the city's setting is as majestic as ever and dazzling Moorish and Renaissance monuments remain. There may even be one or two of the nightingales noticed by Baedeker still singing amid the elms and cypresses clothing the slopes below the Moorish fortress. No matter how many times you see the old city with the Sierra Nevada crouching above, its snows changing hue by the hour, the scene is guaranteed to take your breath away.

Early last century the Romantics went into eulogies over the city's attractions, and the magic they saw survives. Théophile Gautier commented: "This mixture of water, snow and fire gives Granada a climate unmatched in the world, a true paradise on earth." Intoxicated by his stay amid singing waters and halls seemingly spun from air and light, Washington Irving unleashed his imagination in *Tales of the Alhambra*. About the same time, Victor Hugo wrote: "The Alhambra! The Alhambra! Palace which the spirits have gilded like a dream and filled with harmony." More recently, maestro of the guitar Andrés Segovia, who studied here, described Granada as "this place of dreams, where Our Lord put the seed of music in my soul."

Students are an important part of Granada life today, injecting youthful spirit and rebellion into an otherwise staid provincial centre. Some 40,000 of them attend the university, a good number of whom appear to dedicate their time to daubing slogans on walls. Their zeal does not always go down well with the solid citizenry.

Near the cathedral, in a square where teenagers puff exotic-smelling cigarettes and strum guitars, painted appeals for respect for lesbians and homosexuals assault the eye. "We have to pay to clean all that up," mutters Manolo, a middle-aged shopkeeper. "They should cut the arms of the kids that do it, cut them off at the shoulders! That would teach them a lesson!"

His reaction seems restrained for somebody running an establishment called *La Casa de las Matanzas* (The House of Slaughter). Actually Manolo is a peaceful enough fellow, who happens to sell spices for preserving hams and sausages. But his testy words do give pause for thought.

Although Granadinos live in one of Spain's most beautiful cities, they take a perverse delight in confirming many of the slanderous stories spread by envious rivals. "We have never had a good press," admits native writer Francisco Izquierdo. A Granadino "does not worry too much if you call him *malafolla* (cantankerous) or stingy, simply because he really is *malafolla* and mean," he says, adding that this capacity for self-criticism denotes a high degree of education in the citizenry.

"It's true that we are careful with money," one professional woman told me. "Remember the famous quotation that nothing is worse than being blind in Granada, because of its beauty? Well, one joke says there's no worse luck than having an aunt from Granada, as you can expect no gifts."

Commanding a province that varies from semi-tropical coast to semi-desert and includes the fabled Vega, Granada retains the atmosphere of a self-sufficient dominion. It sits more than 2,000 feet above sea-level, conscious of its superiority and – according to its critics – complacent and inward-looking.

If Seville is symbolized by the *caseta* and Córdoba by the patio, Granada is summed up by the *carmen*. This is the typical Moorish-style house, set in a garden of flowers and tinkling fountains, surrounded by a high, impenetrable wall. It is a tranquil, beautiful scene, the inner paradise beloved by the Arabs. But it is also sealed off from fresh influences.

"This is a city of small businesses and many convents, of aristocrats and priests," says young author Antonio Muñoz Molina. "It suffers from having a middle class which does not invest creatively. They don't know how to multiply their money, unlike the people of Málaga or Cádiz who have a different mentality. There, the *burguesía* invested in industry.

"It is a centre for the military and bureaucrats, with little trade of any scale. The great sense of self-satisfaction and limited horizons — Granadinos don't travel much — have created an introverted society. At the same time, Granada feels overtaken by Seville and by Málaga. It is always comparing and commiserating with itself. But at least the coming of democracy has been healthy, because it has awakened young people and produced more movement and flexibility."

Muñoz, it should be said, is from the neighbouring province of Jaén. For some years he organized cultural events on behalf of Granada city council, which he found a frustrating task.

"Lorca's case was a perfect example of what this city is," he maintains. "He had to go away to make a name for himself and, when he returned as a success, he was too different to be ignored. He was a thorn in the side. They had to eliminate him."

The poet's death is the cross that Granada has to bear. Just as Dallas is for ever associated with John F. Kennedy, Granada will always be remembered as the city that killed its own, Federico García Lorca, one of the brightest and the best of the writers and artists known as the Generation of 27. Some amends have been made. His birthplace at Fuente Vaqueros, amid the poplars and tobacco fields of the Vega, has been converted into a museum. Close to the village of Viznar, by bubbling waters known to the Moors as the Spring of Tears, a plaque marks the spot where he is believed to have been shot on August 19, 1936.

Exactly how Lorca died was the subject of a cover-up by the Franco regime, which blamed "unknown assassins". Several investigators, including Gerald Brenan, unearthed embarrassing details, but it took an Irish academic to prove beyond doubt who was responsible. With superb detective work, Ian Gibson demonstrated that Fascist supporters of the Nationalist rebellion executed the poet.

Gibson, now a Spanish citizen and a full-time writer, sees Lorca as essentially Andalusian for he had "a primitive, mythical vision with roots deep in the ancient cultures and religions of the Mediterranean". He comments: "If it is true that poets are the last animists in our industrial society, then Lorca is surely one of the greatest. Reading him, or seeing his plays, we enter a prelogical world, presided over by the moon, where man is one more strand in the intricate fibre of life."

In Granada, however, Catholic traditionalists hated Lorca as a dangerous agitator and a *maricón* (homosexual). They could not forget his description of the Catholic Monarchs' victory as "disastrous", nor how he criticized their city as "a wasteland populated by the worst bourgeoisie in Spain today". Even now his memory arouses fierce passions.When director Juan Antonio Bardem, filming Lorca's life story, sought local co-operation, one Granadino told him, "I want nothing to do with that *maricón.*" Fresh winds have blown through democratic Spain, but in Granada some things cannot be forgiven.

Yet Lorca had great affection for his native city, and appreciated its influence on his art. He noted: "The hours are longer and sweeter there than in any other Spanish town... Granada has any amount of good ideas but is incapable of acting on them. Only in such a town, with its inertia and tranquillity, can there exist those exquisite contemplators of water, temperatures and sunsets that we find in Granada."

A contemporary Granada poet and playwright, José Heredia Maya, points out that the inhabitants are fundamentally different to those from other areas of Andalusia. Because this was the last hold-out of the Moors, attracting thousands of fugitives, an extraordinary blending of Catholic, Jewish, Arab and Morisco blood and cultures occurred.

"Granada people are deeper and less folkloric than those of Seville and Cádiz," he says. "It's the difference between Alberti (from Cádiz) and Lorca. Just compare the poems each wrote about the death of the matador Ignacio Sánchez Mejías. *"A las cinco de la tarde..."* that was Lorca, with so much mor depth of feeling.

José spent 10 years directing Granada University Seminary of Flamenco Studies and plans a definitive work on this music whose passion and verve pump adrenalin through the arteries of Andalusia. Flamenco has developed from gypsy, Andalusian, Arabic, Jewish and oriental influences. Today, José points out, it comes in two distinct types. There is the melodic, musical side with its *malagueñas* and *tarantos.* Then there is the far more complex and emotive category which emanates from the gypsies — "this is rhythmic, danceable, it has *duende,* it is the flamenco of the *soleas,* the *siguiriyas,* the *bulerías* and it is evolving all the time."

He dances a few steps on the sunny terrace of his *carmen.* Set amid the narrow streets of the Albaicín (the Falconers' Quarter), it has one of the western world's most memorable views, looking across the Darro river valley to the red-brown walls of the Alhambra. José is one of the minority of Spain's gypsies who through good fortune and talent have managed to rise above their humble beginnings.

Another is Mario Maya, who has been described as "the wizard of flamenco" for his uncanny abilities as dancer and choreographer. As a child he lived in a cave on the cactus-dotted Sacromonte hillside and danced for tourists. An English painter was impressed, created several paintings of him and sold them in London. She sent the cash to help Mario in his studies and he started a climb that would take him to international fame.

Few of Granada's 4,000 gypsies are that fortunate. They largely remain undereducated, scraping a living on the fringes of society. Harsh treatment has always been the gypsies' lot. In 1499, Ferdinand and Isabel ordered the "Egyptians" — so-called because they apparently arrived from Egypt in the 15th century — to settle down and get regular jobs within 60 days. If they did not do so, first offenders received 100 lashes and exile. If they were caught again, the order was "that their ears be cut off and they be permanently expelled."

There is no longer legal discrimination against gypsies, who account for less than one per cent of Andalusia's population, but *payos* (non-gypsies) still have mixed feelings about these nomadic nonconformists. Often there is hostility, sometimes mob violence, against families blamed for criminal acts.

Yet gypsy influences have undoubtedly added spice to Andalusia. Indeed, Lorca was lyrical: "The gypsy is the most distinguished, profound and aristocratic element of my country, the one most representative of its way of being and which best preserves the fire, blood and alphabet of Andalusian and universal truth."

Wide-eyed tourists continue to be lured to the caves of the Sacromonte quarter to watch flamenco dancing, although most of the gypsies now live elsewhere in apartment blocks.

"Hombre, if you want to see real flamenco, come to the cave tonight," appeals Rosa, full-lipped and full-hipped. A pronounced lisp adds to the sensual rhythm of her speech. Smartly dressed in the latest style, she takes the morning sun in the Albaicín with catlike languor. "In our show, the whole family dances, all 30, aunts, uncles, cousins, and my little girl too. She's only three, but she dances as well as the rest. *Hombre,* it's in our blood."

Payos (non-gypsies) find themselves hassled for hand-outs if they stray over Sacromonte, but once a year thousands of Granadinos flock up to the abbey on the hilltop to pay homage to San Cecilio. He is Granada's patron saint, although so turbid is the history of this spot that it seems quite possible he never existed. Heretics in Granada suggest that the highly venerated saint's bones are actually those of a dog. What do exist in the decaying abbey are priceless documents and art works, including manuscripts signed by Maimonides and Averroës. Others are known to have been sold off at give-away prices in Granada by thieves or poverty-stricken clergy. Books banned by the Inquisition are said to gather dust eternally in the Secret File of the Four Keys.

Hopes for a total renovation of Sacromonte Abbey, after years of neglect, were raised when it was proposed as the site for a Euro-Arab university, sponsored by the Arab League, the European Community and the Spanish government. That prospect later faded, but a resurgence of interest in Granada's history has encouraged the return of Islam. The Al-Murabitun community (the name derives from the Almoravides, primitive Berber tribes from the Sahara who swept across Andalusia in the 11th century) holds prayer meetings in the Albaicín and has ambitions to build a mosque. Potters, leather and metal-workers are among its members.

"Granada has *baraka,* it is blessed," says a young craftsman earnestly. "We believe that from here Islam will spread throughout the region once more." Commenting on the number of *chorizos* (petty thieves) in the Albaicín — one street has even been dubbed "Thieves' Alley" with warnings painted in several languages — one convert displays a fundamentalist zeal. "Cut their hands off," he advocates. "After the second example, there would be no more trouble."

Some Muslims dream of resuscitating the glories of yesterday through an independent state called Al-Andalus. The Andalusian Liberation party picked up 6,000 votes in 1986 regional elections. They demanded that Spain fulfilled the surrender conditions signed by Boabdil, the last Moorish ruler, and the Catholic Monarchs. These recognized Muslims' rights to follow their own religion and customs and to bear arms; promises that were swiftly broken.

A rosy aura surrounded Granada under the Moors, but it was hardly a Utopia. Slavery was common. It did not pay to offend a sultan. One Granada king reportedly rewarded intrigue by lopping off the heads of 36 members of the powerful Abencerraje family in a hall of the Alhambra. And there was occasional intolerance: in the 12th century, 4,000 Jews were massacred at Granada.

Under the Christians, things improved. Trials were held first. On the Bibrambla plaza, crowds were entertained by the sight of heretics being burned alive while luckier ones escaped with a few hundred lashes. Later came bull-fights and other tasteful spectacles. Today Bibrambla is the haunt of flower stalls, gypsy peddlers, shoppers, confidence tricksters looking for victims in from the country, and snapshooting visitors. The last time I was there the haunting notes of flutes from the Andes filled the square as five Peruvians played for their supper, which the "stingy" *granadinos* readily paid for.

Not far away, opposite the post office on Puerto Real, I visited a sanc-tuary for the weary, a club for debaters, a trysting place for youngsters, which had been operating for more than 100 years. The Gran Café Granada was a spacious place of columns and mirrors. Ambassadors served at its marble-topped tables, or at least so it appeared, for the waiters, in black suits and bow ties, often looked more distinguished than their clients. One of the junior waiters, José Fernández, who had only been there 35 years, showed me a chair, its leather seat embossed with the letter "S".

"This dates from when the café was first opened, by a Swiss. That's why the place is always known as *El Suizo,*" he commented. "The history of Granada has passed through here. Why, many people started their careers in the Suizo. In the past, when they had nowhere else to study, the students would use these tables for hours at a time, poring over their books. Some have come back years later, full of nostalgia. And one day the king himself came in. He was just a prince then. He sat right over there, against the wall. There are only two other cafés like this left in the whole of Spain, you know. It would be a tragedy if El Suizo disappeared."

Even this sanctum, however, seemed doomed in the name of progress, just as many other irreplaceable Granada buildings have been swept away in favour of soulless glass and concrete. In 1983, city hall stepped in to save El Suizo from demolition, declaring it of historical interest.

Demolishing the Suizo would be akin to destroying the plaza of Mariana Pineda, a Granada heroine martyred last century. At a time when the monstrous King Fernando VII was crushing all liberalism, the authorities heard that somebody in the city was preparing a revolutionary flag. Mariana, a beautiful, blue-eyed widow, was caught embroidering the subversive banner. At her trial a call was made for "the most exemplary punishment", by none other than her defending lawyer. So it was that, on May 26, 1831, Mariana died by the garrotte.

Lorca and his boyhood friends used to sing songs about the woman whose death "made the stones cry". Later, his family moved to a house from which he could see Mariana's statue and he eventually wrote a play about her. It was grim irony that he too would fall victim to hate and oppression, when Civil War madness enveloped Spain.

Mariana's statue is still there and Lorca's play lives on. It is about love and liberty, in Granada, where "the hours are longer and sweeter than in any other town."

Dusted by snow even in warmer months, the 11,400-foot-high Sierra Nevada looms over the town of Cadiar. As the snow melts, it filters down into the valley below to gush up at springs such as those at Lanjarón.

Olive groves carpet Granada province, and the Sierra Nevada, the "roof of Spain", looms in the background. Right: Granada's famous Alhambra Palace.

Youths play their own version of water polo in a cascade near Canjayar in Almería province.

The Forgotten Land

A WAKENING on the summit of El Lucero is like having a balcony seat at the birth of the world. The stark limestone fist juts 5,800 feet above the Costa del Sol, far enough to soften the view of man's banal attempts to improve on nature. Instead, the eye is filled with panoramic grandeur.

On one such purple dawn, Granada province's pine forests swam in the mists to the north. At our feet, the crags of the Sierra Almijara soared out of dark valleys to catch the first light. A thin column of smoke from a distant village climbed vertically in the still air. On the horizon, beyond a sea of flushed silver, rose the mountains of Africa.

El Lucero looks down on La Ajarquía (also spelled Axarquía), a triangular wedge of country bordered by the Mediterranean east of Málaga and the mountains of Granada. A tortuous path leads to El Lucero's peak, which is crowned by the roofless ruin of a Civil Guard post. Years ago, patrols spent weeks at a time on this lonely perch while they scanned the area for outlaws. Occasionally, they found them and gunfire sent the hawks and buzzards wheeling over the sierras. Not until the early 1950s did the last of the post-Civil War rebels end their resistance.

Hunger, intrigue and sudden death were part of daily life for the people of the Ajarquía. "They were hard times, *hombre.* By night we would creep down to seek food which relatives had left us near their farms," recalled El Duende, a shrivelled ghost of a man who once ran a bar in the resort of Nerja.

"How do you think I got this?" he asked on one occasion, abruptly ripping open his shirt to reveal a ghastly scar across his stomach.

"When you served in the Spanish Navy?"

He shook his head.

"Afterwards, when you fought for the Republicans?"

He scoffed.

"In the sierras when you were an outlaw?"

"No, señor!" he chuckled. "In the prison hospital after the Civil Guards caught me. Appendicitis!"

Later, after El Duende had passed on to other battles, somebody told me that he had been a feared guerrilla who allegedly collected the ears of his victims.

Facing page: *oxen are used to plough the terraced fields of the Ajarquía region.*

Peace has come to La Ajarquía but, largely ignored, it still suffers from neglect and lack of amenities. Nevertheless, these 1,100 square kilometres offer some of Andalusia's finest sea and mountain secenery, a fascinating history, a welcoming people and a superb subtropical climate.

Along the coast, from Rincón de la Victoria to near the border with Granada province, where miles of swaying sugar-cane once testified to the wealth of the aristocratic Larios family, developers have planted more profitable crops. They have raised concrete walls at Torre del Mar and Torrox-Costa and constructed villas and replica Andalusian pueblos amid the olive groves.

Inland, however, La Ajarquía mostly still slumbers. Its huddled, white-washed villages echo to the plod of mules, the hills are terraced with vines, and goatmen doze in the shade of spreading carob trees.

"What unifies the Ajarquía is what all these villages have in comon, the total abandonment they have suffered, from the authorities, from everybody," believes Antonio Jiménez, a voluble, live-wire writer based in the market town of Vélez-Málaga, the area's major centre. "This is a privileged region, with great possibilities. But it's still raw material and it will take maybe until the year 2000 to make something of it."

Although Antonio regards himself as "a universal man", he has dedicated himself to raising the consciousness of his native region. He and other enthusiasts formed a study centre with this in mind and in the mid-Eighties the region's first newspaper was launched under his direction.

"I realized people knew nothing of their roots. We didn't know where we had come from nor where we were going," says Antonio.

Traditional dances and other festivities are held now to celebrate the annual Day of the Ajarquía, held usually on the nearest Sunday to March 21. On that day in 1983 a plaque was unveiled on the ancient Moorish castle that dominates Vélez-Málaga. It commemorated the 500th anniversary of the Battle of the Ajarquía, which most local people had never even heard of.

In fact, the battle occurred during the death throes of Moorish rule when Christian forces trying to close in on Málaga suffered a humiliating defeat in the Vélez district. But in 1487 the Catholic Monarchs finally ousted the Moors. Five centuries later there has been a resurgence of interest in Islamic culture and a new readiness to give the Moors their due.

"We're all *moros* here," cheerfully commented a council employee in Comares, an ancient fort and a cluster of houses dramatically glued to a seemingly inaccessible hilltop within sight of Vélez. Comares is famed for its *panda* (gang) of music-makers. They play *verdiales,* lively skull-blasting stuff which — some say — sprang from the olive-pickers' songs in the Moorish era.

It was the Moors, too, who instigated the complicated system of irrigation that feeds the dense network of fields along the coast and valleys. Some of Europe's earliest strawberries come from this zone and plantations of avocados, custard-apples, even mangoes and papaws are replacing less profitable potatoes and tomatoes, as drip-feed irrigation spreads across terraced hillsides.

The lush Vélez valley was renowned for its fruit in Moorish times. Its figs were said to have been prized as far away as Baghdad, and six centuries ago the chronicler Ibn Batouta recorded a desert Berber's comment: "Don't ask me questions about those figs, just toss a basketful down my throat."

Ibn Batouta noted that Vélez, the Ajarquía's capital (Ajarquía means "the oriental zone", as opposed to Algarve, meaning "the west"), was "a beautiful city with a fine mosque and an abundance of fruit trees". Today, the market town (population: 42,000) retains its atmosphere of old Spain, and some of its old craftsmen.

Manuel Ruiz Bonillo, in his sixties, one of four artisans still turning out rustic chairs of poplar wood with rush seats, did not halt his work as he remarked: "There used to be a hundred of us. In the old days everybody ordered chairs when they got married. Now they want three-piece suites. There..." he pointed to a sturdy chair with carved decoration, "...that's one I made for my own wedding."

Vélez-Málaga is proud of its cultural life. Contemporary painters like Evaristo Guerra and Francisco Hernández have made names for themselves. María Alarcón Zambrano, an anti-Fascist intellectual who spent her early years here, has won a conspicuous place among Spanish thinkers of this century.

The town is also a centre for a sport that is banned in most of Europe. On Sundays during the winter, spectators cry encouragement as two cocks rip into one another in a wild flurry of feathers, pecking beaks and gouging spurs.

Manuel González Casanova, a leading member of the local Cock Breeders and Exporters' Association, denies any cruelty, even as the blood flies.

"This breed — we call it the English cock — is born to fight. It's his instinct and he starts fighting other cocks at only two months. Besides," González claims, "when he's in the ring, he feels no pain."

Palm-trees whisper in the breeze, geraniums splash colour outside wayside cottages as route C-335 winds inland beyond Vélez-Málaga. More land in this fertile valley will be assured of water when a massive dam is completed near the village of Viñuela. To the right a side-road snakes off beneath the shadow of the Sierra Tejeda to places whose very names sound like an Arabic poem: Canillas de Aceituno, Sedella, Salares, Canillas de Albaida, Cómpeta, Corumbela...

While every village produces its wine and boasts of its quality, that from Cómpeta, an archetypal Andalusian pueblo 26 kilometres from Vélez-Málaga, has the greatest renown. Any of the bars around the plaza next to the church will serve you a glass of *vino del terreno*. It tastes like crushed sunshine, and its alcohol content is a heady 18 per cent. That is because sun-dried muscatel grapes are used.

Trek through the hills of the Ajarquía in autumn and you will come across farmers crushing the grapes in the traditional way, with their bare feet. As one extracted the last juice with a primitive press consisting of a beam and a heavy stone, he confided: "My wine is pure, not like the stuff they sell in bars, full of chemicals. But you must be careful during fermentation. If a woman in menstruation goes in the same room as the barrels, it spoils the wine. Remember that if you ever make wine!"

Thousands of people squeeze into Cómpeta's main square every August 15 for its *Noche del Vino.* The all-night party includes flamenco, *verdiales,* and free wine for all. Among the connoisseurs mingling with the crowd are likely to be a fair number of Danes and British who have settled in and around the village, which until recently was regarded as being off the beaten track.

Pasas (raisins) are another local speciality, but, in the words of one leathery farmer tending his vines: "Phylloxera destroyed the industry last century. Now low prices make it hardly worth picking the grapes some years."

In winter snow caps the great bald dome of Maroma, which rises to more than 6,700 feet in the Sierra de Tejeda, and a brisk wind sweeps down on the sierra villages. Often enough, when there is bright sunshine on the coast, mists swirl about the Zafarraya pass through which runs the Vélez-Málaga to Granada road. Once, too, trains from Málaga reached this cleft. The line, known as the *Suburbano,* was built in the early years of the century. It was supposed to run all the way to Granada but ran out of breath at Ventas de Zafarraya.

The stations still exist, converted into restaurants or warehouses, as do the tunnels and embankments. From Ventas it is possible to walk (or drive, with care) along the old track to Periana. It is easier by road, turning west off the main Granada highway just before the ruins of Zalia, a Moorish fortress believed to occupy the site of an old Phoenician city. Zalia's defenders were put to the sword in 1487 in the last days of the Moors.

Peaches and olive oil are two of Periana's claims to fame. A third is *anís.* José Manuel Pasca carries on the family tradition in producing this potent liquor. The effects can be powerful, although there appears to be no truth in the claim by a local wit that the word "anis-thetic" was spawned here.

Curving over the hills beneath bleak peaks, the C-340 carries you to Ríogordo. In Holy Week, the streets may be blocked by Roman centurions and the bars full of boisterous Galilean shepherds, because, reviving a 16th-century tradition, this is the week the village stages a Passion Play. While it may not match the fame of Oberammergau, the Paso of Ríogordo is a remarkable event.

About 350 villagers take part. Some, who can't read, learn their lines by word of mouth. The action roams over a hillside, with a flock of sheep among the extras. One of the plum parts is that of Judas. One Easter when I witnessed the Paso, his role was played with villainous relish by a ginger-wigged truck driver. When he finally hanged himself, the rolling of his eyes brought murmurs of horrified appreciation from the audience.

I enjoyed a close-up of this performance because I had asked to take pictures.

"Certainly," said the organizers cheerfully. "Just put on this robe and mix with the crowd." Thus, that Easter, one of the unruly biblical mob wore spectacles and carried a camera.

Last century, the British traveller Richard Ford recommended other travellers to these parts to carry "a decent bag of dollars". Even more important was a watch, preferably one with a gaudy gilt chain and seals.

"Not to have one exposes [a traveller] to more indignities than a scantily filled purse. The money may have been spent, but the absence of a watch can only be accounted for by a premeditated intention of not being robbed, which the thief considers as a most unjustifiable attempt to defraud him of his right," he wrote.

This was *bandolero* country and north of Ríogordo, beyond the great black buttress of the Tajo de Gomer, stands a lonely *venta* (inn) which testifies to that. Located in the Ajarquía's northernmost corner, 50 kilometres from Málaga on a crossroads on the old Málaga-Granada road (C-345), the Venta de Alfarnate was catering to travellers at least as long ago as 1691.

On a hot summer's day about 160 years ago, some customers were enjoying a cooling gazpacho when a dusty horseman strode in and asked if he could share the meal.

"No spoons left," he was informed. Unabashed, the newcomer shaped a spoon from the crust of a loaf and, ignoring the others' protests, polished off the gazpacho. Then he produced a pistol and revealed who he was — El Tempranillo, one of the most notorious highwaymen. But one with a sense of humour.

As the group quaked in terror, he smilingly told them, "Now you will do the same as I do. Eat your spoons!"

It was no problem for him to eat his bread implement, but the others had to crack their teeth chewing at their wooden spoons.

The old building, which once accommodated 60 beasts of burden and their masters, has been converted into a popular eating place. Girls from the nearby villages of Alfarnate and Alfarnatejo serve such fare as partridge, smoked pork and roast kid. In winter, clients move closer to a great stone fireplace over which hang gleaming copper pots — a scene which cannot be much different from that of El Tempranillo's time.

Alfarnate, left-wing, and Alfarnatejo, right-wing and smaller, maintain a long-standing rivalry. They find it difficult to co-operate on anything — each has its own television repeater station, for example. And locals say they think twice before visiting the rival community, whether for a fiesta or a funeral.

"They did nearly get together once," recalled the *venta* landlord, Fernando Sánchez, with a roguish twinkle in his eye. "They planned to celebrate the San Isidro festival together on neutral ground, with a Mass here at the inn. But at the last minute, at midnight, Alfarnate said they weren't coming."

Highwaymen are not too common these days among the inn's clients, but within living memory they were a danger for anybody crossing the sierras. For instance, they added to the risks of an elite band of muleteers, known as the *corsos* who used to transport up to 180 kilos of fresh fish from the coast to inland towns, travelling by night over precipitous paths.

"It was running all the way. I used to pick up the fish at the beach in the evening, then make tracks for Granada," recalled Miguel Castillo, a veteran *corso* whose route lay across the Sierra Almijara from Nerja.

"If I stopped at a wayside inn, I only had time to sink an *anís* and then I was off again. We had to reach Granada market by dawn to get a decent price. Men burned out fast and so did the mules. They were big, strong animals but they'd only last about three years. And sometimes they'd slip and fall into a chasm in the dark, even though mules are sure-footed and see better by night than by day.

"On top of that, there were the *bandoleros*. I always carried a revolver just in case, but once when two fellows held me up with shotguns I didn't dare use it. I would have been dead before I'd pulled it from my belt. But I was lucky, I handed over four big fish and that satisfied them."

Miguel came from Frigiliana, an impeccable cluster of interlocking cubes and crooked streets, wandering over a ridge above a mosaic of terraced fields. For a long time, the village (900 feet above sea-level) was untouched by changes taking place along the coast. But now the inhabitants have acquired flush toilets, videos and late-model cars and foreigners are busy buying up old houses.

Frigiliana was the scene of one of the last, great battles between Moors and Christians, which occurred long after the Catholic Monarchs had conquered Granada in 1492. Persecution provoked the Moriscos (Muslim converts to Christianity) to rebel in the Alpujarras, as recorded in the chapter on that part of Granada province.

Soon the revolt spread to inhabitants of the Bentomiz range which reaches the sea near Vélez-Málaga. Moriscos rallied to the green-and-crimson banner raised by Francisco Roxas at Canillas de Aceituno, a sleepy sierra pueblo 17 kilometres from Vélez-Málaga.

When King Philip II ordered reinforcements from Italy and thousands of men began disembarking on the beaches of Torrox, 8,000 Morisco men and their families dug themselves in around the Frigiliana fort. But they were not equipped to tackle cavalry and well-armed troops. They resisted desperately, even hurling rocks at the attackers, but were routed on June 11, 1569.

Two thousand Moriscos and 400 attackers died, and if you wander over El Fuerte, the mountain behind Frigiliana, you can still turn up whitened bones and corroded weapons amid the thyme and rosemary. The tale of the great battle is told on 12 ceramic plaques, placed around the village's old quarter. One cobbled street is called Hernando el Darra, after the Morisco leader, and at Nerja, six kilometres away on the coast, a street is named after Hernando de Carabeo, one of the most courageous Christian soldiers.

Many travellers have been smitten by Nerja, whose Arabic name "Narixa" means "abundant spring". Local guidebooks like to quote the rapturous feelings of the poet Ibn Saadi, writing around 917:

"Stretched on a carpet of magic colours
While sleep closed my eyes,
Narixa, my Narixa sprang from the flowers
To bathe me in all her beauty."

Silk weaving and sugar production brought the community some prosperity in Moorish times, but until a few years ago Nerja barely scraped along on fishing and farming and was little visited. Until a day in 1959. Then, five boys went on a bat-catching expedition in the hills behind the hamlet of Maro. One felt a current of warm air issuing from a crack in the wall of a small cave. It led to vast caverns of extraordinary beauty, and suddenly Nerja was on the map.

According to archaeologists, the Cueva de Nerja throws significant light on the western Mediterranean's prehistory. Up to 20,000 years BC, palaeolithic man used it as a sanctuary, daubing images on its walls. Human skeletons, weapons, tools and pottery have been found and more almost certainly await discovery, for the hills around are honeycombed with caves.

Thousands of visitors now tramp through the Sala del Cataclismo and the Sala de los Fantasmas, gazing in awe at the spectacularly lit fairy castles, Gothic cathedrals and organ pipes that the steady drip of water has built over the millenniums. In summer, ballet performances are held in the cave, where bats wheel over the spectators' heads.

As in many coastal towns, the tourist avalanche spelled the death of innocence, a sharp change in values and the growth of a new middle class. Today it is easier to find an English pub than a fisherman in Nerja. The British have dominated the rush to buy property there and the opening of large hotels has brought an influx of package tourism.

But, despite the fast growth, high-rise blocks have been kept out of the old centre and some of Nerja's intimate charm remains. The Balcón de Europa, the town's beautiful, palm-lined promenade, is a favourite spot for strollers, flirting teenagers and people-watchers. It owes its name to an incident in January 1885, when King Alfonso XII visited Nerja. He walked out on to the rocky promontory and gazed spellbound at the spectacular coastline, with the mountains plunging abruptly into the glittering Mediterranean. Here and there, crumbling watch-towers stood guard, relics of the time when pirates ravaged the coast.

"This is the Balcony of Europe," the king allegedly declared. Brochure-writers love to quote him usually forgetting to mention the reason for the king's visit. He was actually relaxing after touring communities devastated by an earthquake which struck southern Spain on Christmas Day 1884. Stories circulated that the sea had rolled back two kilometres all along the coast. Certainly for a week after the tremor fishermen's nets were empty.

Although many visitors think that the Costa del Sol runs only from Estepona to Málaga airport, the eastern section of the coast — lying in the Ajarquía — appears certain (doomed, some might say) to experience a similar development boom. Already, in summer, the beaches from Nerja to Málaga are crammed with sun-worshippers and the rich odour of barbecued sardines mingles with that of toasting human flesh.

At Torrox-Costa, German is a more useful language than Spanish since most of its apartments have been sold to natives of Hamburg and Bremen. Earlier invaders were the Romans. They established a thriving settlement around where the lighthouse stands and traces of baths, villas and a fish-curing factory have been unearthed. A few kilometres inland lies "the Very Noble and Very Loyal Town" of Torrox. High-rises have fortunately not crushed this agricultural and administrative centre, which struggles for space in a narrow valley.

Just down the coast, however, uncontrolled development has created a second Torremolinos, but without the "charm" of the original. Foreigners bought the first apartments in Torre del Mar, and later large numbers of Jaén and Córdoba families took advantage of new prosperity to acquire holiday accommodation in the soaring blocks. Belatedly, a clean-up began and streets were paved and a promenade built on the wide, dusty beach.

The insatiable demand for villas and apartments is converting the 30 kilometres between Torre del Mar and Málaga into one long development strip. In July and August, only masochists drive the clogged coastal highway, the N-340, which runs from the provincial capital through its dormitory town of Rincón de la Victoria to Torre del Mar and beyond. Yet, only a slight deviation brings one to the Ajarquía of old, to villages where the locals claim "nothing ever happens". Each of those inland communities has its story, however, and sometimes it is more remarkable than one could imagine.

There is no better example than Macharaviaya. Málaga is 26 kilometres away, but seems a lot further. A perilous, corkscrew road leads to the village, straggling over a ridge amid almond and olive trees. Only a hundred or so people live in the village itself. The only unusual aspects about it are a noble, but crumbling church and the street names; names such as Pensacola and New Orleans. They are all that is left of the briefly glorious epoch when Macharaviaya was known as Little Madrid.

Two hundred years ago the village hummed with industry, thanks to the establishment of a playing cards factory which was granted a monopoly in exporting cards to the New World. The church was rebuilt in neo-classic style and stuffed with art treasures. Roads were built, streets paved, public fountains installed, a school was founded. This prosperity was all due to members of the Gálvez family, who became favourites of King Carlos III. Soldiers, diplomats, adventurers, they left their mark on Mexican and American history. They opened up new regions, including California, for colonization and played a significant part in the struggle for independence of the United States.

A large vault beneath the church holds the marble and alabaster tombs of Macharaviaya's illustrious sons. The most impressive structure is a grey marble mausoleum where the ashes of José de Gálvez rest. As an eight-year-old orphan, he was noticed by the Bishop of Málaga and given an education. He rose to become private secretary to the prime minister and came to the king's attention. Gálvez was brilliant and ruthless and showed such flair that King Carlos made him Marquis of Sonora and Minister of the Indies.

Sent to the Indies as visitor-general, José masterminded the controversial expulsion of the Jesuits and crushed a revolt with summary justice. When he learned that the Russians were planning to push into California, he dispatched military and religious expeditions to extend New Spain's boundaries as far as San Francisco Bay.

José's nephew, Bernardo, was wounded in campaigns against the Apache Indians. Later he was appointed governor of the vast territory of Louisiana and a new settlement, Galveston, was named after him. During the American War of Independence, he marched on such Redcoat outposts as Baton Rouge and Mobile. He crowned his career by becoming Viceroy of New Spain.

The Gálvez dynasty rained benefits on little Macharaviaya, but the golden age did not last long. Bernardo and his relations died, the playing card factory closed and the village sank back into poverty and neglect. In the 1980s, the mayor, an energetic young man named Eugenio Claros Gallardo, struggled to revive its fortunes and win recognition for its place in history. Robert Harvey, an American painter who has made his home there, aided efforts to hold an annual cultural week.

But Macharaviaya has no money, only a gloomy pantheon of alabaster sculptures, and the melancholy reminder of an anonymous poet, who recorded:

The Gálvez melted away
Like salt in water,
And like sparks from the forge
They disappeared.
They went down as they came up,
Like a sigh;
May God forgive them,
And may we not forget
That this world conquers
Those to whom it gives adoration.

Journey Into Prehistory

THICK, Sulphurous steam coiled about me as I lay back in the hot bath, lulled by distant echoes of what sounded like an angelic choir. My skin tingled agreeably and I thought of all the good that the minerals in the water must be doing... iron, magnesium, potassium sulphate, calcium, selenium, arsenic. The last ingredient was a little disturbing, but had not Byron, Dumas, Doré — even royalty — all sought cures here for everything from carbuncles to dropsy?

Drowsing in the baths of Carratraca, it is not difficult to imagine oneself a Roman emperor, or at least a centurion, relaxing after a hard campaign (even though that background music is issuing from nothing more celestial than a tape recorder). The atmosphere carries not only the faint odour of rotten eggs from the curative waters which bubble from the rock at 700 litres a minute. There is a sense of antiquity too.

All in all, the *balneario* (spa) is as pleasant a spot as any to gather one's forces for a journey into the interior of Andalusia. It stands on the threshold of an area of Málaga province neglected by many travellers but offering a variety of attractions, including Bronze Age enigmas, throat-catching vistas, traces of a lost kingdom and legends of lost love. And at the heart of the region lies the noble city of Antequera, a strategic crossroads since Roman times.

In the old days, the approach to Carratraca was a painful business, from whichever direction the coaches of the rich and famous came. The road from Málaga, 58 kilometres to the south, is paved now, but it still rocks and rolls erratically through the Guadalhorce valley's leafy sea of citrus orchards, before climbing past ancient Alora's long-vanquished castle and twisting into the dry hills. Improvements to communications with the Costa del Sol may eventually bring the spa within easy reach of mass tourism.

It took a beggar or a smuggler, depending on which story you favour, to put Carratraca on the map back in the 17th century. The man was Juan Camisón (so named because he wore a long shirt to cover the sores festering all over his body). When he saw a goatman treating sick animals by dousing them with water from the Carratraca spring, he decided to try the same cure. After bathing himself, all his ulcers cleared up.

The *balneario* enjoyed its heyday early last century when King Fernando VII ordered an inn built to accommodate himself and his retinue. It is not clear whether the royal head ever rested there, but the creaking, rambling building remains. Now it is known as Hostal del Príncipe. Three gambling casinos and an active social life attracted a select clientele, including Empress Marie Eugenie, Countess of Teba and wife of Napoleon III.

Today you will see few blue-bloods, but in the season from June to mid-October a steady stream of visitors arrives. Many stay at the Hostal del Príncipe. Swathed in towels, they flit across the street to the solid, stone *balneario,* to bathe in private cubicles or try the chillier delights of the "temple of healing", an oval, pillar-lined bath in a tiled patio.

They are greeted by white-garbed attendants and a cheerful young man named Emeterio Benavides, whose family is one of the owners of the baths. Emeterio comments: "Many people come for a week or two weeks' treatment, under medical supervision. The waters help with skin diseases, nervous troubles and many other complaints. And, of course, they are just plain relaxing. Now, how would you like your bath? Natural temperature? That's 18 degrees centigrade. Or would you prefer it a bit warmer, 30 or 38 degrees?" In the evenings, Emeterio deals in more potent liquids when he works in his family's lively bar in the village centre.

Carratraca is the archetypal sleepy pueblo, but it does boast two unusual structures. The stylish town hall was the residence last century of a well-known Málaga figure, Doña Trinidad Grund, who gave her name to nearby caves discovered in 1821, which feature enormous chambers and palaeolithic paintings. And just outside the village stands the bullring, one side of which is hacked out of the rock. It is the scene during Easter Week of a passion play in which 130 (out of the 1,000) inhabitants take part. Everybody looks forward to the climax when those playing Christ and the two thieves are crucified, though not with nails. Oddly enough, it was a Canadian, James Blaine Rutledge, owner of a local supermarket, who first organized the play in the early Seventies.

North of Carratraca, placid waters spread a turquoise carpet amid the hills. This is Málaga's lake district, a playground for picnickers and campers who plunge into the cool waters, cast lines for bass and carp, and enjoy the shade of pine-fringed slopes.

Inspired engineering has created three large reservoirs. A series of dams holds back the deluge that comes with winter rains, then rations it out to provide year-round hydroelectric power, irrigation and drinking water for the city of Málaga, 60 kilometres to the south.

Just north of the lakes, the ruins of La Estrella castle jut from a rocky escarpment, down one side of which straggles the town of Teba. Near here a Scottish warrior fell in battle against the Moors. It took more than 600 years for a monument to be raised to his heroism, but now a memorial in white Scottish granite stands in the Plaza de España. The Black Douglas, so called because of his dark complexion, was trying to fulfil the deathbed request of King Robert the Bruce that his heart should be buried in the Holy Land.

On his way through Spain in 1330 he became involved in the king of Castile's siege of Teba. The Black Douglas was said to have been so valiant that he could "turn the worst coward into a leopard by his example" and, when he was surrounded by Moorish horsemen, he defiantly hurled at them the casket containing the royal heart before he was sliced to death. When the octagenarian Earl of Selkirk, kilted leader of the Douglas clan, unveiled the monument to his ancestor in 1989, Teba threw a mighty party, wine and whisky flowing freely and the skirl of pipes echoing through the streets.

Below the Guadalhorce dams, the river cascades through Los Gaitanes pass, a ravine whose sheer walls soar 600 feet. At the southern end, it knifes through a massive buttress of rock. This is the gorge of El Chorro.

El Chorro is more than impressive. It is awe-inspiring and daunting. The main railway line traverses this chasm, offering glimpses of tumbling water and dizzy precipices as it snakes in and out of tunnels. But it is possible to obtain a more dramatic view by negotiating the gorge on foot... possible, but not advisable unless you are suicidally inclined or have iron nerves.

Look up from the El Chorro railway siding and you will see a thread cutting across the cliff face. This is El Camino del Rey (the King's Path). It was built during the construction of the dams early this century. When King Alfonso XIII came to open the great enterprise in 1921, his inspection tour included a walk along this path. Overcome by the project's daring and per-haps suffering from vertigo, he named the chief engineer the Count of Guadalhorce.

Pinned to the bare rock, the catwalk leaps the gorge by way of a bridge. But it badly needs repair. In many spots the handrail has vanished. At others, alarming gaps have opened up underfoot so that one gazes straight down into the yawning abyss to the water foaming below. When Alfonso's son, Don Juan (father of Spain's present king) inaugurated sophisticated new turbines at El Chorro in 1987, he did *not* take a walk along the Camino del Rey.

During off-peak periods, the turbines use stored power to pump water up to a reservoir sited on a flat-topped mountain. Later, the water runs down again to generate more electricity. But the hilltop, known as the Mesas de Villaverde, is not just a technological curiosity, it is believed to be the site (though some researchers dispute this) of Bobastro, capital, 1,000 years ago, of a rebel kingdom.

From this virtually impregnable stronghold, Umar Ibn Hafsun is said to have challenged the might of the Caliph of Córdoba, and controlled large areas of present-day Málaga, Granada, Seville and Córdoba provinces. Hafsun, a convert to Christianity, held sway over the fortresses of Teba and Mijas, over Ardales and Archidona and beyond. He died in 917, but Abd ar-Rahman III took 11 years more to conquer Bobastro. Now there are some tumbled ruins and a unique Mozarab church hewn from the rock, where it is claimed Hafsun was laid to rest.

A dusty track weaves east over the mountains from El Chorro to Valle de Abdalajis, which sits below a bleached wall of rock where a small shrine is lodged. It shelters a venerated figure of the Virgin, patron of the village. Other images found nearby speak of religious cults stretching back into the misty past, and to judge by finds of terracotta goddesses with infants, fertility rites were once common. In Roman times, when the settlement was called Nescania, a temple to Jupiter stood here.

East and south of Valle de Abdalajis, towards Villanueva de la Concepción and Almogía, lies a part of Andalusia that seems to have been forgotten. Mules are still an important means of transport, for there are few roads. Running water and telephones are unknown in hamlets tucked into remote valleys where the soil offers only a bare living.

"This is the other Andalusia, the Andalusia some prefer to hide, the Andalusia of the disinherited," declares one villager, bitter in his poverty.

The ramparts of El Torcal frowning down from a lofty escarpment on Villanueva and these depopulated ranges have an appropriately forbidding aspect. Closer inspection reveals, however, that the turrets and belfries were not constructed under the lash of some power-hungry conqueror. The architect was nature. Wind and water have sculpted outlandish imagery in the limestone terrain off route C-3310, 15 kilometres from Antequera. Vultures and hawks circle over a strange jumble of obelisks and alleyways, reptile and animal forms.

The 1,200-hectare El Torcal natural park is under the protection of the Andalusian government. Protection was necessary to stop quarry work which threatened irreparable damage, and eager tourism promoters who planned to scale the heights with a cable-car. El Torcal's wonders have been saved for those who have the energy and curiosity to wander the well-marked trails.

The road north cuts through the mountains, then dips towards a green-and-brown chessboard of fertile farmland. This is the *vega* (plain) of Antequera and at its rim three remarkable dolmens (burial sites) indicate the skill and ingenuity of a people who inhabited the region around 2000 BC. One of these dolmens (the word comes from the Celtic for "a table of stone") is the largest and best-preserved prehistoric relic of its type. Known as Menga, it sits incongruously a few metres from a petrol station on the Granada road out of Antequera. The tree-lined approach leads to a mystery, for we still know little about the people who created this monument or how they managed the immense construction task.

Slave labour was probably necessary to haul the 31 stones, weighing a total of 1,600 tons, to the site from a quarry in the mountains. No doubt the slabs, weighing up to 180 tons, bore the bloodstains of those who stumbled and fell beneath them as they were levered into position. Somehow, a "cave" 12 feet high and 80 feet long was built.

Menga is empty now, looted long ago, but inside it is surmised that the bodies of leaders and warriors were laid with their weapons and most precious possessions. Then the chamber was sealed and covered with earth. Nearby is the chamber of Viera, similar but smaller. A third dolmen, the Romeral, stands a short distance away. It is entered by a corridor and ends in two circular chambers.

Menga's position has particular significance, believe archaeologists. They theorize that it is related to the early Iberians' magic rites and that the first light of the sun rising over the nearby Peña de los Enamorados on a particular date decided the dolmen's alignment.

There are several legends about the Peña, an oddly-shaped peak jutting from the plain east of Antequera. Some people see in its contours the outline of two lovers embracing; others a human face gazing skywards. One story tells of Tayzona, daughter of the mayor of Archidona, who fell in love with the governor's son. But she was a Moor and he was a Christian. Neither family could permit such a liaison. The desperate couple climbed to the top of the mountain, embraced and hurled themselves off, to be united for ever in death. It is a melancholy tale, but fitting in its way, for the people of this region have a reputation for seriousness, which they themselves confirm.

"We are different from the people of the coast. We're sad, closer in character to Granada people," says José Muñoz Rojas. "The reason lies in our history. For 200 years Antequera was a frontier town, the point of the Moorish lance surrounded by Christian forts. That leaves a mark."

José, poet, academic and member of one of Antequera's oldest landowning families, points out that, unlike many Andalusian towns, Antequera was never dominated by a single noble house and so developed on less feudal lines.

Until the Civil War, it was known for its weaving, tanneries and metal foundries, but these industries have vanished. Today, the main highway swings around the town, which preserves the subdued air of a prosperous agricultural centre where everybody seems to know everybody else. *Antequeranos* have a name for being businesslike and one of Andalusia's largest savings banks is headquartered here. Smart shops have opened along the main street, where drivers jostle their cars for parking space.

The street is named after Infante Don Fernando, Regent of Castile and one of the most significant figures in local history. After he crushed a Moorish army at the nearby Boca del Asno (Ass's Mouth) gorge, Antequera was virtually isolated from the kingdom of Granada and in September 1410 Christian forces entered the town. Fernando gave it a coat of arms, consisting of a vase of lilies, a lion and a golden castle. The initials "P.S.A." on the escutcheon stand for *"Por Su Amor* (For Your Love)", a title awarded Antequera for its help in ousting the Moors from Málaga and Granada.

Several ballads recall the severe blow the loss of Antequera represented for the Moors. One, possibly making the best of a bad job, tells of the king of Granada sighing not for the lost town but for a 16-year-old damsel imprisoned there. He would give Almería to rescue her and, if that were not enough, "I shall go to Antequera, where they hold you, pretty one, and I shall act as hostage, just to gaze on your face."

Romance took a back seat when the Christianizing process got under way. Dozens of churches were built, religious orders arrived in force — at one time more than a tenth of the population was composed of clerics, monks and nuns — and the Inquisition began examining the habits of Antequera's citizens.

The Holy Office knew how to extirpate heresy, witchcraft and bigamy. In 1582, a *morisca* (a Moorish woman converted to Catholicism) was burned for having revered a large bone, worked on holy days and eaten meat on Fridays.

An old clothes dealer got off more lightly. For refusing to go to Mass because "I prefer to make love to my mistress," he was fined.

Although modern touches have come to Antequera, monastic life continues behind closed doors much as it did in medieval times. Of eight convents for nuns, in five the inmates have no contact with the world beyond their high walls. And monks pray in sealed-off tranquillity in two monasteries.

"Are we particularly religious?"

Antequeranos smile at the question.

"Well, you should see the Corpus Christi procession. Many of us go to Mass, particularly the womenfolk. And we do have a lot churches..."

In fact, at the last count Antequera had 24 churches, quite a number for a community of 28,000. Several are national monuments, including Santa María la Mayor, a 16th-century edifice with an imposing Renaissance façade, which stands high above the town.

Higher still rises the *alcazaba,* a Moorish fort raised over Roman foundations. The Roman settlement of Antikaria gave the town its name, but recent excavations to the west have revealed the existence of a bigger colony named Singilia Barba. An amphitheatre there could accommodate 8,000 spectators and naval battles are believed to have been simulated on an artificial lake.

One of the most magnificent relics of Roman civilization in the peninsula is to be found in the municipal museum. Efebo, a 58-inch-high bronze statue of a boy, was turned up on a local farm in the 1970s. It dates from the first century AD and was probably brought from Rome to decorate a wealthy resident's villa. A million dollars would not buy it, as a hopeful American purchaser discovered.

The building housing the museum started off as the palace of the Marquis of Nájera in the early 18th century. Later it housed Civil Guards and, in the Civil War, Moorish troops. It is a stately building, but not unique in Antequera. On the higher levels of the town, titled families struggle to maintain palatial dwellings, although from the outside it can be hard to guess at their splendour.

Much of these families' wealth came from great estates on the Vega. Holdings are smaller these days, with few over 250 hectares, but they are more intensively farmed. Machines have moved in to plough and harvest the rippling fields of corn and lop the golden heads of a lucrative new crop, the sunflower. Irrigation has been extended, so that on a hectare where only 80 olive trees survived before, three times as many now flourish.

Even as production has improved, job opportunities have shrunk. As one farmer notes, "Back in 1940 I employed 30 *jornaleros* (casual workers) but today I need only nine permanent staff."

Antequera was the target of the first move by the Andalusian government to launch a controversial agrarian reform programme which planned to expropriate properties judged to be under-utilized and hand them to co-operatives. Landowners fought back through the courts, alleging the scheme was unfair, unviable and unconstitutional. Although the reform programme finally went ahead, radical changes in the structure of land ownership were highly unlikely.

Antequera's traditional ways and the steady pace of rural Andalusia are reflected in its weekly newspaper which is the oldest in Málaga province (true, there is little competition). *El Sol de Antequera,* founded in 1918, is located in a printshop just opposite San Sebastián church. A linotype clatters in one corner, setting hot lead as real newspapers always have been set, and editor Angel Guerrero comes in to handle editorial and advertising details in the evenings, after he has finished work in a bank. A thousand subscribers, including a few in the New World, impatiently await *Sol's* arrival.

One story which should rate attention is the future of Fuente de Piedra, a saline lagoon to the north-west of Antequera. Every spring some of nature's most graceful creatures come winging in to this reserve to perform their annual breeding ritual. It is one of the few places in Europe where flamingos nest and up to 25,000 of the pink-legged birds can be seen paddling in the shallow waters in an exceptional season.

But flamingos, herons and other species compete with man's needs. Expanding agriculture and new crops — the 1980s brought an asparagus boom to nearby Sierra de Yeguas — require more irrigation. More wells siphon off water that would feed the lagoon, as well as increasing the danger of salt ruining subterranean reserves. Ecological groups and Andalusia's *Agencia del Medio Ambiente* (Environment Agency) battle to protect the 1,400-hectare wetland, but the flamingos need all the help they can get.

Sol de Antequera also rises over a town that once wielded considerable power. The 7,000 inhabitants of Archidona, 17 kilometres away, feel over-shadowed by their larger neighbour. After all, it is hard to accept a minor role when, in Moorish times, you had your own Emir. Emirs have been out of style in Andalusia for several centuries, but Archidona still has something special, a beautifully-proportioned, eight-sided plaza, built 200 years ago in Mudéjar style.

On the wall of the Café La Posada, on one side of the square, a 1968 plaque sets out to break Andalusian records for floral elaboration: "Archidona, Country of Magnolias," it proclaims. "You have a meeting point which focuses and gives form to the attitudes of this heroic land. The octagonal square: store-place of history, statement of yearning, flower that adorns... cup of nostalgia, virginal flask, mortar of the stars, inverted crown, dish of amber..."

After that, it is something of an anticlimax to explore the adjacent hill, the Sierra Virgen de Gracia, site of the old town. Columns inside a hermitage, which houses Archidona's patron saint, date back to the era when a mosque stood here. From the hillcrest, where the breeze whips over castle ruins, you can peer at distant sierras, olive groves running to the horizon, and even reflect on the brimming cup of nostalgia below.

And, just possibly, over there, beyond the Peña de los Enamorados, you may catch sight of a long fluttering line; flamingos rallying above the heroic land before setting course for Africa.

A youngster shows off his baby goat;
a sea mist lends an air of enchantment to
the crags and valleys of the Ajarquía;
aficionados bet on a cock-fight held at
Vélez-Málaga.

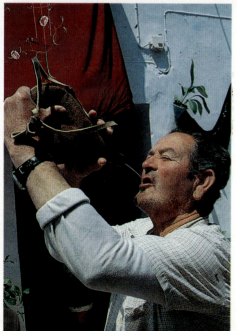

Clockwise: *a villager hoists his wine-skin to sample the sweet, powerful wine from the Ajarquía region; a farmer ploughs a field near the remains of Teba castle; Malagueños relax beside the Guadalhorce reservoirs; limestone pillars take on strange shapes at Torcal, near Antequera.*

Clockwise: *hot chestnut sellers in a Málaga street; the colourful headgear of a Verdiales musician; a horse-drawn carriage outside Málaga cathedral.*

The Singing City

P OETS and parsons, captains and consuls, remittance men and penniless wanderers share the terraced, insect-humming slopes at the foot of Málaga's Gibralfaro hill. They sleep peacefully, sheltered from the snarl of passing traffic by a forest of shrubs, of cactus, carobs, pines and cypresses. They lie not in wall cavities, as is the usual custom in Andalusia, but beneath shadow-dappled gravestones and the inscriptions are in several languages, in Spanish, Dutch, German, Hebrew, English.

Small mounds, studded with sea-shells, testify to the scourge of fever and consumption that carried off children in the mid-19th century. Solid monuments recall stalwarts of the foreign community. A series of graves commemorates the crew of a German frigate wrecked in 1900. Jorge Guillén, one of this century's most respected Spanish poets, lies here. Gamel Woolsey, South Carolina-born poetess and wife of British writer Gerald Brenan, rests beneath an inscription reading, "Fear no more the heat o' the Sun."

Nostalgia and sweet melancholy permeate the air in Málaga's English Cemetery. Visiting the spot in 1862, Hans Christian Andersen rhapsodized: "I walked in a paradise of myrtle hedges and tall geranium bushes. Passion flowers twined their tendrils over many a gravestone and there were pepper trees with weeping branches."

At one time, the only burial place available to non-Catholics in Málaga was on the beaches. Often the dead made ghastly reappearances when the waves washed away their shrouds of sand. But in 1830 Spain ceded some land to William Mark, the British consul, to found a Protestant cemetery, This carefully-tended corner has its own small church, which is regularly attended by an Anglican chaplain.

In greater demand than ever today, due to the increased number of foreign residents on the coast, the English Cemetery underlines the fact that Málaga has always been remarkably cosmopolitan. Foreign names such as Gross, Schneider and Scholtz, Higgins, Bidwell and Bevan, mingle with native ones in the local telephone directory.

Throughout its long history Málaga has been open to influences, traders, and invaders, blowing in from the Mare Nostrum, cradle of western civilization. In many ways it is the least Andalusian of the region's cities, thanks to the ceaseless friction of outside ideas breaking in waves on its wide bay. It is the city of *pronunciamientos* (declarations of rebellion), of liberalism, of tolerance. And of *alegría* at all costs.

Sometimes the *malagueños* seem set on outdoing the flamboyance and *gracia* (charm) of Seville. Easter Week processions rival the Andalusian capital in their baroque extravagance and pagan pomp. During the round-the-clock revelry of the annual fair in August's sticky heat, the citizens spend like there is no *mañana* and sing until it arrives. The province has developed its own style of *cante flamenco*, including *verdiales, rondeñas, malagueñas, jaberas.*

Poet Manuel Machado defined Andalusia's cities thus: *"Cádiz, sala claridad/ Granada, agua oculta que llora/Romana y mora Córdoba, callada/Málaga, cantaora* [Cádiz, salty clarity, Granada, hidden water weeping, Córdoba, Roman, Moorish and silent, Málaga singing]."

Quoting the lines approvingly, a *malagueño* comments: "We like to live to the hilt. If somebody hasn't got enough money to enjoy himself then he will find a way. He needs cash for a party? He'll borrow from his friends or ask his bank manager for a loan. We don't believe in depriving ourselves."

"Why should we?" asks another. "We *malagueños* like to spend. We live for the day. We can work as well as those *granadinos,* but we're not solemn like them. We're Phoenicians!"

Blessed with Europe's mildest climate (the February day in 1954 when snow briefly carpeted the streets has become the stuff of legends), Málaga can afford to act the carefree, singing cricket while Granada in its mountain fastness busily squirrels away fodder for the winter. Conservative Granada may sniff at Málaga folk as being unreliable but, as long as the sun shines, the *malagueños* will retain their zest.

"Málaga," points out Julián Sesmero, local historian and broadcaster, "is less chauvinistic and more open to new ideas than other areas because it is a port, which has meant a lot of contact with outsiders. We have all the virtues of past invaders and all the defects too, but, to tell the truth, I don't know which dominate.

"One of our — and the country's — problems is that we are not interested in nuances. Here you must be *"o carne o pescado"* (fish or fowl) and we admit nothing in between. Andalusia is a place of extremes. It comes from our history as a melting pot of Phoenicians, Romans, Arabs and all the others."

To the Phoenicians goes the credit for establishing ancient Malaka, a name said to derive from the settlement's importance as a fish-salting centre. During the long reign of the Moors, from 711 to 1487, it was praised by scribes and emirs as an earthly paradise. With the fall of the kingdom of Granada, however, Málaga, which served as its seaport, slumped into a torpor which only the turbulent 19th century could shake.

Initiative on the part of a dynamic middle class brought a new era of prosperity last century, short-lived though it may have been. Families such as Larios and Heredia, both from the Rioja region in northern Spain created textile factories, sugar mills, shipyards and steelmills. From Málaga to Motril, the Larios dynasty held feudal sway, commanding a chain of sugar refineries and vast tracts of coastal plain. Although the industry has declined, the land has soared in value beyond anybody's imagining.

Málaga's main shopping street bears the name of the Marquis of Larios in recognition of his financial help in its construction. Opened in 1891 after years of work, it slashed through a warren of narrow, squalid alleyways, frequented by rogues and vagabonds. Later came the handsome, tree-shaded Paseo del Parque on land reclaimed from the sea.

The rich constructed palatial mansions in the Limonar and Caleta quarters. Reflecting Málaga's character, these were totally unlike the walled-in *carmens* found in Granada or the secretive dwellings centred on a private patio found in Seville and Córdoba. They stood on the hillsides, open to the admiration of the passing public and to the breezes from the sea.

Hans Christian Andersen was charmed by the city, remarking: "In none of the towns and cities of Spain did I feel as happy and as comfortably at home as in Málaga." Forty years later, in 1901, Baedeker may have muttered about the dust, the dirt and the drainage, pointing out that the annual death rate was just under 40 per 1,000 inhabitants, but Málaga was growing in popularity as a winter resort.

In Victorian times, too, Málaga dessert wine reached a fashionable peak. Known as the perfect "lady's wine" it was a major export and vineyards flourished on the heights around the city. The sweet, heady liquid has had illustrious addicts through the ages. Pliny and Virgil sang its praises. The Sultan of Samarkand and Catherine the Great of Russia were among those who ordered it by the shipload.

But a small, greenish-yellow bug from America, the phylloxera, destroyed the vines, tastes changed, and today lovers of sweeter wine have to endure the scoffs of the wine snobs. Only 15,000 hectares of the province still produce grapes. Many are dried, particularly in the Ajarquía area, to make delicious raisins, but there too Málaga has lost out. Maybe the crickets were too busy playing in the sun to anticipate the trend, for the market has been lost to Israel and California, which long ago taught the public to demand seedless raisins.

Lost causes appear to be a Málaga speciality. Changing times and sharper competition sank its industries. Always ready to fight for liberal principles, the city was the flashpoint for various revolts. In the Plaza de la Merced (in one corner of which stands the house, Number 15, where Pablo Picasso was born), an obelisk pays respect to the memory of General Torrijos, who, in 1831, led a rising against the tyrannical King Ferdinand. Lured from Gibraltar, Torrijos and 52 companions were shot on San Andrés beach, next to the humble Barrio del Perchel, traditionally the home of fishermen and the breeding ground of dangerously democratic ideas.

The Civil War left deep scars. Republican supporters burned churches and convents; much of Larios — Málaga's proudest street — went up in flames; Italian planes bombed the city and reprisals were taken against bourgeois prisoners. Living up to the slogan on its coat of arms, *"La primera en el peligro de la Libertad"* (roughly "The leader when liberty is in danger"), Málaga stood virtually alone for seven months against Franco's rebel forces.

Abandoned by the government in Madrid, poorly organized, the city fell in February, 1937. As swastikas were paraded about its streets and executions of *"Rojos y anarquistas"* began, aircraft and warships strafed thousands of refugees fleeing along the coast road towards Almería. (Among those who aided the wounded were three heroic Canadians led by Dr Norman Bethune.) It took decades to get over the nightmare.

Finally, tourism helped heal the wounds as Málaga's insignificant suburb of Torremolinos blossomed into an international resort. Although *malagueños* have a rare level of tolerance — "They have seen so much, they accept anything, *too* much," believes Julián Sesmero — even *their* eyebrows shot up at some sights. I recall the traffic stopping in the city centre in 1966 when a foreign girl paraded past in a mini-skirt.

New styles came in architecture too. Fine old buildings were ripped down. Tiles and latticed ironwork gave way to concrete and glass. Belle époque cafés charged with memories disappeared; they were not glossy enough for modern tastes. Almost too late, the *malagueños* began to react, alarmed at their vanishing heritage.

Prosperity brought the automobile to choke streets and nostrils, threatening to turn Málaga into another Los Angeles. Some see positive similarities, arguing that the climate, the fruits of the hinterland, the prospects for high-technology industry could make this another California-style boom area. Optimists who know the pleasure-loving Málaga character are confident that such a catastrophe will never happen.

Although the city is the capital of the Costa del Sol and feeds off it, it retains its individuality. While other municipalities are dominated by tourism, Málaga is surprisingly untouched by the phenomenon. Most of its half a million inhabitants have little or no contact with the package tourists, who are whisked straight from Jumbo charters to hotels along the coast.

To the west of the city towards the airport, new workers' suburbs bristle with ugly high-rises struggling for elbow room. The more affluent residents live in hillside villas and apartments east of the bullring. High-decibel music rings out until the early hours from Pedregalejo, the beach quarter once inhabited only by poor fishermen but now abuzz with trendy bars and teenage motor-cyclists.

But the area around the central market is a reminder that Málaga remains a true Mediterranean crossroads, pungent, colourful, bustling, timeless as an old print. The narrow streets are crowded with shoppers, bootblacks, sellers of illegal lottery tickets, walnut-faced gypsies, country bumpkins, sly beggars, vendors of contraband butter and cigarettes, legionnaires just off the boat from Africa, Moroccans in jellabas, off-duty whores, bemused foreign sailors, sleek commercial travellers, Senegalese trinket-pedlars.

In odd corners, dead-eyed youths offer *"Chocolate, chocolate"* (hashish) and the *timadores* (tricksters) lure the gullible by paying out wads of notes to accomplices who pick the right card or the cup with a pea under it. "Some of these types are amazingly ingenious and the pickpockets can be true artists. They aren't like the new breed of *chorizos* who are completely without finesse," say the police, nostalgic for the days when Málaga was so backward that mugging was an unknown concept.

The city still has dark, odorous bars where they draw Pedro Ximenez, Lagrima and Seco Añejo direct from the barrel and chalk the price on stained wooden counters. The customers gulp gratefully at the golden liquid and crunch crab legs and prawns, and kick aside ankle-deep shells on the sawdust-covered floors. There is always time for a joke, an *aperitivo,* a coffee, and more talk.

Malagueños admit they don't know where paradise is. "But," they add, "it must be near here." And on this point they are not joking at all.

Happy Hour in Paradise

A puzzled magazine researcher once called me from Toronto to ask: "You mention Marbella in your article, but I don't see it on any map. Where exactly is this island?"

Canadians are not the only ones uncertain of the whereabouts of the Costa del Sol. Many a Spaniard wonders whether it belongs to his country at all. To a Bilbao steelworker, a Madrid bank clerk or an Andalusian olive-picker, the name conjures up visions of sybaritic delights, of a pulsating Sodom and Gomorrah adrift in the Mediterranean. He regards it with the same mixture of fascination, envy and distaste that a Midwestern farmer would reserve for California.

He has heard about the all-night parties, the beaches packed with half-naked females, the affairs and scandals of the rich and famous. His wife has an even clearer picture of this never-never land, because she reads the *revistas de corazón* (gossip magazines) which give heavy coverage to the doings of jaded playboys, aristocrats on the spree, criminals on the run, dodgy financiers, and show business celebrities.

A colourful cast. But a minor part of the industry that has brought wealth to the Málaga coast. The humdrum truth is that an overwhelming proportion of the two million or so foreign visitors who flock here for their annual skirmish with the sun are package tourists fleeing from the rigours of Dusseldorf and Leeds. They are distant spectators of the so-called jet set. The bronzed Don Juan they spy strolling along the seafront is more likely to be Paco Rodríguez, tile-layer from Córdoba, trawling for pliant foreign girls, than professional heart-throb Julio Iglesias. The closest most visitors get to the "beautiful people" is a wide-eyed stroll through Puerto Banús.

Around this luxury pleasure port near Marbella, where the easiest way to be labelled an exhibitionist is actually to put to sea, a clunky symphony of gold jewellery tolls the news that good taste has also taken a holiday. Few of the several hundred thousand retired expatriates who have taken up permanent or semi-permanent residence on the coast play any part in this flashy consumption. They have other excitements. Fluctuating exchange rates or a hand of bridge can set their pulses racing. Mostly, however, they are content to soothe their rheumatics (the coast averages 320 sunny days a year) and utter thanks, over yet another round of drinks, that they are escaping winter's blasts.

Officially, the "sun coast" runs from the border of Almería province to within cannon-shot distance of Gibraltar. The Costa de Granada, and the stretch between Málaga and Nerja, known as the Costa Oriental (see the chapter on the Ajarquía) has been slower developing. It is the 110-kilometre strip from down-market Torremolinos to deluxe Sotogrande which has gained most fame, or notoriety.

This section embraces more contrasts than most visitors can assimilate. Developing at phenomenal speed, the narrow coastal plain has grown into a subtropical pleasure ground, sheltered by bony ranges from winter frost, soothed by the Mediterranean through the summer heat. It veers abruptly from the tacky to the exquisite, from the strait-laced to the amoral. Critics sneer and decry it as a gaudy Disneyland, as a paella-and-chips nightmare. But they are only partly correct.

True, the poverty-stricken fishing villages that dotted the coast until the 1950s have been submerged in concrete, and rows of tombstone blocks often bar any view of the sea. Thousands of villas spread like measles over hillsides that once knew only olive trees and wandering goats. Neon rainbows light up resort skies, advertising gambling casinos, "sexy shows" and all-night discos, not to mention Dortmund Bier and Watney's Ale. There are belly-dancers and gigolos, bawling children and blistering parents.

Yet there are also, at least for the moment, uncrowded beaches and tranquil residential areas. And the "real Spain", unvisited by most tourists, is close at hand, in the saw-tooth sierras rising behind the coast. There you can wander for hours and meet only shepherds and hawks. In villages older than Cervantes, people actually speak the native tongue and worry as always about the potato or the citrus crop.

About the worst thing that can happen to a visitor is that he finds himself in the wrong resort. A Marbella person lost in Torremolinos would consider it a nightmare. A Torremolinos person in Fuengirola would be bored out of his mind. Not that some visitors would know the difference: such as the man who waited at a stop for the next bus to Ibiza, or the tourist who solemnly declared he had left his watch at home because it did not show Spanish time.

One non-Spanish-speaking tourist hailed a taxi at Málaga airport, alighted at a hotel, spent two weeks there and then complained when he was presented with a bill.

"Outrageous! I paid for the whole holiday before I left home," he stormed. "This is the last time I shall come to Estepona!"

"Indeed, sir?" replied the hotelier. "You appear to have stayed in the wrong hotel. This happens to be Marbella!"

It was not always thus. Earlier travellers usually knew just where they were, although they did not always like it. Some got as far as Málaga but few considered the coast to its west worthy of comment. Richard Ford, writing about Spain in 1835, noted that it was a land "where the all-wandering foot of the all-pervading Englishman but seldom rambles. The beef-steak and the

119

tea-kettle which infallibly mark the progress of John Bull are as yet unknown in the *ventas* and *posadas* of the Peninsula."

Mark Twain glimpsed the coast, but quarantine restrictions stopped him going ashore at Málaga in 1867. He applied his usual quirky humour: "Shipped my newspaper correspondence, which they took with tongs, dipped it in sea-water, clipped it full of holes, and then fumigated it with villainous vapours till it smelt like a Spaniard. Inquired about the chances to run the blockade and visit the Alhambra at Granada. Too risky — they might hang a body."

In those days visiting any part of Spain was regarded by such caustic guides as Karl Baedeker as an adventure in a semi-barbaric world. He warned in his 1901 edition against inns where "the sanitary arrangements are abominable. The servants are frequently lazy, disobliging, and wholly deaf to all requests involving the slightest deviation from the usual national routine."

While recommending the Mediterranean coast, he remarked: "The climatic advantages of such places as Alicante, Almería and Málaga are largely counterbalanced by their dirt, dust, and general lack of comforts. An increase in the number of foreign visitors is the surest way to bring about a change for the better."

The changes were to come, but not for several decades. The year 1932 is regarded as a turning point. Then, the story goes, a lady named Carlota Alessandri bought an empty tract of land at Montemar, west of Torremolinos. When a friend asked what she was going to plant, she replied: "Plant? I shall plant tourists! This could be the beginning of a Spanish Riviera."

It took time. When English writer Laurie Lee walked along the coast just before the Civil War, he found "a beautiful but exhausted shore, seemingly forgotten by the world" which was dotted with "salt-fish villages, thin-ribbed, sea-hating, cursing their place in the sun. At that time one could have bought the whole coast for a shilling."

After the war, the Marquis of Najera arrived to give development a boost. Wealthy Spanish families built stylish villas overlooking the sea; retired colonial officials and diplomats (and a clutch of Nazis on the run) found a refuge. By the 1960s, the word had spread. Torremolinos became the "in" place for artists, runaway heiresses, writers, eccentrics, film stars, matadors.

The living was cheap and the life was easy. Wine was one or two pesetas a glass. Houses overlooking the sea rented for 4,000 a month. Hash-smoking flower people staged "happenings", a word redolent of the age. Café society — or "Nescafé Society" as some wits described it — circulated around the old Bar Central and James Michener lumbered portentously in to eavesdrop and write *The Drifters*. Sourly, English critic Kenneth Tynan commented, "This is an open township, inbred and amoral, after which the next stop is Tangier, followed by a suicidal leap from some high peak in the Canary Islands."

Soon, this lotus land sank with hardly a trace under the tourism boom. All along the "costas", the beef-steak and the tea-kettle took their rightful place, next to the ceaselessly grinding cement mixers. In 1946, 83,000 foreigners visited Spain; in 1951, 1.2 million. Encouragement of foreign investment, removal of visa restrictions and the demand for a cheap playground from a newly-affluent Europe swelled the figure to six million in 1960. By 1980, the number was 38 million and in 1987 it topped 50 million, of whom 33 million were officially classified as tourists (those staying more than 24 hours).

The "thin-ribbed" villages got their share. Ploughboys became head waiters. Shopkeepers became supermarket millionaires. Bricklayers became real estate tycoons. One had his first break when some Málaga businessmen put up the cash to build apartments to accommodate their mistresses. He made enough to throw up another block, and another, and another. They were ugly, poorly built, but cheap, and West Germans bought them eagerly. The builder swiftly died, "from wine and women" said his neighbours. But the blocks remain.

Compared to other Spanish coasts, the Costa del Sol initially was regarded as somewhat exclusive. But the avalanche of foreign and Spanish visitors made that image difficult to retain. By the late 1980s it had more than 50,000 hotel beds, as well as thousands of villas and apartments, more tourist beds altogether than the whole of Greece. Tourist arrivals had swollen from about one million in 1968 to more than five million. British accounted for about one third of foreign visitors, with the Germans, Scandinavians and others some way behind.

The North European obsession for sunshine and proximity to azure water appears unlimited. Thousands of foreigners have bought property on the Málaga coast. Building regulations have buckled under the weight of cash, greed has flourished, and many a sun-dazzled purchaser has thrown caution and his life savings to the winds. Sharks and swindlers of all nationalities gratefully scoop up this bounty. They mingle easily with law-abiding pensioners and vacationers, for the coast's easy-going ways and general laxity make it a happy hunting ground for them and other rogues, from tax-dodgers to bank-robbers hunted by Interpol.

The villains benefit from the coast's unwritten rules of discretion. It is not good form to enquire too closely into another's background. This is not so much because of suspected delinquency, but because a dream machine only functions if individual fantasies are respected. So it is that a greengrocer can claim he was in "import-export", a fireman becomes a "writer", and nobody is to know that the neighbour who was "Something in the City" actually unblocked the Bank of England's drains.

Many of those who settle semi-permanently make little attempt to integrate into Spanish life or learn much about it. They form ghettos of their own countrymen, read papers in their native language, drink in bars where Spanish intruders invite a frosty reception. If they are British, they can tune in to Gibraltar television or eat steak and kidney pie at the British Society. Americans bewail local plumbing and the state of the dollar when they meet at their club. Danes and Swedes import furnishings to the last fork. There are Belgian butchers and French patisseries. The Japanese come to get married and plan to build their own retirement villages.

An amazing aspect of this process is the lack of friction with the local people, although as services are strained their tolerance wears thin. "Spending a holiday around here is like going abroad," some Spaniards mutter. "In many bars and restaurants you need to know a foreign language to make yourself understood. We've sold our birthright."

During the first years of the boom, the free-spending ways of the visitors and their relative sophistication silenced the doubts of the simple coastal inhabitants. Everybody wanted a share of this lucrative trade, even though they were shocked by the sun-worshippers' antics.

In 1960, only footballers wore shorts in public and for a couple to merely hold hands on the beach was an offence. Many men were never alone with their girl until the marriage day. The Franco regime and the Church had embalmed Spain in the past, but the invasion of the body-exposers turned rigid moral codes on their heads and helped awaken Spain to what was happening beyond the Pyrenees.

Today, Spanish girls toss off their bikini tops with as much abandon as their foreign counterparts. Tourism has shattered old traditions and taboos, creating family friction, corrupting and liberating at the same time. A fisherman's son will defy his father's authority. Why should he suffer hours at sea when he can gain twice as much by playing Romeo to some middle-aged foreigner?

A teenage girl, engaged to be married, shows the sort of resignation expected by the macho society of her mountain village: "I won't see my boyfriend during the summer. He's on the coast. But he will be back in October, when all the foreign girls have gone home."

And a young man comments: "I go to Torremolinos every weekend. I can be myself there, but in the pueblo they just insult me as a *maricón* [queer]."

Torremolinos has its respectable residential areas and even an old quarter, El Calvario, of whitewashed houses and black-clad septuagenarians. But it has acquired a honky-tonk reputation, characterized by Calle San Miguel, the pedestrian mall chock-a-block with illuminated signs, glib touts, bleeping electronic games and sparsely-clothed holiday-makers. Its nights are haunted by teenage ravers, transvestites, drug-pedlars, street musicians and flower-sellers. After the golden days of the sixties, the town slumped into tattiness and blamed the decline on Málaga's failure to reinvest the taxes gathered there. The recent creation of an autonomous Torremolinos town council could reverse the trend.

Whatever its critics say of it, Torremolinos has no pretensions. It tried to be Greenwhich Village, but ended up the coast's good-time girl, bawdy, cheerful, always ready for a party. Fuengirola, on the other hand, just up the road, is like a maiden aunt. How Bournemouth was transferred to the Mediterranean coast I shall never know. The fishing village has been crushed by the high-rise apartments that line the sea promenade. New ones are shoehorned in by the day. In summer, it is popular with tightly-budgeted families, who cook their meals in those endless apartments. In winter, the loudest noise is the click of walking sticks and pace-makers.

Pegged to the mountain above Fuengirola, picture-postcard Mijas has barely changed — apart from the vast car-park built to accommodate hundreds of tour buses, the quaint burro taxis, the museum of miniatures, the souvenir shops, the boutiques, the town hall fit for Roman emperors, and the thousands of expatriates enjoying simple village ways. At Happy Hour, ice rattles in so many highballs, this could be a Long Island suburb.

Since more than half the residents within Mijas boundaries are non-Spaniards, expatriates could one day take control of the Town Hall. The European Community allows its nationals to vote in municipal elections and hold office in whichever European country they reside.

English is the lingua franca along the coast. So great has been its advance that authorities of San Roque (the town formed by Gibraltar's original inhabitants who fled the Rock when the British took it in 1704) tried to ban its use in advertisements. At Marbella, however, Arabic script competes for attention on billboards and business signs, announcing the power of oil money. A glistening mosque close to the king of Saudi Arabia's mansion rubs the message in.

If Torremolinos is the good-time girl, Marbella is the courtesan, the Madame Pompadour of the Costa. Until the 1950s, her charms were unpublicized and iron mining was an important industry. The pleasant old quarter and the Moorish walls remain, but the blast furnaces and ore-loading port are gone. Ricardo Soriano, Marquis of Ivanrey, pioneered Marbella as a high-class resort for his well-heeled friends. Later, his nephew, Prince Alfonso von Hohenlohe, of Liechtenstein, founded the Marbella Club. When it opened in 1953 in a converted farmhouse, a room cost a hefty 100 pesetas a night, but it soon became a watering hole for hosts of celebrities.

Today Arab princes, bankers, wheeler-dealers, stockbrokers, the upwardly mobile and their hangers-on are among those who pay court to Marbella, snapping up million-pound penthouses and filling more than 130 bank branches with a sultan's ransom in petrodollars, Swiss francs, riyals, sterling and gems. Marbella sees itself as a second Monte Carlo, with the advantage that the winters are warmer.

Several hundred Rolls Royces glide smoothly between the casino, luxury hotels, golf courses and costly housing estates girding the town and neighbouring San Pedro. Those with the right connections move in a smug world filled with yachts, tennis, riding, backgammon, gossip and parties. In the words of one party-giver: "We like fun people. Marbella can forgive anything but a bore."

Some of the fun people are no joke. They live behind high walls and electrified fences. Bodyguards and slavering hounds keep well-wishers at a distance. Occasionally they welcome *tout* Marbella to lavish parties. Everybody has lots of fun and avoids asking where the money comes from. Gate-crashers may include plain-clothes policemen trying to crack down on the heavy traffic in drugs on the coast.

"The coast is a gateway for drugs," says a narcotics detective. "On any moonless night, we know that tons of hashish are being unloaded on Costa del Sol beaches. Speedboats can make the run from Morocco in 30 minutes. Often the smuggling of hashish, cocaine and heroin is financed by the proceeds of robberies in other European countries. We know who the leaders are, but loopholes in international law make it difficult to seize them."

To the west lies down-to-earth Estepona, and beyond — in Cádiz province — the golf courses, marina and polo fields of Sotogrande, poshest of all. Close by, Gibraltar, crouching under its plume of cloud and Union Jack, provokes continuing friction between London and Madrid. The *llanitos* — as the 19,000 natives are known — slip easily between Spanish and English and many have bought themselves homes on the Costa del Sol. But they brook no talk of Spanish sovereignty.

Any concessions to Spain are viewed as treachery. Indeed, after Madrid and London agreed to joint use of Gibraltar's commercial airport, the colony's government defiantly refused to permit such a move. Gibraltarians viewed with mixed feelings the departure of the Royal Green Jackets in March 1991. They formally handed over defence responsibilities for the Rock to the locally-recruited Gibraltar Regiment. For the first time since 1704, when Britain seized the territory from Spain, there is no British battalion based permanently in the two-and-a-quarter-square-mile territory.

Looking up at the Union Jack flying over The Convent, the Governor's residence, a policeman asks: "She's still flying, but for how long?"

Traces of Gib's warlike past abound in the crowded, claustrophobic colony, with its grim ramparts and old cannon. In King's Chapel, the garrison church, hang the fading colours of nine regiments of the line entitled to bear the battle honour "Gibraltar". Joe Bossano, the colony's Chief Minister, trying to shake off the garrison town image, has sought economic independence by making Gibraltar a second Hong Kong. Some four million visitors flock into the colony yearly and it has taken off as an offshore financial centre. More than 30,000 company plaques line lawyers' walls and a score of banks do business. Tourists and financial wheeler-dealers are more frequently to be seen these days in the typically English pubs than Jack Tars and Tommy Atkinses.

But there are still British servicemen in Gibraltar and it continues to have strategic importance. The 1,400-foot-high Jurassic limestone Rock is honey-combed with secret installations. From here the Atlantic and Mediterranean are electronically surveyed and traffic through the Straits checked.

Legend says that when the apes — believed to have first arrived with the Moors — leave the Rock, the British will go too. Winston Churchill made a monkey out of that story during the Second World War. Hearing that the Barbary Ape *(Macaca sylvana)* pack was diminishing, he ordered that the number should never fall below 35. Ever since, the Army, whose responsibility the apes are, has made sure that ape numbers are maintained. A strict health food diet was ordered for them after it was found that junk food fed by tourists was making the apes fat and uninterested in sex.

General Franco, sadly uninformed about the simian myth, tried to win Gib back by closing the frontier. But the 19-year blockade backfired by making the Gibraltarians more determined to avoid Spanish sovereignty. Spaniards claim that the Rock is a nest of smugglers — sneaking cheap tobacco into Spain is still a local pastime — and a haven for drug money. In return, Gibraltarians look askance at their neighbours, comparing their own tranquil, almost puritanical atmosphere and the shenanigans in crime-ridden La Línea, just across the frontier.

This British colony appears a strange anachronism in the 20th century, but no stranger than the multinational escapist paradise developing along the coast. The Costa del Sol is a cosmopolitan colony, where new settlers can live out their fantasies under few restraints; but some people have difficulty acclimatizing. Cut off from their roots and the pressures of their home environment, they cannot handle the freedom. They drift into alcoholism, marriages break up, they go home.

While appreciating the material gains, some Spaniards feel they have been exploited by the pale-faced arrivals, although the exploitation has surely come from both sides. In the process, through inevitable intermarriage and interchange of cultural values, a new hybrid society has been spawned, one which Andalusia will probably assimilate in time as it has so many others.

Integration is already well under way. A friend who split his childhood between Andalusia and an English public school demonstrated that as we drove through a town. "Slow down a moment, old chap," he cried in his best cut-glass English accent, then leaned out to address a passing female in broad Andalusian: *"¡Hola, guapita! ¡Que ojos tan bonitos! ¡Bendito sea el día que tu naciste!* [Hello, pretty one! What beautiful eyes you have? Blessed be the day you were born!]."

Less a place, more a state of mind, the Costa del Sol goes its own hedonistic way. Maps are no help in locating this wonderful, wacky island in the sun, somewhere off the coast of Spain.

Realm of Eagles

L OST in the sierras, the cluster of dwellings sits amid tree-girt slopes and tumbled limestone crags. Newspapers rarely find their way in and only one bus a day connects the village to the outside world. It is a fitting refuge for the last of the guerrilleros.

Manolo "El Rubio", officially reported dead half a century ago, lives here in Genalguacil. Though nearing 80, he is robust in mind and body, a revolutionary who fought and lost but has not surrendered, the sort of man you would prefer to have on your side. His is a remarkable story, and an appropriate one to introduce the eyrie guarded by the sierras of Ronda and Cádiz.

In 1949, when General Franco's soldiers and Civil Guards were hunting down the last of the Communist-led rebels in Andalusia, Manolo's group was trapped in an ambush. Six men were gunned down, and Manolo was identified as one of the dead.

Scanning press cuttings about his exploits, Manolo smiles grimly: "The body was somebody else's. I was far away, hiding out in a cortijo."

Afraid that showing himself would mean instant execution, he stayed in his hideaway for 27 years. Most of his days were spent sitting on a pile of cork in a pine-branch shack. Only at night did he venture out for some exercise. He read little, rarely having the chance to see a paper. A shortwave radio gave him some news and once a year he had a special treat — through binoculars he could watch the Virgin being carried through the streets of Genalguacil.

"These were my only luxury," recalls Manolo, lighting a cigarette packed with pungent black tobacco. "But I had to hide my butts and be careful about the smell because the Civil Guard came by on patrol. Sometimes they would sit a few metres away in the shade, and me in my shack hardly daring to breathe."

All those years, Ana "La Oveja", the sturdy, spirited woman who looked after him, kept his secret. Finally, a betrayal led to his arrest. He emerged into a transformed, post-Franco Spain and was promptly pardoned. With friends and relatives, including a son he had never seen, he held joyful reunions.

Under his real name of Pablo Pérez Hidalgo, Manolo returned to live peacefully with Ana in Genalguacil. But he says that, under circumstances similar to those in his youth, he would still be ready to take to the hills as a guerrilla.

Hermits and bold spirits have always found sanctuary in these bristling ranges. The phantoms of outlaws, smugglers and rebels tread the lonely paths, and myth and fact interweave inextricably amid the misty heights. To this day, they remain a realm of eagles.

The people of the sierras that stretch from Málaga province into Cádiz inhabit a separate, isolated world from that of the frivolous lowlands. Can urbane Jerez be in the same province as Grazalema or Ubrique, locked in their mountain fastnesses? What does colourful, cosmopolitan Málaga have in common with sober, self-contained Ronda?

Ronda — poised on a 600-foot cliff — was once the centre of a Moorish kingdom ruled by Abu Nur. A thousand years later, the old town still has an independent air. By day, bus tours flock in from the coast, but, when they have departed and the sun dips below the amphitheatre of surrounding mountains, Abu Nur's stronghold withdraws into its private self again.

It took cunning and a seven-day siege by an army of 13,000 cavalry and 25,000 infantry to oust the Moors in 1485. Fooled by King Ferdinand into thinking that the main Christian attack would be against Málaga, Ronda's governor Hamet el Zegri marched away with most of his army. Later he wailed to his lost city: "Oh unfortunate one! Why did I leave your strong walls? You were beautiful and impregnable."

Since those times many a bloody drama has been played out around El Tajo, the awesome void which splits the town in two. Attempts to span the gorge have had their quota of tragedy. The lowest bridge is a much-restored Arab structure. Next comes the Puente Viejo, dating from the 17th century. The so-called Puente Nuevo (New Bridge) now the main entrance to Ronda, is a mere 200 years old. This bridge is the second built at this point. An earlier one went up in eight months and fell down within six years. Determined that such a scandal should not recur, the builders took 40 years over the next attempt. When the last stone was in place, in 1793, architect Martín Aldehuela had himself lowered over the abyss to make an inspection. His hat blew off, he tried to grab it and plunged to his death.

Macabre events dot the history of the Tajo. Picadors' horses killed in the bullring used to be tossed into the chasm, until a 1929 decree ordered better protection for them against the bulls' horns. At the start of the Spanish Civil War, the rocks choking the bed of the Guadalevin river claimed many more victims. Priests and right-wingers were forced to run the gauntlet, then were tossed into the gorge, an incident referred to in Ernest Hemingway's *For Whom the Bell Tolls*.

"So many awful things happened that you accepted it as normal," recalls Paco, a veteran *rondeño*. "After the left-wingers murdered their enemies, the Nationalists captured the town and they had their turn. We all went to the Casino, the gentry's club, to watch the court martials and every day there were executions."

The Tajo continues to exercise a strange fascination on visitors who gape awe-struck into its depths. Unfortunately the Puente Nuevo also exerts the same magnetic effect as San Francisco's Golden Gate Bridge. Regularly, somebody arrives on the bus from Málaga, walks calmly to the Puente Nuevo and launches himself into eternity.

The bridge was completed thanks to help from the Real Maestranza de Caballería, which was eager to improve access to the new bullring. The Maestranza dates from 1573, when Philip II ordered a chivalrous brotherhood to be formed to encourage manly arts among a decadent nobility. Similar organizations were later formed in Seville, Granada, Valencia and Zaragoza. The nobles used the ring for equestrian training and practised the art of fighting bulls from horseback, but the Romero family established Ronda as the cradle of the modern corrida, which is contested on foot.

Francisco Romero invented the killing sword and cape, and on the golden sands of the new, circular plaza, still the largest of any in Spain, his grandson Pedro (1754-1839) perfected the skills of the sober, classic Ronda style. Goya immortalized the exploits of Romero, who killed 5,600 bulls during his 30-year career and is regarded as one of the greatest matadors of all time. Every September Ronda commemorates that epoch with a *corrida goyesca,* in which the participants wear costumes in the style designed by the painter. The *goyesca* is organized by Antonio Ordóñez, the Ronda matador who followed Romero's classic style.

Although he is retired, Ordóñez is still addressed as *maestro* by aficionados in recognition of his skill in the ring. Ernest Hemingway, a close friend, praised Ordóñez as "a genius with the cape", and the maestro thinks that the American author was quite a fellow too. "There should be more recognition of what Ernesto did for Spain," asserts Ordóñez. "His writings helped to make this country known to a whole generation of Americans."

Another American with a soft spot for Spain and Ordóñez was Orson Welles, so much so that he asked for his ashes to be laid to rest on the matador's estate near Ronda. Ordóñez agreed and at a simple ceremony in May 1987, the film-maker's remains were interred on Spanish soil.

Bullfight fans who make pilgrimages to Ronda make a point of visiting the Bullfight Museum, housed under the plaza's terraced seating. Posters for the first corridas, held on May 19 and 24, 1785, are on display. Another poster, from September 1799, advertises that Pedro Romero, Josef Delgado and Antonio Romero would fight 16 bulls, and adds: "So that the public receives as much entertainment as it desires, two of the most arrogant bulldogs will be made ready to subdue the bull designated by the judge." Nearby, an exhibit from more recent times is a reminder of the perils faced by those who seek glory in the ring. It is the last ear cut in Ronda by the matador Paquirri, shortly before he himself met death in the afternoon in 1984.

The bullring stands in Ronda's more modern quarter, El Mercadillo, where bars, banks and shops are concentrated. Courting couples linger in the Alameda park, which looks out over a precipice to undulating farmland and the encircling mountains. The park's construction had an original source of finance: it was paid for by fines imposed on persons guilty of blasphemy and

Far above the coast, the summit of El Lucero offers an unrivalled view of the rugged scenery and fertile valleys of the Ajarquía in Málaga province.

Two Rondeños enjoy an impromtu dance outside the plaza de toros in Ronda.

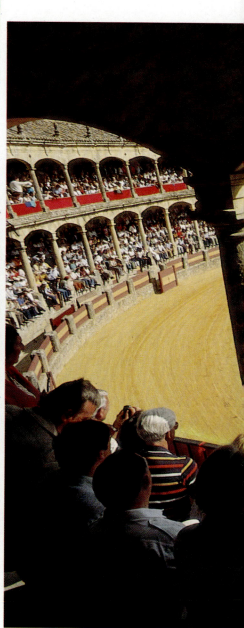

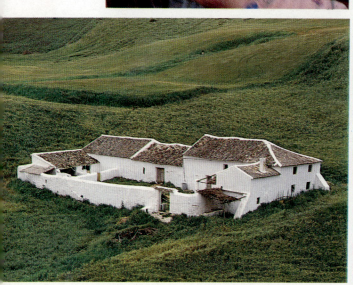

Lush spring grass frames the archetypal farmhouse near Setenil.

Carriages parade through Ronda's ancient bullring to the applause of an enthusiastic crowd.
Overleaf: Pablo Pérez Hidalgo, craggy as the landscape he fought over as an anti-Fascist guerrilla, stands with wife Ana outside the farm where he hid from the Civil Guard for 27 years.

indecency. *Rondeños* like to stroll through the Alameda, past the bullring and along the Carrera de Espinel, a lengthy, traffic-free shopping street which owes its name to Vicente Espinel, a 16th-century poet and novelist. He is Ronda's most famous man of letters, but fame is fleeting and most *rondeños* know the street as the Calle de la Bola.

The strollers often pause for a *yema,* a sweet Ronda speciality made from egg yolks, or for a beer or a *fino* sherry. One port of call is the Casino, the same club where summary justice was administered in Civil War days. Today the Casino, on the Plaza de Socorro, is a more democratic establishment. It is called the Circulo de Artistas and has a bar open to the public.

Ronda's streets reach a height of animation during the May and September fairs, when they are thronged with whippet-lean shepherds from the hills, gossiping village folk, visitors from the coast and pedlars of herbs and trinkets. The livestock market, held at the same time at the edge of town, attracts shrewd-eyed gypsies carrying loaded sticks who play an important part in fierce haggling over sales of mules, donkeys and horses.

For sheer architectural interest, the zone known as La Ciudad, with its narrow streets and noble buildings, has most appeal. This is the old town, through which visitors arriving by route C-339 from coastal San Pedro de Alcántara pass before crossing the Puente Nuevo into El Mercadillo. Mudéjar, Renaissance and Gothic styles are to be found in the churches and palaces in La Ciudad. Mondragon Palace, said to be built on the site of a 10th-century Moorish potentate's residence, once sheltered the Catholic Monarchs. Today it is an exhibition centre. The restored minaret of a mosque, long ago destroyed, is another reminder of the Moorish era. Nearby, the palace of the aristocratic Salvatierra family presents an elegant Renaissance façade, complete with two curious figures supporting the pediment over the balcony. Meetings of the Real Maestranza have often been held in this mansion.

Legends swirl about a residence on the edge of the gorge. Though it is called the House of the Moorish King, it dates only from the early 17th century. Behind the house more than 300 steps, cut out of the rock, lead down to the river. Christian slaves, held captive in rock dungeons, are said to have been forced to carry water up these steps for their Moorish masters. Nobody can vouch for the truth of the story. However, a curse once commonly used in the region — "May you die humping water bags in Ronda!" — adds credence to the tale.

The thousands of day tourists who arrive by the San Pedro road, an impressive piece of modern engineering which has made Ronda more easily accessible, rarely get futher than the old quarter, the Tajo and the bullring. Speeding past, they see the surrounding country only as a blur of mist-girdled mountains and obscure villages. Yet there is interest enough for those who care to explore. To the east of C-339, for example, rises Torrecilla. At 6,200 feet, it is the highest peak in the region and dominates the Sierra of the Snows. This range lies within the 23,000-hectare Serranía de Ronda national game preserve, which extends to the wild country behind Marbella.

Ornithologists scan the heights for cruising eagles, falcons and vultures. Hunters stalk the ibex in season. But the range has something else to offer:

on its rocky slopes the *pinsapo* thrusts down thirsty roots. This curious, short-needled fir is unique in Europe. The only other stands are in northern Morocco. The tree can grow to a height of 100 feet and thrives in the coldest, dampest spots more than 3,000 feet above sea-level.

To the west of the San Pedro-Ronda highway, a series of villages slumber as though in another century. In spring, wild sweet pea and rock-roses splash purple and white along the sides of the roads that wander erratically by. Grass grows between the cobbles and flowers sprout on rooftops in hamlets like Cartajima, which nestles amid chestnut and pine trees. Only in the local bars, which may double as post offices or grocery stores, will you find modern touches. A jumbo-sized television may be blaring soap opera and a fruit machine jingling while spare men in worn clothes concentrate on their domino games.

The Moors pinned a series of fortress villages to the precipitous slopes of the Genal River valley. As its Arabic name reveals, Benadalid was one. It sits next to the C-341, the Ronda-Algeciras highway, and offers a curiosity: ranks of cemetery niches lining the walls of a fort built in the days of the caliphs. Close by lies Algatocín, near which occurred the ambush in which El Rubio was wrongly identified as one of the dead. He and his comrades were accustomed to sneaking into a farmhouse at dusk to eat. El Rubio had left the group that day Civil Guards laid the fatal trap which claimed the lives of his guerrilla companions.

Route C-341 wanders on, to Jimena de la Frontera, Castellar, and Algeciras bay. But first it calls at Gaucín, in the past a favourite haunt of smugglers. In the old days, travellers between Gibraltar and Ronda often made overnight halts here, staying at an hotel which still exists under the name La Nacional. Many entries in the hotel register are in English, like that of one guest who, in 1881, had ridden from Ronda in nine hours and commented, "The saddles were invented by the Inquisition."

A 13th-century castle still looks out over Gaucín, but not much remains since a powder magazine exploded in 1848. The castle receives attention in Spanish history because in 1309 Guzmán El Bueno, who had made himself a hero by sacrificing his son to Moors besieging Tarifa, was killed in battle here.

North-west of Gaucín, Málaga province projects like a pan-handle into Cádiz. In this remote corner lies the Cortes de la Frontera game preserve. Abundant rainfall encourages thick forests of cork-oak which shelter red deer and roe deer. A variety of hawks and eagles play the air currents over the rugged terrain, seeking prey. One potential victim they would do well to avoid because of its ability to defend itself against all comers is the small, catlike carnivore which makes its home here: the Egyptian mongoose, the only mongoose found in Europe.

From the C-341, a road twists spectacularly to lonely Cortes de la Frontera. En route it crosses the Ronda-Algeciras railway, which darts in and out of tunnels as it follows the Guadiaro river. Not far from Cortes the river plunges through the Angostura del Guadiaro, a narrow canyon with walls more than 300 feet high.

Riding the train from Ronda as it threads its way through the mountains can be a magical experience, with ever-changing views of rushing water, chasms, and crags sliding out of the mists. The line was built by a British company last century. ("Excellent carriages, fare Bobadilla to Gibraltar, including ferry, 11, 18 or 25 pesetas," reported the 1901 Baedeker, noting that even Spanish *express* trains rarely travelled at more than 25 mph.)

From Cortes, a road climbs and weaves through the forest, edges into the game preserve and emerges in Cádiz province. This is depopulated country. Most of the people who once lived by charcoal-burning, rearing pigs and running flocks have moved away. Finally, at the Monjon de la Vibora crossroads, a road swoops down to Ubrique, with breath-taking views all the way.

Ubrique, sheltering under the mass of the Cruz del Tajo mountain, looks nothing special. But since the 1960s it has experienced a big jump in population and I witnessed one reason for the boom when I entered a modern building in a back-street. A worker deftly sliced supple hide to size and hammered it with a wooden tool known as a *pata de cabra.* Around him scores of men and women were engaged in similar work. Soon the elegant leatherware, handbags, purses, wallets, they were producing would go on sale under such names as Balenciaga and Dior. I was asked to avoid photographing finished articles, possibly because part of Ubrique's prosperity stems from "pirate" products.

Trade with outlaws and *contrabandistas* — nearby Gibraltar was a centre of tobacco-smuggling — stimulated the growth of Ubrique's leather industry in the 18th century, when the locals began making belts in which muleteers could keep tobacco and flint.

"We have our own trade name these days, Piel de Ubrique," they told me at the town hall, where they laughed at the idea of "piracy".

Ubrique has only a handful of factories with more than 50 workers. The rest are family concerns, tiny enterprises to which a special holiday is devoted on the last Monday in May every year. Exhibitions and entertainment are held then, on the Day of the *Petaqueros,* makers of *petaques* (tobacco pouches). But one of the best times to be in Ubrique is during the first week of May when each quarter lights a street bonfire and throws a party to celebrate an ancient festival, the Crosses of May. Children get a particular kick out of the *fogonazos,* an odd ritual in which a *gamón,* an asphodel stick, is heated in a fire, then whacked against a stone to produce a sharp bang.

A traveller can easily stumble on other ancient rituals if he traverses the sierras. At nearby Villaluenga del Rosario, with its *plaza de toros* cut into the rock, the biggest annual excitement is a bull-run. Grazalema, just up the road, has a similar event known as the *lunes del Toro,* which draws large numbers of visitors. Every July, on the Monday after the fiesta devoted to the Virgen del Carmen, youths dance defiance before the horns of a bull which careers madly along the narrow streets. Although five centimetres are shaved from its horns and the half-ton beast is restrained by a long rope, the game can still be lethal. But most damage is self-inflicted as panicking runners elbow one another aside. Signs warn runners not to mistreat the wild-eyed bull during this mini-Pamplona which dates from Moorish times and was later adapted by

Carmelite monks as a Christian festivity.

Although the sun usually blazes down during this fiesta, for a good part of the year it is a different story in Grazalema. The town, more than 2,800 feet above sea-level, crouches in the mighty shadow of El Torrejón, one of the army of peaks which form a solid barrier against which clouds sailing in from the Atlantic collide. The clash causes rain to tumble down in winter as though it will never stop. With a claimed annual rainfall of more than 3,000 litres, the village is said to be the wettest spot in all Spain.

"Once 290 litres fell in nine hours and the water came bubbling up in shops and houses, lifting the tiles," recalls Mario Sánchez Roman, pausing over his account books.

Mario's family for long kept alive the last trace of the weaving industry that once spread Grazalema's name as far afield as South America. Products from its half-dozen woollen mills brought fame and prosperity to the pueblo, and in Argentina shepherds still wear the heavy ponchos made here, while local brides treasure the thick, natural-coloured blankets which never wear out. But early this century economic factors almost wiped out the business and Grazalema's population has halved to fewer than 2,000. In the 1980s, however, government aid encouraged a revival. An old mill was renovated as a working museum and local youngsters trained in traditional methods.

Mario's own mill, out in the Ribera valley, is about as traditional as you can get. A 40-foot-high iron water-wheel creaks outside, powering century-old machinery inside the rambling structure which is supported by colossal wooden roof beams. Wool is combed, cleaned and spun in the same manner as it has been done for hundreds of years. Two of the weavers, Manuel Campuzano and Juan Valle, work at a large hand-loom, to the clatter of the flying shuttle.

Thousands of merino sheep roam the heights where sudden storms can blow up, catching the unwary. It is hardy country, fit for eagles and *pinsapos.* And it is trout country, too, and the crystal waters that gush from these mountains have been exploited to establish hatcheries for rainbow trout at Benamahoma and El Bosque.

Many of the sierra villages look as though they were made for brigands and smugglers. Olvera is a striking example. Of this community, it was once written: "Olvera, one street, one church, one castle... but what a Street, what a Church, what a Castle!"

And Zahara, not far from Olvera, appears even more dramatic as it tumbles about the foot of a fortress-crowned outcrop. These days, the village is re-nowned for its Corpus Christi procession, and during the celebration, the streets are decked with greenery. In the past, however, they ran with blood. In 1481, under cover of darkness and a wild storm, Muley Hacen, ruler of the kingdom of Granada, urged his men up Zahara's walls. They butchered the Christian garrison and marched a column of slaves off to Granada. There, one ancient sage bewailed this offence against the powerful Christian lords, cry-ing: "The ruins of Zahara will fall on our heads. The days of our empire in Spain are numbered." And so it was — Granada fell 11 years later.

Violence marred life in Zahara again in the turbulent last half of the 19th century, when this region was a stronghold of anarchy. One local outlaw, Juan Villaescusa, or "El Cristo", was said to have belonged to the Black Hand, a secret society allegedly plotting to assassinate all landowners. In those desperate times, thousands of labourers, angered by the selling off of common land, were ready for anything. Their miserable situation pushed many into banditry and provoked the creation, in 1844, of the Civil Guard, whose specific task was to protect the persons and property of the more privileged.

As Gerald Brenan pointed out (in *The Spanish Labyrinth)*, in Andalusia the outlaw often acted as a safety-valve for popular discontent. "In the eyes of the country people he was a hero, the friend of the poor and [a] champion against [their] oppressors," he noted.

The caves and ravines of Ronda's sierras were ideal bolt-holes for runaways, and *bandolerismo* was an accepted trade until comparatively recently. Old-timers will tell you that, apart from El Rubio and his fellow rebels, the last true *bandolero* was *"Pasos Largos"* (Big Steps), a poacher born near the village of El Burgo, on the Ronda-Málaga road. Quick-tempered and fast on the trigger, he took to the mountains after murdering a father and son. Agile as a goat, cunning as a fox, Pasos Largos became a legendary figure. He served 16 years in gaol, but fell foul of the law again and once more went on the run. Mystery surrounded his last moments. Officially, Pasos Largos died in a shoot-out with the Civil Guard in 1934, when he was cornered in a cave. But some accounts suggest that the last of the *bandoleros* was murdered by a treacherous companion.

If any runaways are to be found in the mountains of Ronda and Cádiz these days, they are likely to be escaping from the stresses of city life rather than the long arm of the law. In turn, youngsters escape from the hard existence and limited opportunities of remoter communities to seek excitement and more money in the cities. Those who stay complain about the difficulties of scraping a living from a harsh land, but they still manage to keep themselves entertained. The people of the village of El Gastor, within easy reach of Olvera and Zahara, are a case in point. Wander through El Gastor's quiet streets and you may hear strange melodies issuing from the houses. If you are around at Corpus Christi, the sound swells into a symphony when 20 or so cow-horn players compete in an annual contest. Most of the instruments are made by farmer Manuel Gómez.

"This was a lost art until I started making these instruments in 1983," he says. "Now dozens of people have started playing. The horns of wild bulls are best as they are finer. I clean them, file them, then insert a walnut-wood mouthpiece. A piece of cane forms the reed. Now listen to this!" Cheeks bulging, Manuel and his young son, Francisco, demonstrate the somewhat limited capabilities of these rustic music-makers.

From El Gastor an idyllic country road undulates towards Setenil (19 kilometres from Ronda). This village is an amazing tribute to man's optimistic nature, for the glowering lips of rock that form the roofs of many houses look ready to crush the lot at any moment. Setenil is unusual in that it is built in a cleft rather than on a ridge as is the usual Andalusian habit. Rock blocks the sky in one street, yet the villagers appear unaffected by claustrophobia.

Between El Gastor and Setenil, a side-track leads up to the escarpment occupied by the ruins of Ronda La Vieja. Once this was the site of the Roman settlement of Acinipo. The wind whistles about a reconstructed theatre with a Doric door and a semicircle of seats. The famous Battle of Munda, between Julius Caesar and Pompey's army, is supposed to have taken place near here in 45 BC, although some historians claim it occurred elsewhere.

What nobody can deny is that man made some of his earliest attempts at artistic expression in these mountains. A Stone Age art gallery awaits those who drive 29 kilometres from Ronda along a winding route that passes the villages of Montejaque and Benaoján. A sign indicates the Cueva de la Pileta. The entrance to the cave sits above a secluded valley, occupied by a farm-house, home of the Bullón family. (the name is a reminder of Napoleon's invasion, when a French soldier married a Ronda girl). Sooner or later, one of the three Bullón brothers notices your presence and climbs briskly up the hillside to act as guide. They are not the bored professional guides you find in some spots.

"We're all well read and naturally we're interested in history because here in this cave we have the story of man. You can see 14 distinct epochs of man's past," says Eloy.

He issues oil pressure lamps to visitors — no multicoloured illumination or background music here — and leads them by their flickering light into a series of vast caverns believed to have been hollowed out by an underground river. Amongst stalactites and stalagmites signs of palaeolithic Man abound. His campfires dusted the walls with soot in some places. There are animal bones, tools, shards of pottery and paintings in charcoal and red and yellow ochre.

"It would take five years to see all the paintings. After Altamira, this is Spain's most important cave for art work," claims Eloy, indicating an archer, a goat, a deer, and a pregnant mare, which is believed to be related to a fertility cult. A striking outline of a fish dates back at least 15,000 years. In the same chamber abstract signs and symbols, hinting at magic ritual, have been the subject of archaeological debate. Did the young woman, whose fossilized remains were found, die in human sacrifice?

Eloy's grandfather, José Bullón Lobato, discovered the cave in 1905 when searching for guano to use as fertilizer.

He noticed a pile of bat deposits and lowered himself on a rope through an opening in the rock. After descending 30 metres, he found himself in a small chamber. His flickering acetylene lamp revealed that he had stumbled on an astonishing treasure trove of primitive art and artefacts. First, he saw pieces of pottery and blackened rock, then a series of chambers with vivid wall-paintings. Later, an English veteran of the Boer War, Colonel Willoughby Verner, visiting the district on a hunt for birds' eggs, was persuaded by Bullón Lobato to take a look at his great discovery. The colonel's enthusiasm sparked outside interest and later exploration turned up a number of fossilized skeletons, some at the bottom of a 200-foot-deep gallery.

Other traces of prehistoric man must certainly lurk amid the sierras. So far, man has only nibbled at the surface of this wilderness. There are clefts and chasms which remain almost impenetrable. Only in 1929, for example, did an expedition solve the mystery of a disappearing stream. Descending into the Hundidero cave, not far from La Pileta, near the village of Montejaque, the explorers discovered that the stream continued underground and emerged after four kilometres in the Cueva del Gato (Cave of the Cat). Nobody had known the two were linked.

The discovery was made by men working on an ambitious project close by. A dam 200 feet high was constructed to block a valley, but the expected reservoir failed to materialize. To the chagrin of the engineers, the water was not trapped by the dam but leaked away through crevices in the rock. They abandoned the project in disgust. Now climbers find the dam wall useful for practice.

The tortured ranges of the Serranía de Ronda do not yield easily to man's endeavours, nor willingly give up their secrets. Only a rugged breed can survive here, in the realm of eagles.

A Taste of Sea Salt and Wine

IT is 5 a.m. on Good Friday and they are playing a lullaby to the Virgin in Arcos de la Frontera. The heavy float of Nuestra Señora del Mayor Dolor y Traspaso rocks gently from side to side as it descends Bethlehem Hill in time to a soothing melody. Its 10 bearers strain to keep their footing on the wet paving, which is spattered with melted wax from hundreds of candles. In about nine hours' time they will be back this way, muscles cracking, heads ringing, struggling up the Cuesta de Belén with the Virgin on their shoulders for a final delirious welcome at her home church.

Amid the drumbeat solemnity of Holy Week in Andalusia even unbelievers experience a tingle up their spines, and this is particularly so in a town like Arcos where a medieval fervour breathes through the streets. Streets so narrow at some points that the Easter processions come to a halt while images are edged past close-leaning walls inch by inch.

Sometimes there is light relief. When a sudden rain squall interrupted one procession, a hooded penitent hammered on the nearest door with his staff.

"Open up! Open up!" he bellowed. "El Cristo must have shelter."

Black-robed members of the brotherhood rushed inside with the lifelike image of a blood-streaked, suffering Jesus nailed to the Cross. He was safely installed in a corner of a room, which proved to be a bar. Customers and penitents mingled cheerfully until the storm eased.

Later, in the early hours of the morning, in a thronged, hushed street, a procession halted while a *saeta* singer launched his flamenco lament at Christ's sacrifice. As the voice died, the penitents resumed their march, staves thudding, bare feet rustling on the cobbles. It was an eerie, throat-catching moment.

It is hardly surprising if the past weighs heavily on towns like Arcos de la Frontera, for often they seem burdened with too much history. Legend says that Noah's grandson founded Arcos. Since then a good deal has happened in this archetypal Andalusian fortress community which clutches to its soaring crag for security. The Moors stayed for centuries, until King Alfonso the Wise of Castile swept them out 600 years ago.

In the bitter wars of that era, a number of towns in modern Cádiz province acquired the "de la Frontera" tag. Arcos, Jerez, Chiclana, Conil, and Véjer were Christian towns on the frontier with the Muslim kingdom of Granada.

Today's "Frontera" territory, in Spain's wind-ruffled south-west corner, has a character all its own and enough myths and legends for a whole country. There is an open, spacious feeling about much of Cádiz province. Maybe it is the rolling landscapes with swaying crops of grain and endless cattle pastures, or the big skies over limitless beaches, or the exposure to the relentless surge of the Atlantic.

From the sea have come both treasures and troubles. Tarifa was the starting point for the Moorish invasion. Tarif Ben Malik stepped ashore on the Isla de la Paloma in 710 to reconnoitre. The following year his compatriots hit the peninsula in earnest. Now the Spanish military occupy La Paloma, but bleached and buffeted Tarifa, a garrison town with streets named after dead warriors, seems part of Africa. And indeed Tangier, gleaming white across the Straits of Gibraltar, is only 30 minutes away by hydrofoil.

Until recently, Tarifa did not take much interest in attracting tourists, although local historian Francisco Terán Fernández points out: "You won't find better beaches anywhere, or more history. Look at the Arab fortress: one thousand years old."

It was in Tarifa castle that Alonso Pérez de Guzmán created a legend in the late 13th century. Moorish besiegers threatened to cut the throat of his nine-year-old son, who was in their power, unless he surrendered the town. He replied by tossing a dagger down to the enemy from the castle. This act earned him the name Guzmán el Bueno. Presumably, nobody asked his son's opinion...

When the *levante* wind is not blowing day and night about Tarifa's private streets, the *poniente* is likely to take its place. Visitors find it annoying, but researchers hope to harness Tarifa's wind and put it to practical uses: a hilltop just outside the town has been chosen for a government-sponsored experimental wind-power project.

A flock of vultures soared and glided effortlessly on the air currents as technician-in-charge José María Escudero López explained: "Three 10-metre blades of polyester reinforced with glass fibre are placed atop a 20-metre tower. They start revolving once the wind speed rises above six metres a second. This turbine can produce 100 kilowatts and that should be sufficient to supply Tarifa's street lights, making it Spain's first town to benefit from wind power."

He looked dreamily out over the stormy landscape.

"Who knows how much power would be available if all these hills were covered with hundreds of similar towers?"

Thousands of birds migrating to and from Africa battle — some sometimes unsuccessfully — the fierce winds near Tarifa, but another lean, weathered breed comes here from all over Europe precisely because of these hard-blowing winds. Just along the sandy, 10-kilometre sweep of Los Lances beach on one particular day when ships were heading for port, windsurf fanatics were having the time of their lives on a thundering, white-flecked sea. Riding tremendous breakers, they occasionally performed somersaults just for the hell of it.

"It may look crazy but it's fantastic fun," said a young instructor. "Everybody comes here because the conditions are among the best in Europe. It appeals because it's something you do by yourself — there's just you and the sea."

Men have been challenging the sea, and sometimes winning, along the Cádiz coast since craft of the fabled kingdom of Tartessus plied these waters. More than 2,500 ships are estimated to have come to grief off the city of Cádiz, from Roman galleys to Spanish galleons loaded with Inca gold. An ancient amphora is sometimes washed up on a beach and dredgers have turned up such articles as Phoenician images. Thick mud protects the wrecks, but controversy has raged about who has the right to disturb that mud before dredging operations wipe out the secrets of other ages.

Some of those secrets are slowly being unearthed alongside the white sands of Bolonia bay, just north of Tarifa, where archaeologists have laid bare the bones of Baelo Claudia, a prosperous Roman settlement at the time of Christ. Here fish were salted and "garum" was prepared for export. Although the Cordoban philosopher Seneca called this thick, dark paste "salted putrefaction", it was highly prized.

"It was made from the entrails of such fish as tuna and mackerel. And the garum from here was of such good quality it was renowned throughout the Roman empire," declared Isidoro Otero, guardian of the ruins, as we climbed the steps of Jupiter's temple.

"It was in demand because it was a stimulant and a reconstituent, containing lots of vitamins. They used to take it with water or wine. As far back as 500 BC we know the Greeks came here seeking this sauce."

Isidoro, a stocky, amiable Castilian who came to Bolonia in 1948 to work on military fortifications, pointed out a market, a theatre and the columns of the court building revealed by excavations started early this century. He talked with the authority of somebody who lives with history, and indeed he runs a café next to the ruins when he is not showing visitors around. We walked along Decumanus Maximus, the main street whose worn paving testifies to heavy traffic back in AD 100.

"There has not been much work on private houses so far," said Isidoro. "But there must be some grand ones because some very rich people lived here. They did business with Rome, so you could say they were the multinationals of those times."

They still hunt tuna off these coasts and methods have changed little in 2,000 years. From April to June, shoals of blue-fin tuna, which can reach a weight of 800 kilos, skirt the coast as they head for spawning grounds in the Mediterranean. They make the return run in July and August.

Relentless hunting around the world of this superbly streamlined fish — plus sea pollution — has cut back catches. In 1541, 141,000 were said to have been caught between Conil and Zahara de los Atunes. Now the annual haul is down to a few thousand. The privilege of setting *almadrabas,* the walls of netting used to trap the tuna, was first granted to Guzmán El Bueno and his descendants, the Dukes of Medina Sidonia (one of whom led the Great Armada against England).

At dawn, one perfect May day, I joined the fishermen of Barbate as they set out to check the seven kilometres of netting attached to the ocean floor by more than 500 massive anchors. Rows of bobbing floats marked the site of the *almadraba,* three kilometres offshore.

A modern touch was the frogman who dived to ascertain the number and the movements of the tuna. Some 90 men, sweating under the rising sun, hauled lines and dragged in the net under the cool direction of el Capitán, Vicente Zaragoza, a shrewd, middle-aged man distinguished by his white trilby. Twice the tuna swerved and dodged back towards the open sea, but there was no escape and they were slowly squeezed towards the *copo,* the sealed-off end of the net.

The frogman surfaced, giving the thumbs-up signal. A cheer went up from the exuberant fishermen.

"We've got 'em. And there are more than 300 down there," said one of the men, José Tortoza, stripping off an oilskin and producing a wicked-looking steel hook.

Abruptly, as the boats surrounding the net drew closer together, a gleaming torpedo broke the smooth surface. Then another, and another. And suddenly the sea erupted into a lather of foam as hundreds of fish leaped and plummeted before us in a despairing dance of death.

Leaning over the side of their craft, two or three men at a time hooked into the flesh of a struggling tuna and hauled it aboard. Within minutes, scores of 200- and 300-kilo monsters were smacking their tails against the timbers as life ebbed away.

The blood-bath lasted an hour. By midday, the men were exhausted, their boats low in the reddened water with a catch of 320 tuna.

Back in Barbate, the boats delivered most of their catch to waiting Japanese vessels. Spaniards, Japanese and Koreans worked quickly and skilfully, gutting, washing and slicing the tuna into mighty fillets for immediate storing in a freezing room with temperatures at minus 50 degrees Celsius. Soon those tuna would be on dining-tables half-way around the world.

It was near Barbate that Nelson's fleet routed a Franco-Spanish force in the Napoleonic War. Today, a lighthouse guards Cape Trafalgar, a low headland, near beaches where summer visitors work indefatigably on their all-over tans. Up the coast, past beaches and pine forests, close to Chiclana, stands another *almadraba* (tuna fishery). But Sancti Petri, next to marshes and salt-flats, has fallen into disuse. It is a ghost town, its church locked, its streets sprouting weeds. Nearby, next to La Barrosa beach, a luxury tourist resort called Novo Sancti Petri has sprung up.

In Chiclana, over a glass of chilled *fino* which the locals claim is as good as any sherry, I watched the sun dip into the purple ocean beyond a small offshore island said to have been visited by Hannibal to consult the priests of the Temple of Hercules before his elephant march on Italy. The Phoenicians were certainly here, for historians accept that they came from Tyre (Lebanon) around 1100 BC and founded Gadir.

The *gaditanos* (inhabitants of modern Cádiz) claim their city is the oldest in the Western world. Cádiz is an island in itself, a narrow, crowded peninsula with the sea at the end of almost every street. The site of shipyards and a naval base, it has always lived from the sea. Visigoths destroyed it, the French besieged it and Sir Francis Drake — an unprincipled pirate in Spanish eyes — sailed into the harbour to "singe the king of Spain's beard."

Tons of gold and silver from the Americas arrived at Cádiz in colonial times. Between 1810 and 1812, Cádiz was the capital of all Spain not under Napoleon's sway and the constitution proclaimed in the church of San Felipe Neri, in the heart of the city, became a rallying point for liberals. The city briefly boomed again in the 1970s when Spanish shipbuilders headed world production.

In the crypt of the yellow-domed cathedral rests the body of one of Spain's most popular contemporary composers, *gaditano* Manuel de Falla. *Nights in the Gardens of Spain* and *The Three Cornered Hat* are unmistakable evocations of Andalusia. (Music on a brassier, deafening level rules Cádiz every year at Carnival, celebrated here with a colourful, almost deranged gusto.)

Gaditanos love fresh seafood, from succulent squid to solid-fleshed swordfish. Puerto de Santa María, just across the bay, prides itself on its selection and, like the locals, I took "El Vapor", the ferry, to reach there. In one of the quayside bars they weighed out my order in paper bags which I took to a table. There, I savoured fat prawns and *percebes,* black barnacles resembling miniature elephants' feet and ordered my sherry from the waiter.

They are all sherry connoisseurs in the Puerto since it swims in the stuff. The town stands at one corner of the triangular sherry district, with Sanlúcar de Barrameda and Jerez at the others. In the cool twilight of one of the Terry company's bodegas, José Jiménez Heredia, better known as Pepe el Gitano, was demonstrating that the simple way is not always the best. Using a whippy rod with a cup on the end to extract wine from a barrel, he deftly filled a handful of sherry glasses with a showman's flourish.

"I use a *venencia* because it gives *alegría* (happiness) to the wine. This way the full aroma comes out," explained Pepe, who has travelled the world serving Terry wine. "There's more to it than just filling a glass. Above all, you must have *gracia* (graciousness), to please the people and make direct contact with them."

The *venencias* used to be made of whalebone, but today they are of plastic and stainless steel. And other things have changed in sherry land, too, as Fernando Gago, Terry's public relations chief, noted. "Some years ago I was much criticized when on a hot day I arranged for some visitors to be served a 'Hemingway' — crushed ice, lemon and sherry. It was regarded as sacrilege. But since then the bodegas have become less rigid about their wine... as long as people buy it and enjoy it."

Such an attitude amounts to a revolution in the sherry industry which until recently was dominated by about 15 families who were at pains to emphasize the exclusiveness of their product and the mystique surrounding its creation. The "snob" image went down well with the British, who are deeply involved in the business and still the biggest consumers, but it wasn't helping sales in the rest of the world.

Fast-talking marketing men and sharp-eyed accountants may have moved into the business, but sherry production still follows the old ritual. In a vineyard near Jerez de la Frontera, I watched a team of men harvesting Palomino grapes under a burning September sun. The heat bounced up from the hardened, white Albariza soil, one of the keys to quality sherry wine. Bending again and again over the vines and carting away the crates of golden grapes was hard labour, and far from overpaid. But these seasonal workers were glad of the opportunity to earn something.

"The harvest only lasts a couple of weeks and after that there's hardly any work around here, just odd jobs in the cotton fields or picking sugar-beet," said 20-year-old José García, as he squinted against the sun.

Fewer permanent jobs are available in the bodegas because they were forced to streamline operations after a financial crisis in the early Eighties. Following over-ambitious expansion, they sank into debt when exports stagnated.

Even a giant like Pedro Domecq was rumoured about to fall into the hands of a local wheeler-dealer named José María Ruiz Mateos, who had acquired one-third of sherry production.

Few of the sherry elite shed tears when the government abruptly seized his huge holding company, Rumasa, alleging fraud. Other bounders have moved in, however, like the Canada-based multinational, Seagrams, who now control the old English firm, Sandeman Brothers.

Ultra-modern equipment handles the grape before the fermented juice is deposited in barrels of American oak, each containing 500 litres. Jerez has a million of those barrels. They are stored in tiers, the youngest wine on top. Tier by tier, this is transferred to the bottom layer and blended with older vintages, until finally the mature wine is tapped. It is known as the *solera* system and, in Spain, to "have *solera*" means to have character.

Every year around 100 million litres of *finos, olorosos, amontillados* and *manzanillas* are exported. Spaniards themselves do not drink much sherry but they are addicted to Jerez brandy; not a prestigious drink but a highly profitable one for the bodegas.

Bartolomé Vergara, of the Sherry Exporters' Association, pointed out, "They say Jerez is full of *señoritos* [literally 'little gentlemen']. Sure, but what have the *señoritos* done? Produced one of Spain's most profitable export industries."

Bartolomé was not on his best form. Until 6 a.m. he had been entertaining important guests visiting the annual horse fair. If anybody goes to bed before dawn at this spring spree or at the September wine festival, *jerezanos* consider the party has been a flop.

"Our fair is not like the one in Seville," said Bartolomé. "It's an intimate affair, when friends who haven't seen one another in months meet and pour their hearts out about things they would never normally mention."

In the pulsating early hours of the morning, as jeans-clad teenagers, gold-jewelled matrons and little girls in vivid gypsy dresses swirled to flamenco music, accompanied by strict tempo hand-claps and the pop of corks, talk and wine flowed.

"Everybody — rich or poor — comes to the feria because they all dream of living like a *señorito,* if only for a moment," confided a *jerezano.*

True *señoritos* are easy to pick out at the fair. They wear flat-brimmed Córdoba hats and finely-tooled leather chaps and look suitably haughty and aristocratic as they ride magnificent thoroughbreds in the afternoon parades.

With their female counterparts, soft-eyed debby types, they throng the *casetas* (entertainment booths) of the major bodegas. Paris perfumes mingle with the odour of horse sweat in a world reminiscent of the English shires.

Nobody better typifies this squirearchy than the Domecqs. One chuckled: "Of course my English is good. I learned it from my nanny."

Wine comes first in sherry country, but bulls and horses are not far behind. At Dehesa Bolanos, the Osborne bull ranch, breeder José Luis explained some of his difficulties.

"Breeding is very complicated work and you need a lot of luck. It's not profitable — it's an *afición.* So many factors affect a bull's performance. It can take two days to get to the plaza. For the first time the bulls tread on cement, which heats their feet up. Then they run on to the sand of the ring or pick up a pebble and they're finished.

"Too much emphasis can be put on weight. Each cattleman breeds according to his own style and temperament, so that it's very difficult to have all bulls of the same weight and type. Apart from which, the suitable weight depends on the *plaza.* You know, when a bull enters the ring, it is like a small kid going to school for the first time. It has come straight from the country and seen nothing. A good *torero* is a true *maestro* because his task is to show the bull what to do."

At the sprawling property known as Los Alburejos, Alvaro Domecq rears his Torrestrella bulls. Once he was a noted *rejoneador* (mounted bullfighter). His son followed in his footsteps, but now devotes much of his time to the Escuela Andaluza del Arte Ecuestre, of which he is technical director. In a lofty arena built in the grounds of Las Cadenas, one of the numerous palaces of Jerez, Alvaro junior leads his team of "dancing" horses through a superb display of equestrian skills.

The fiery, silky-maned horses descend from the Cartujano breed, once bred by Carthusian monks at a nearby monastery. They train for three years, to the relaxing strains of classical music, until they are ready to learn such movements as the spectacular *cabriolé,* a kick while having all four hoofs off the ground. The school's high standards raise classical horsemanship to an art-form, and youngsters compete fiercely for a place there.

While Alvaro Domecq's mastery wins admiration, some local figures are objects of adoration. Like the *sevillanos,* the *jerezanos* like to create myths. Singer Lola Flores could stop the traffic with her voice, but her fans worship her as "The Pharaoh". When melancholy-faced gypsy matador Rafael de Paula, faces a bull, they say the sun stops and the wines stop breathing.

To some Spaniards, all this represents a feudal throw-back. They regard Jerez as a caricature, but there is a trace of envy in their griping. For it has to be admitted that Jerez does have style.

Away from sherryland, amid vast estates, the feudal aspect is unmistakable. Ancient hilltop towns, like Medina Sidonia and Alcalá de los Gazules, doze in whitewashed inertia, with traces of past splendour and with their quotas of dispirited landless labourers, jobless most of the year. Some things do change, of course. At Alcalá the old bullring is a disco.

They do not bother with a bullring at Vejer de la Frontera, a dazzling pyramid of white houses near Barbate. Every Easter Sunday a full-grown fighting bull chases taunting youngsters along its narrow, immaculate streets. His horns are padded, but in a similar ritual at Arcos the same day the bull is not *embolado* and blood often runs.

"Americans from the naval base at Rota get themselves killed by running with the bull after a few wines. They seem to think his horns are made of cardboard," commented Manuel Pérez Regordan.

Manuel, an Arcos native, is a schoolteacher who cannot stop writing.

"So far, I've written 24 books and I must know more about this province than anybody. Once I finished a book in one week, between a Saturday and a Sunday, but that was after months of research. My latest volume, about the anti-Franco maquis in the sierras after the Civil War, took five years' work. I've written a lot about Arcos and its history. There's so much here.

"For example, one legend involves the castle. Once it belonged to the Dukes of Arcos, the Ponce de León family. Now an English lady lives there, the Marquesa de Tamarón. In Moorish times, the king had to leave his favourite there to go to war. He never came back and she died of a broken heart. The story is that Nanafassi, as she was called, turned into a big black bird and every Friday she comes back. Our mothers used to frighten us with the story: 'Nanafassi is coming!' "

A cooling breeze wafted up from the Guadalete river to the plaza at the top of the town, but I saw only circling hawks near the battlements of the adjacent castle. Crossing the plaza, I climbed the tower of Santa María church. A shrivelled woman, as daunting as any Nanafassi, emerged from the depths to demand "a contribution", muttering as she peered at my coin.

Sunset brushed the tight, tiled roofs of Arcos and its soaring churches, casting into relief the panorama of green crops and ripening barley. The bells of Santa María sounded the hour, setting the stonework atremble. Far below in the plaza, oblivious to all, a make-believe matador spun and postured before an invisible bull in the golden twilight of the land of "la Frontera".

I descended the tower slowly, skirted the plaza and the wild-eyed bull-fighter challenging horns that nobody could see, and squeezed through the narrow, twilight streets of Arcos. The atmosphere was oppressive in the tight hilltop town. Sealed off from the expansive land about it, memories of past tragedy seemed to lurk at every corner. I left Arcos and headed for the wilderness. It was time to return to the source of the Great River, to the distant Sierra de Cazorla where a bubbling of clear water beneath the pines heralds the start of the Guadalquivir's long run through history and Andalusia.

*Isidoro Otero guards the ruins of Bolonia,
site of a prosperous Roman settlement at
the beginning of the Christian era.*
Below: *tuna thrash themselves into a death
frenzy in the Atlantic waters off Barbate.*

The dancing horses of Andalusia line up during a display in Jerez led by Alvaro Domecq.

Pepe el Gitano "gives happiness to the wine", by serving it with aid of a 'venecia'. Overleaf: pines and rock faces are reflected in the pristine waters of one of the lakes in the sierra of Cazorla.

The Last Wilderness

DARKNESS came early to the valley. Limestone pinnacles locked out the sun as twilight invaded the woods and the pine trees pressed closer. Beyond a squadron of poplars at the water's edge, the stillness was broken by a leaping fish.

Somewhere, a stray cow lamented its fate.

Except that this was no cow. From the dense shadows behind my campsite came a deep-throated response. A stag raised its cumbersome weaponry and let out a mighty bellow that bounced off the valley walls before being picked up by the proud leader of another harem which sent its own challenge echoing through the woods. As an overripe pumpkin of a moon sailed clear of the surrounding crags, working its alchemy on the dark head-waters of the Guadalquivir, the thundering chorus redoubled.

It continued all night, one rutting stag after another proclaiming his power and domination. Every September the ritual is repeated, an eerily impressive performance in one of Andalusia's — and Europe's — last wildernesses.

Wedged into a corner of Jaén province, the Sierras of Cazorla and Segura shelter a hoard of nature's treasures. Eagles and hawks circle peaks rising to more than 6,000 feet, while below wild goat, boar and deer roam abrupt escarpments and forested glens. Heron and otter picket the pools and tumbling streams for lurking trout.

This 80-by-30-kilometre zone of stunning natural beauty has escaped man's worst depredations, saved by the same isolation that has tested the powers of survival of its independent-minded inhabitants. A man from one of the remoter hamlets sees nothing odd in remarking, "I'm off to Andalusia to look for work."

And, indeed, these sierras hardly appear a part of the Andalusia we know.

Yet the familiar Andalusia is close at hand, lapping at the battlements of Cazorla and Segura in the form of wave upon wave of olive groves. Amid the olives sit two towns celebrated for their history and architecture: Ubeda and Baeza offer visitors a glorious past, luring them off highway NIV which links southern Spain with Madrid via the Despeñaperros Pass. Eternal wonders are enough to persuade some to detour a little further, to the birthplace of the

145

River Guadalquivir.

Springing from the rock beneath 6,650-foot-high Cabañas, Cazorla's second biggest peak, the Guadalquivir rushes northwards at first, swelling the Tranco de Beas reservoir before making a U-turn to begin its progress towards Córdoba, Seville and the Atlantic. Increasing numbers of campers and sightseers flock to the long river valley. In fact, the annual flow of more than 700,000 visitors has provoked concern about damage to the zone's flora and fauna.

This was one reason nature-lovers welcomed the February 1986 decree by Andalusia's Agencia de Medio Ambiente (environmental protection agency) making 220,000 hectares of Cazorla and Segura a "natural park". Some sierra folk were hostile, afraid that traditional activities such as cattle-raising would be restricted. But park director Juan Garay, a young biologist and agricultural engineer, points out that the project is firmly committed to improving the quality of life of local people.

"Development and conservation are always linked. The people are one element more of the park," he says.

In the past, Cazorla was viewed chiefly as a hunting reserve, 70,000 hectares being set aside for this purpose in 1970. General Franco visited the valley several times to indulge his taste for fishing and shooting. An outsize pair of antlers displayed in the museum-cum-information office at Torre del Vinagre testifies to his marksmanship. They are from a red deer, killed on September 24, 1959, which registered 210.13 points on the hunter's scale.

Antonio "Calavera" (the skull) — "everybody knows me by that" — recalls meeting Franco and a succession of other VIPs needing guidance on fishing the lakes and streams near his simple woodland home. On a spring evening, when a late snowfall still lies deep on the heights, Antonio warms his hands at a log fire on which his wife is cooking *gachamiga,* a floury, gut-filling porridge with fried peppers and bacon. Occasionally the electric light dims.

"Water-powered," explains Antonio, a wiry man in his fifties. "It fades now and again, but the power is free. And so is the air. You won't find any purer. My rent's only 110 pesetas a year. I built this house myself, on Forestry Commission land. I've worked for them since 1970, but I've always lived in the sierras."

Neither Antonio nor his wife Eugenia, born in a remote *cortijo* near his family's, went to school, but they are far from ignorant.

"A teacher used to come tramping around all the farms so we had two hours' tuition a week. Life is different for our children. They go to school in the town of Cazorla," says Eugenia. "A lot of the old *cortijos* are abandoned now, but you won't find better people than the sierra folk."

Antonio spends his days looking after a 60-hectare fenced-off reserve where goats, deer and other species are bred. Many are sold to restock other wilderness zones, and fetch good prices.

Not far from his home, a track loops downwards by a busy stream to the pine-fringed lakes of Valdeazores and Aguas Negras. Their placid waters reflect clean blue skies and distant peaks. In spring the hiker comes across patches of primroses, and vivid splashes of colour in rock clefts provided by the tiny violets native to Cazorla. Heavy-horned wild goats and timid mountain sheep graze the upland meadows. After one hard winter, I found numerous remains of these goats which had been caught without food in the heavy snow.

One species I did not see was the rare brown and tawny lammergeyer, or bearded vulture, highly elusive even though it can have a wing-span of up to 10 feet. In Spain, only one or two exist in Cazorla and a few more in the Pyrenees. It is known as the *quebrantahuesos* (bone-breaker) because of its habit of smashing bones on rocks to get at the marrow.

"It's better that not many people know the location of the *quebrantahuesos* because of the danger from egg collectors. Professionals from some Northern European countries have despoiled the park looking for eggs," comments Diego Navarrete, member of a youthful co-operative of guides offering their services to Cazorla visitors. "The forest guards do a good job, stopping poachers. The worst are not the local folk, who just want something for the pot. It's the outsiders who kill a fine stag for the trophy, then leave the meat."

In spring the park is filled with the clamour of running water and, in good years, the water laps near the top of the 92-metre El Tranco dam. But by autumn when the hunters make their appearance, the picture changes. Sometimes it is possible to walk across the reservoir bed to the islet crowned with a castle which once dominated the long-disappeared settlement of Bujaraiza.

East and north the Segura ranges are dotted with slumbering villages, ruined castles and ancient churches. One of the most spectacularly situated is Segura de la Sierra, topping a 4,000-foot-high hill on the edge of Andalusia. One tourism brochure claims it "intoxicates the visitor with the witchery of its medieval atmosphere". Certainly, Segura breathes antiquity. Phoenicians and Romans are said to have mined iron and silver around here. Visigoths ruled until 781 when the Moors converted it into a stronghold of the Emirs of Córdoba.

Napoleon's forces burned Segura for its presumptuous resistance but the Arab fortress remains, though over-restored. Its walls command a stirring view of hills and chasms and pine and olive-clad slopes. At its base sits a rectangular bullring, partly carved out of the rock. It sees action during the annual fiesta in the first week of October when Segura rings to the lively music of the *seguidillas,* which originated in La Mancha.

Neighbouring Orcera boasts an unusual 16th-century church and is home for a community of loggers and woodcutters. Once Orcera men trekked the roads of Spain as muleteers and the waterways as expert log-rollers. These days local youths exercise their urge for adventure running before the horns of the young bulls they release in the streets during the August fiesta.

These *encierros* are a feature of festivities in this corner of Jaén province, close to the Guadalimar river valley and the Albacete-Jaén highway. September is bull-running month in such villages as Chiclana, Genave, Villacarrillo and Iznatoraf. And they will all assure you their *encierro* is better than anything you can witness in Pamplona.

The Sierra de Segura has one particular claim to fame. It is one of the handful of olive-producing areas which has qualified for a *Denominación de Origen* label. A fine, low-acidity oil comes from those thousands of trees running to the horizon.

Average yield from a single tree is 30 kilos of olives, but one monster near Beas de Segura has produced, according to its owner, up to 900 kilos. It is 50 feet high and takes four men, arms outstretched, to circle its trunk. One story has it that it sprang, 100 years ago, from an olive twig which had been blessed on Palm Sunday. Clearly a case of divine intervention, although the 40 kilos of fertilizer fed to it every year by its owner could do no harm.

Olive oil is the life-blood of Jaén province. At Ubeda, Manuel Berlanga, president of the 900-member Unión de Ubeda co-operative, explains how quality oil is processed in the 50-day picking season that begins every December.

"We produce a stupendous virgin oil here. It retains the taste and the vitamins because it is made by natural methods, not like refined oil which is treated to get a nice colour and has other things added," he declares, as we walk to the yard where load after load of olives are arriving.

"Olives must be freshly picked, otherwise they have higher acidity. The best oil has 0.5 to 1 per cent. Having the right soil is important, but so is care in manufacturing. We only accept ripe black olives and we treat them fast."

Picking olives is still a laborious operation in which whole families participate, but at the plant machines speed the process of stripping away leaves and stalks, washing, and extracting pips. The fruit flows along channels to a grinding machine where it is mashed to a pulp. This is fed into *capachos,* circular containers once made of woven esparto, but now of artificial fibre. Piled under presses, the *capachos* are steadily squeezed for one and a half hours as the air grows ever heavier with the rich odour of the new oil. Once filtered, the product is ready for frying and adding flavour to salads.

"In a good year this co-operative produces eight million kilos, but 80 per cent of our members earn under the minimum wage as the average holding is only five hectares and I'd say you need at least double that to live on olives alone," says Manuel.

"The Italians are more commercially-minded than us. They even buy our oil and sell it as their own! We are too dependent on a couple of private companies which sell our product. But here in Ubeda we're marketing our own brand of virgin oil. It's called Oro de La Loma [gold of the ridge]."

Ubeda has been sitting on its *loma* for a millennium and more, but gold — apart from this special liquid variety — has not been over-abundant since the 16th century. That was when a number of citizens reached dizzy heights of prestige and position, and churches and palaces blossomed. Today the magnificence of these structures contrasts sharply with the provincial dullness of Ubeda's dark, narrow streets.

The group of buildings around the Plaza de Vázquez Molina is particularly outstanding. Step out of the Parador Condestable Dávalos, a gracious mansion which is now a State-run hotel, and turn left to El Salvador church. This is a Renaissance wonder built as the family pantheon of Francisco de los

Cobos, Secretary of State to Holy Roman Emperor Charles V. Turn right on leaving the Parador and one comes to the Casa de las Cadenas, a majestic structure housing the town hall. It was constructed for Francisco's nephew, secretary to Philip II, after whom the square is named.

Immediately opposite stands Santa María church whose architecture tells something of Ubeda's history. It is built on the site of a mosque, for under the Moors "Ubbadat-al-Arab" was an important centre, famed for its esparto and ceramic products. In the beautiful cloister the castles and lions of a royal coat of arms are a reminder that Alfonso VII, king of León and Castile, conquered the city in 1157.

The city changed hands several times before Ferdinand III, "The King Saint", finally expelled the Muslims in 1234. His victory is recorded in the cloister, where another plaque warns: "If you want your pain to turn to joy, don't pass, sinner, without saying 'Ave María'." It is worth bearing in mind if you have an appointment next door, at the courthouse.

Outside the walls of the old town runs the Calle Valencia, worth a visit for anybody interested in the potters' art. The bowls and jugs of Ubeda are easily recognized for they are usually well-glazed with a deep green hue. And Ubeda continues to export, as it has done down the centuries, its esparto baskets and mats.

If you like Ubeda, you will surely love its twin just nine kilometres away, Baeza, one of the best-preserved and least-spoiled of Andalusia's monumental cities. For centuries Baeza was in the front line of the Wars of Reconquest. It was a regional capital under the Moors and, after its fall in 1227, held a key position in the Christian assault on Andalusia.

An old Moorish ballad has the king of Granada haranguing his men in the 1407 siege to "destroy Baeza, that city of towers, bring back the children and the old folks in cavalcade, and put all the youths and men to the sword". Baeza, however, survived gloriously.

The old university is still there — it functioned for nearly three centuries until 1824. Now it is a high school. One of this century's leading poets, Antonio Machado, taught French grammar in the ancient classrooms from 1912 to 1919.

The Jaén Gate is still there too, built to commemorate the passing of the Emperor Charles V on his way to Seville to marry Isabel of Portugal. Around the town, plateresque windows, Romanesque arches and Gothic vaulting in golden stone recall the prosperous past.

"Do you want to see the monstrance that is carried during our Corpus Christi processions?" asks shopkeeper Federico Garrido, who acts as cathedral custodian in his spare moments. "It will cost you 25 pesetas."

He activates a lever and slowly a thick iron shield slides back and a light flicks on to reveal the niche where the monstrance sits, an amazingly ornate piece of baroque silver.

"You must see the cathedral archives," says Federico, leading the way to a hall with an intricately-worked ceiling which once formed part of a mosque. "See, here is an illuminated hymn-book from 1547. Scholars come to consult the hundreds of old volumes."

A faded 1788 document advertises for a cathedral organist, required to play morning and evening. The annual income: 2,750 *reales* (about 700 pesetas) and 24 *fanegas* (38 bushels) of wheat. It is one of the insights offered by the archives into Andalusia's rich history, with all its quirks and drama.

There is no exterior sign to indicate the presence of Baeza's archives. Those who are interested will find them. Information is a rare commodity in Andalusia, not given away casually to any stranger, unless he strikes up conversation. Then, mutual confidence established, doors swing open.

In this way, by word of mouth, customers arrive at José the Birdman's home. Those who need him find him. He lives in a modern, geometrical settlement not far from Baeza, near the Guadalquivir. In his workshop he is surrounded by owls, ducks, pheasants, pigeons, gazing mutely at his fingers' skilful movements.

José Molina Torral and his sons Vicente and José Antonio make birds, and buyers come from all over Spain. Sitting on a low chair, José thrusts straw into a plastic bag, binding it tight with thread — "That's the egg." He bends wire to form a framework and wraps it with dyed sisal imported from Canada. Other pieces of sisal are glued on to represent feathers.

"The womenfolk paint on the final markings. We check the colours for accuracy in a book, but I only need to look once and I know them," says José. "I've lived in the country all my life and I respect birds. But there are far fewer now. They're killed by eating insects in the olive groves after the trees have been sprayed with poison."

It takes José close to a day to make a lifelike replica of an eagle; longer for a proud, strutting peacock. His models sit on thousands of mantelpieces and tables.

"I started this as a hobby in the early Seventies after my father-in-law made a bird for a grandson to take to school." He shakes his head. "I never dreamed it would grow into a business."

The sierras are a short drive away for those eager to spy living birds of prey. They wheel about the heights near Tiscar, Huesa and Quesada, on the edge of the Cazorla and Segura National Park. Tiscar, commanding a spectacular pass, is the home of a much-venerated Virgin. Every spring the people of Quesada transport the Virgin to their town, returning it to its sanctuary amid much revelry at the end of August.

In December, when the mists creep down from the sierras, the village of Huesa stages a celebration to itself. On the night before San Silvestre (December 31), bonfires of pinewood blaze in the streets. They are known as "the saint's castles". Watching the fire outside one house, the owner confides: "This is my way of thanking San Silvestre. I asked him to cure my wife of illness and he did."

Inside the parish church, women make offerings of *roscos* (white, ring-shaped cakes) to the saint's image while outside three bonfires send sparks shooting above the rooftops. Excited children whoop and race between the flames while gossiping elders warm themselves to keep out the evening chill.

A drizzle falls on San Silvestre's day, but it does not deter the villagers as they march in procession with the saint's image through the damp streets.

Children race to pick up the spent rockets that spin down from the heavens and a posse of farmers pauses from time to time to blast away with their shotguns, loaded with confetti.

Ahead of the procession proudly walk *"Los Cargos"*, four middle-aged men dressed in 18th-century red and blue soldiers' uniforms. Manuel Marin leads. He is the Captain. Blas Herrero, carrying a nasty-looking pike, is the Sergeant and Estefanio Martínez, Lieutenant, bears the flag. Domingo Monje solemnly thumps a drum.

"I've been the *tamborero* for 18 years. It's a great honour to have the chance to pay respect to the saint," explains Domingo. He is the only permanent *cargo,* the others having to pay 10 pesetas each year to take part in the draw for their coveted role.

Outside the church, the *cargos* march up to the priest, who is standing before the saint's image, and ceremoniously pay their respects by doffing their caps and bowing. Then the flag-twirlers take over, young and old eagerly taking their turn to whirl the colours about their heads and between their legs as shouts ring out of "Long live San Silvestre the Great!" After mass, everybody warms themselves in the bars on anise and brandy.

North, through the rain, along crazily curving roads lies the village of Cazorla, gateway to the natural park. It is a friendly, up-and-down town, harmoniously blending stone and whitewash. Castles and towers brood from precipitous crags. In early times Cazorla is said to have been the seat of the bishop San Isicio, who helped bring the gospel to Spain. Certainly the town is dotted with plenty of old convents.

Down narrow, roller-coaster streets lies a broad square. One side is dominated by the ruins of Santa María church. Next to it stands a building with massive stone walls. After a varied history, the structure now houses a restaurant. It's a cosy place to be on a winter's night when Cazorla is shrouded in mist and the wind tugs at the sierras.

On one New Year's Eve, I watch the owner, a perky little lady called Mercedes Díaz del Barco, briskly grilling trout and lamb chops on an open fire as her pretty daughter Chelo serves the clients.

"This place goes back to 1560," Chelo informs me, as she slides a pan of red-hot coals under the table to toast my feet. "Once the priest from Santa María church lived here. Then it was part of the town hall and after that, an inn."

Fortified on thick bean soup and grilled chicken, I leave the restaurant as the bells ring out to herald the start of a new year. The streets of Cazorla are wet and empty and far above, in lofty fastnesses where the snowflakes are drifting down, the herds of deer and goats are huddling together for warmth, dreaming no doubt of springtime in the sierras.

A Confirmation of Life

THE first rocket goes off about 9 a.m. on San Antonio's Day. The programme says 8 a.m., but Eduardo has his own schedule. Bleary-eyed but steady, he clasps the artefact in his left hand, nonchalantly applies a lighted cigarette to the fuse, and at the right moment — just before it blows his hand off — releases it skywards in a shower of sparks.

Then, somewhere off at the other end of the village where the players have braced themselves with coffee and *aguardiente,* the band starts. The brassy notes echo through the narrow streets, growing in volume until the enthusiastic, bulging-cheeked musicans are right beneath my window and the neighbours emerge on terraces and balconies to gaze down. This band has a special sound, one that cannot be counterfeited. Whether it is rendering *"¡Viva España!"* or a *paso doble,* it is gloriously and joyously out of tune. Its cracked harmony has a nostalgic quality, reminding one of past festivities, or other times. It is a band perfectly suited for the village fiesta.

Turn any corner in Andalusia and the chances are you will stumble across a fiesta. They come in all shapes and sizes... *romerías, ferias, veladas, verbenas, encierros, concursos de arte, flamenco.* Flower-decked bullock-carts struggle towards lonely shrines; sherry-sipping grandees guide steeds as elegantly groomed as they; fishermen wade into the waves with their patron saint; Moors battle Christians; bare-chested legionnaires strut to thundering drums.

The religious, the pagan, the commercial, and the political mingle without inhibition. Elsewhere, the Industrial Revolution and materialist cynicism may have wiped out such exuberant manifestations of folk culture. In Andalusia, they are thriving. So much so that, far from the fiesta dying out, old ones are being revived and new ones invented.

Oddly enough, television has helped to breathe life into old customs. The arrival of a film team so impresses a community that it shows new interest in something it had previously neglected. Fiestas have always had social importance. They marked the changing season in an agrarian society and allowed friends scattered in remote hamlets and farms to meet and make merry. Fiestas continue to be the one time in the year when many fathers go out with the whole family.

Large numbers of Andalusians live in distant cities, in Spain and abroad, and the fiesta is the occasion for a grand reunion. An emigrant will take exceptional measures to attend his local fiesta where he will display his new prosperity, renew ties, settle family matters, but most of all reaffirm his identity with the community.

Strangers from "progressive" societies, where roots are what plants have, are often bewildered by these events. The Seville Fair, for example, consists basically of the same ingredients year after year, with more or less the same people taking part, ritually showing off their horses and costumes, ritually attending the corrida and ritually meeting in the *casetas*.

Ritual, with large doses of spectacle, is the glue that holds many a community together. Ritual expresses a community's personality, draws its members together, underlines its solidarity. Towns splash out vast sums on their fiestas to impress their rivals and to bolster local pride. Citizens often display fierce emotions when discussing the merits of their own festivities.

As an Andújar man told me: "Our *romería* to the Virgen de la Cabeza is far prettier than El Rocío. It's less showy, more genuine. Well, no, I've never actually been to the Rocío. But I know this is the best. Because she's *my* Virgin!"

The Virgin Mary appears in many guises in Andalusia, where religious myth and fact merge indistinguishably. Her praises are sung in ceremonies that vary from the solemn to the riotous.

One of the simplest acts of homage takes place every August 5, high in the Sierra Nevada. Rockets soaring over Pradollano at 4 a.m. announce the start of the *Romería Blanca.* A wavering column of flaming torches marks the progress of a few dozen pilgrims wending their way up from the ski station through the darkness.

When the sun nudges clear of the slopes of the Veleta peak, some 60 people are waiting on a rocky spur 10,500 feet above sea-level. Only pockets of snow linger in crevices in the mountains, but the wind is chill enough even though it is high summer.

The first shards of light strike the dazzling white, carnation-ringed figure of *Nuestra Señora de las Nieves* (Our Mother of the Snows), patron of the Sierra Nevada. Half a dozen doves are released, to swirl and swoop joyfully in the thin morning light. Wild goats gaze suspiciously from a nearby crag as a priest intones Mass to a warmly-clad congregation of climbers, ski instructors and sierra workers.

Afterwards, the pilgrims sip scalding herb tea brewed in a vast pot and collect every shred of rubbish, leaving only biscuit crumbs for the goats. "This ceremony for the mountain people is one I would not miss," notes Father Enrique Iglesias, chaplain for the sierra. "Why is it held here? Well, they say a shepherd found the image during a snowstorm, but it's only a legend."

In the past, shepherds were always stumbling over Virgins. The reason they turned up in strange places is that, during Islam's centuries-long sway, Christians hid them where they could, in wells perhaps, or hollow tree trunks.

However, Almería's *Virgen del Mar* (Sea Virgin) was found in 1502 by a fisherman as he wandered along a sandy beach. This Virgin's miraculous powers were soon recognized, and ever since fishermen have taken her for an annual boat trip. Fishermen all along the coast pay homage in the same way, complete with fireworks, to the Virgin of Carmen.

Flamenco music rings out from a hilltop sanctuary near Cabra, in Córdoba province, when gypsies flock to say mass to *their* Virgin. If some visitors are surprised by that, they are shocked by the brutal manner in which the lads of Almonte "kidnap" the Virgin of El Rocío at the biggest fiesta of all.

"*¡Que guapa!* [How pretty!]" cry the crowds, as though the Virgin were a living creature. But who is she really? In these spring rites, when the Andalusians drink, dance and make love with such abandon, it is possible to see links with ancient orgiastic rites devoted to pagan deities.

Probing into this aspect, in his book *White Wall of Spain,* Allen Josephs remarks that the fiesta formed by the primordial music of flamenco and the veneration of the Queen of the Marshes "provides an unsuspected window on antiquity". In the West we have purged our ability to journey into other dimensions through these Bacchanalian mixtures of devotion and diversion. But, he concludes, "In Andalusia, the old way, the ecstatic wine-dance of antiquity, is still practised as religious ritual."

Religion as spectacle reaches its ultimate in Semana Santa. *Hermandades* (brotherhoods), some with several thousand members, compete to exhibit the most beautifully adorned Virgin on the most sumptuous floats which are paraded through the towns and villages in a daunting, military-religious atmosphere. Considerable prestige goes with the position of *hermano mayor* (the elected leader) of a brotherhood, particularly a wealthy one.

"Holy Week and its significance are something you carry inside you. It's a confirmation of our faith, when we renew the Passion of the Lord," says José Guillermo Carrasquilla, who has been *hermano mayor* of Seville's Hiniesta brotherhood. "People live all year for the brotherhood. By Lent they begin to become emotional. Because in the procession each brotherhood wants to do best. There's great concern about who has the best flowers and how the band plays. But don't think we only bother about that. We do a lot for charity, helping local families, paying their electricity bills, visiting them."

The practice of walking with ball and chain has been banned as exhibitionistic, but many masked penitents go barefoot through the streets, to atone for a misdeed or to seek a favour. Correct comportment is important.

"Look at the way that fellow is carrying his cross," a spectator will comment on a group of passing penitents. "Very sloppy. Now see that one, with it biting into his shoulder. That's the way to bear a cross!"

Nothing is quite what it seems, of course. Many of the Seville *costaleros,* who carry the floats weighing a ton or more, are paid for their services. And the *saetas,* the spontaneous outbursts of faith during processions, are sometimes sung by professionals. Seville city council spends several million pesetas contracting nearly 50 singers to lend emotion to Semana Santa.

Málaga adds a dramatic touch by releasing a prisoner from its gaol on Holy Wednesday. This custom is a "reward" to the prison community and dates from an incident 200 years ago during the reign of Charles III, when nobody would carry the images due to a plague in the city. Gaol inmates asked if they could carry the float of Jesús Nazareno el Rico, promising to return to their cells afterwards. When permission was refused, they broke out, seized the image and bore it through the streets. Then they walked back into gaol. Ever since, the freed prisoner has usually walked in procession to give thanks.

Many spring and autumn fairs, such as those at Jerez and Ronda, have no particular religious significance. They started as horse fairs and markets. Seville's April Fair has swollen into a fashionable extravaganza, where the rhythm of *sevillanas* never seems to stop under the perpetual day of 300,000 light-bulbs. Ambitious politicians, penniless *hidalgos,* show-business personalities, titled landowners join the throng, to see and be seen, and if possible be photographed for the gossip magazines.

Málaga, Córdoba and smaller fry seek to emulate Seville, provoking criticism that Sevillan styles in dress and dance are spreading to the detriment of local customs. Most of all there is the complaint that the *caseta* is proliferating, so that whole areas of the fairgrounds become private clubs, where only those with the right *enchufes* (connections) can gain admittance.

Pagan origins appear obvious in one of the most light-hearted fiestas, the Crosses of May, which takes place on or around May 3. These are most lavishly celebrated in Granada and Córdoba, but are often more attractive in villages such as Añora (Córdoba) and El Berrocal (Huelva). Neighbours get together, adorn crosses with thousands of flowers and surround them with typical handicrafts. A tour of the crosses, which signify life and rebirth, is an excuse for day-long drinking, dancing and singing.

Carnival, which may have started with the saturnalia festival of ancient Rome, is another excuse for letting off steam and nowhere more so than in Cádiz where for days the streets are filled with outrageously-garbed groups. Poking fun at authority is a feature of Carnival, giving the participants, at least briefly, the illusion that they are enjoying a certain freedom. The festival has been banned at various times, most recently during the Franco regime, because of its subversive potential. In fact, it has been the spark for revolts in the past.

Another wild fiesta, with primitive roots, takes place every year on December 28, when thousands of people descend on a *venta* outside Málaga to listen to the wild, driving *verdiales* music. Some 20 *pandas* (gangs) from mountain villages fiddle, strum and rattle their instruments in a cacophonous frenzy, while bottles of potent Málaga wine and *aguardiente* pass from hand to hand.

The *pandas* compete in the volume and fervour of their playing but also with their astonishing headgear. Their hats are festooned with plastic flowers, mirrors, bells and beads, with long, colourful ribbons as a final touch. Nobody knows quite how far back the *verdiales* go, although one theory has it that they sprang from the songs of the olive-pickers in Moorish times.

Superstition and devotion interweave in many fiestas. One of the strangest takes place every October in Moclín (Granada). A standard used by the

155

Christian forces 500 years ago is carried through the streets in procession. Known as the Cristo del Pano, it bears a somewhat clumsy painting of Jesus. The standard has gained a reputation for miracle-making, not least in its ability to cure sterility. Women travel great distances to pray for Christ's help in making them fertile, although more cynical observers claim that the numerous pregnancies announced a few months later have little to do with divine intervention.

Symbols of fertility are explicitly admired in this largely agrarian society which, unlike industrialized Europe, has stayed close to its roots. Apart from its reverence for the Virgin, the fecund earth mother, Andalusia is fascinated by the epitome of strength and life force, the bull. It is not by chance that this region is the heart of the *fiesta brava*.

Bull cults, featuring ritual sacrifice, stretch back into ancient history. The Greeks wove legends around the Minotaur, a Cretan monster, half-bull and half-man, and Cretan frescos depict ceremonies in which men leap over a bull. The Persian cult of Mithra, which flourished under the Romans and spread as far as Andalusia, put great emphasis on a sacred white bull. When Mithra, warrior deity, giver of fertile rain and god of sunlight, slew the bull, holy seed issued from its genitals which gave life to every living thing.

General Primo de Rivera, Spain's dictator in the 1920s and a good Andalusian from Jerez, obviously believed there was something in this. Impulsive, hard-living and always larger than life, he kept himself in form for his drinking bouts by tucking into platefuls of testicles sliced from bulls freshly killed in the ring. Fried *criadillas* (testicles) figure on many a restaurant menu. No doubt their popularity is due to macho-conscious males' concern about maintaining their hormone levels. Another practice alleged to have beneficial physical effects, drinking bulls' blood, is common well beyond the borders of Andalusia.

Bullfighting as practised today, on foot, originated in Ronda two centuries ago and it forms an integral part of most towns' festivities. Andalusia is renowned as the producer of great matadors — the Romeros, Belmonte, Manolete, Ordóñez — and some of the fiercest fighting bulls, which are said to be descended from an African breed. Without Andalusia, it is doubtful if the corrida would exist.

At its worst, bullfighting can be a wretchedly cruel farce, but at its finest it has the majesty and grip of Greek tragedy. Arguments between abolitionists and supporters are inevitably pointless, since one side argues from the standpoint of progressive, 20th-century concepts while the other is talking of myth and soul and primordial emotions. To an aficionado, it is irrelevant and ridiculous to talk about barbarism and equal chances for the bull. This is a celebration of death, where there is no "winning" or "losing". It is a ritual in which all is necessarily pre-ordained. Second-hand, the spectator suffers the fear of his hero, who stands armed with only a cloak and sword before a massive, fire-breathing beast bred to attack. If the matador proves incapable of teaching the bull to play its part "correctly", he risks a maiming or death. If he dominates the bull with skill, on rare occasions he seems to step into another dimension that has nothing to do with sport or art.

The closeness of death gives the spectacle its special drama, and the matador's triumph and the bull's sacrifice exalt the spectator and sharpen his feeling of being alive. Outdated, bloody, barbaric, often corrupt, the *fiesta brava* is castigated as a circus appealing to the baser instincts. The truth is that it appeals to instincts in all of us. The Andalusian sees no reason to conceal the catharsis he experiences. A good performance lifts him into ecstasy. To tell him that he must stop sacrificing bulls is to strike at the essence of his being and invite a revolution.

The ritual corrida apart, bulls or young cows are also featured in numerous village fiestas. Conscious of outsiders' criticism, local authorities try to avoid excesses, but controls are slack, and sometimes indefensible cruelty occurs. *Encierros,* in which young bulls are released in the streets, are frequent. To run before the horns, risking ridicule or a goring, is the supreme test for a youngster on the verge of manhood. Sometimes the bull's horns are padded or it is restrained by a long rope, but the animal can still cause lethal damage.

Sierra villages in Jaén province are a stronghold of this diversion. In autumn, one *encierro* succeeds another, in Segura de la Sierra, Villacarrillo, Torreperogil, Chiclana, Genave, Iznatoraf... Turn any corner and you may be confronted by a rushing, stumbling, hooting, laughing mob and by flush-faced youths eagerly demonstrating their virility before their peers.

Fiestas in Andalusia can be coarse, angelic, pious and riotous all at once. This causes no conflict in an Andalusian's mind, just as he sees nothing grotesque in mixing obscenities with his cries to the Virgin. By going to extremes, by underlining his recognition of himself as a human being, he demonstrates his fervour and that he lives! Who can blame him for treasuring those moments? Every time the drums thunder in Semana Santa and the band blares out on an afternoon at the *toros* and Eduardo puts a match to another rocket, it is a confirmation that, in the face of death, life goes on.

CRAFTS

Tradition on the Cliff Edge

P EDRO Castillo, a frail little man with a gentle smile, is chained to the wheel. He started work when he was seven and, well into his eighties, he still works 10 hours a day. His worn, stained hands nimbly shape pots in his back-street workshop near the centre of Andújar, in Jaén province. Bowls, vases, bulls, horsemen have flowed from Pedro's hands by the thousand, always in traditional style, simple designs glazed in basic colours on a white background.

"I keep working because that is where my bread comes from. It's my life. And I stick to the old ways because that is what I know," says Pedro, peering like a cheerful gnome from under his peaked cap as he prepares another mass of clay.

He represents the last of a long line, the craftsmen who have seen machines, new materials and changes in fashion undermine what they once thought nobody could take away from them, the value of an arduously-acquired skill, the skill in their hands.

Mass-produced products played havoc with the market for handicrafts. Plastics knocked the stuffing out of wickerwork and earthenware. Housewives tossed out plain old artefacts and rushed to buy bright modern articles. The rush-covered chair, so simple, so functional, was tossed on the rubbish heap. It was a symbol of the bad old days, of the poverty-stricken past.

But the wheel turns. An old-timer like Pedro Castillo has become something of a celebrity with the resurgence of appreciation for popular art and concern that old traditions may be lost. Craft skills that died out elsewhere in Europe a century ago, crushed by the Industrial Revolution, still have at least a chance of survival in Andalusia, thanks to private initiative and official aid.

Andalusia's rich heritage from successive invaders is seen through its crafts, from pots moulded in Roman style to carpets woven with Arab designs. The region's native art lives on, under threat but still there, sometimes primitive, sometimes surprisingly sophisticated.

Tourist demand has produced a spate of "medieval" iron keys which never opened a door and "antique" irons which never pressed a shirt. But many rustic articles are genuine enough and in daily use, for Andalusia continues to live from the land.

The farm labourer still relies on his *botijo* (the earthenware drinking vessel which keeps water cool through evaporation) to refresh himself on a hot summer day. In the Alpujarras, I came across a market trader selling mule-saddles made from willow branches, esparto and straw. They could not have changed much from those used 2,000 years ago. Colourful harnesses and oxen's wooden yokes may be "art" to the city-dweller, but to country people they are far from being mere wall decorations.

More expensive articles, such as carved oak furniture, finely-chased silver and embossed leather gear, were bought in the past only by a wealthy élite, the merchants and landowners. It is no easy task to find genuine antique dressers and tables of any quality because most of Andalusia was too poor to afford them.

In contrast, church wealth supported a whole range of skills through the centuries. An army of stonemasons, carvers, gilders and seamstresses toiled to adorn the only buildings of any note in most communities: the churches, and the images they contained.

Today, the number of such craftsmen has fallen sharply. In the town of Priego de Córdoba, for example, which is a showplace for baroque ornamentation, there used to be 50 carvers. Now a dozen remain.

One, Cristóbal Cubero, told me: "The machine has taken over many tasks and it is killing off craftsmanship. We shouldn't let it happen, because Spain is not a country of industry but of crafts. And Andalusia is a treasure-house of these crafts. It's a jewel! Its art has influenced Europe!"

Cristóbal had just completed a *paso,* a religious float carried in processions on important occasions. The carving, polishing, staining and gilding had taken almost a year. Such a float could cost five million pesetas for a small one, or 10 times that sum if it were ordered by the large brotherhoods of Málaga or Seville.

The robe alone for one of the grander images of the Virgin can cost 20 million pesetas. But orders for those are few and far between these days, says José Guillermo Carrasquilla, whose family has one of Seville's few remaining embroidery workshops. Their masterpieces in baroque design add lustre to places of worship from Spain to Peru. In a typical tiled house, complete with flowery patio, in Calle San Luis, 10 infinitely patient women produce sumptuous pieces of gold-and-silver-threaded brocade.

José — whose great uncle Manuel Rodríguez Ojeda started the business a century ago — and his son create their own designs, but doing repairs constitutes most of their work now and he worries about the effects of rising costs. As a member of Seville's *Real Academia de Bellas Artes,* he has called for help to prevent the tradition becoming no more than a memory in a museum.

José points out: "The handicrafts are genuine popular culture, expressions of the traditional identity of a people. Their loss would signify a dramatic deculturization, a lamentable loss of our own roots."

Despite the decline in some fields, Seville remains an important centre for a variety of hand-made articles, including Manila shawls, ornate combs (for your *mantilla*), and tapestries. And guitars.

159

"There are only three guitar-makers in Seville, possibly because it's a demanding job which will never make you rich," comments Andrés Domínguez, whose superb instruments are coveted by such professionals as Paco de Lucía. He works in a loft in a narrow Triana yard, where painters and sculptors have their studios.

"I was taught by Manuel Ortega Sosa, an old maestro. Strangely enough, he himself cannot play the guitar, nor even tune one. I used to play, but now I don't have a guitar of my own because whenever I make one, somebody comes in and buys it."

Orders from Belgium, Japan, Greece and South America flow in to Andrés. He spends five to seven weeks building one of his instruments, much more if it has special features. A classical guitar costs around 200,000 pesetas for a standard version. A flamenco guitar may be cheaper.

Sixty years ago the old Seville quarter of Triana sheltered 40 potteries. Today the number is reduced to three, which produce distinctive, hand-painted products that owe their origins to the Moorish era. Tiles from Triana decorate London restaurants, the Buenos Aires underground, Californian mansions, and Madrid palaces.

At the Santa Ana works, pots are cooked for 24 hours at 900 degrees in wood-fired ovens, a method that has not changed in a thousand years.

"There's more demand than ever, as people realize that tiles made in 1600 have lost none of their quality nor colour," says José Manuel González, son-in-law of the owners. "Our clay comes from the banks of the Guadalquivir and we make our own colours by baking and melting minerals in an oven. The formula is a secret."

In the rambling factory, employees expertly brush some parts of pots and wall plaques with oil-mixed colour and fill in other areas with a water enamel. In this way, paints do not run together and a relief effect is created.

Virtually all these craft industries are family-run, and most firms say they cannot afford to employ anybody outside the family. In Granada, the Morales brothers produce ceramics in a style which has changed little since the time when dozens of Moorish potters congregated around the city's Fajalauza gate. Attractive blue and green Fajalauza designs can be seen in the Alhambra, and its popular emblems, such as a bird or a pomegranate, grace walls and kitchen shelves all over Spain.

"Designs are basically the same but they evolve because each artist puts something of himself into whatever he paints," says Cecilio Morales, professor of Applied Arts at the Granada art school, who runs an ancient establishment that looks as though it dates from the times of Boabdil. Across the road in a former convent, his brother Miguel runs his own Fajalauza factory. The Morales name has been connected with this craft for 400 years.

"Our clay, from the Baira river, is the best, very plastic and very fine," explains Cecilio. "People used to buy our products to use, but now they're mostly for decoration. It's a struggle. Once we had 50 workers, now we're down to five. We get some subsidies, but they're laughable."

Even so, some Andalusian potters can't keep pace with demand. Paco Tito and his father of Ubeda have achieved justified fame with their lustrous,

*Seville guitar-maker
Andrés Domínguez
works on an instrument
custom-made for a
demanding client.*
Below: *veteran weaver
Dolores García works
on her loom in Valor.*

*Sisal, wire and José Molina Torral's years of experience go into the making of peacocks, ducks and owls.
Below: pots are prepared for firing in the Almería village of Sorbas.*

deep green glazes. Santa Inés of Málaga is another potter who works around the clock to keep up with orders.

It does not take much experience to recognize an original design from Cortegana, close to the Portuguese border, or a green-on-yellow *perula* (a pot-bellied water carrier) from Lucena (Córdoba), or a single-baked, rough-textured dish from Níjar (Almería).

Many potters cling obstinately to old ways. Manuel Granados Sánchez, of Níjar, declares: "Of course, we still use wood ovens. My wood oven produces a superior product. Do you get the same taste from microwave cooking as when you roast meat in an oven?"

But "progress" has reached Níjar, where pottery manufacture is dominated by the brothers and in-laws of one family. In response apparently to popular taste, the restrained blue-on-white designs of the past are being squeezed out in favour of gaudy "modern" creations. It is the same story in La Rambla, south of Córdoba. Many potters there have turned to electric ovens and large-scale production. Only a few bother with the traditional styles and techniques.

In a valiant battle against time, the Robles family of Almería — Francisco and his sons, Paco, Jerónimo and Antonio — have set out to preserve the forms of the fast-disappearing *botijos*. Each area has its particular shape. Whenever they come across a new one, they make a miniature of it. To date, their collection includes over 100 examples from all corners of the country.

Apart from its pottery, Níjar is a centre for the weaving of *jarapas,* colourful blankets, mats and bags made from the cast-offs of northern textile factories. Weaving suffers more than most handicrafts from competition from machine-made and cheap, imported products. Granada's Albaicín quarter once echoed to the clatter of scores of looms. But rising costs and lack of interest by youngsters have brought the art to vanishing point. Aurelia Casares, the daughter of a well-known Granada family of weavers, has battled to carry on the tradition in Málaga for half a century, teaching, exhibiting and transmitting her own enthusiasm.

In some places, for instance in the Alpujarras and Grazalema (Cádiz), efforts have been made to revive the weaving art by incorporating traditional and newer designs in carpets, tapestries, blankets and ponchos.

Other arts have declined sharply. Once Córdoba's name rang around the world for the quality of its embossed and polychromed leather and for its fine silverware. Something of the latter remains. Silver filigree is still a local speciality, and Córdoba is said to have more silversmiths and jewellery shops than any other Spanish city.

Leatherworkers are few and far between, however. The high cost of basic materials pushes prices up, reducing the number of clients. Deluxe hunting boots stitched in the Montoro (Córdoba) workshops of the Mohedo Soriano brothers cost from around 22,000 pesetas a pair. Beautifully embossed *zahones* (chaps) can cost 65,000 pesetas. Discriminating customers cut fine figures in this gear and, fortunately for the craftsmen, English and German aristocrats and Spanish sherry barons are ready to pay handsomely for these fine products. Valverde del Camino (Huelva) is renowned too for its leather boots and belts, as Ubrique (Cádiz) is for its elegant bags, purses and wallets.

Across Andalusia, in the most unsuspected places, you are likely to stumble across surprising crafts. In Villanueva del Trabuco, amid the mountains of Málaga, I came across a young man carving artful heads on olive wood walking sticks. Near the Guadalquivir in Jaén province, the Molina family produces realistic models of eagles and peacocks from sisal. Veteran farmworkers think nothing of turning out a neat esparto basket while their wives perch themselves in their doorways to produce delicate examples of lace. It is part of a rural culture, perhaps the last traces of a dying life-style.

Although their children may scorn such old-fashioned ways, Andalusia's handicrafts will surely endure, because they reflect the ingenuity, pride and individuality of a people who shy away from being "organized".

If the region's craftsmen and women have a common trait, it is a spirit of independence. Sometimes they can wax philosophic about it, like Luis Alfonso Salas, patriarch of a sturdy Albox (Almería) pottery family: "Every human being has responsibility for his own actions. To be free is what is valuable in this world, isn't it? To be chained to another, that's not freedom."

Ramón Segura would agree with that. More than 30 years ago, he left his native Níjar and began creating his own distinctive pots in Ronda. He endured some hard times. But now he can smile. "You have to wait for the fruit to mature," he reflects. "All my life I've said, 'I don't want to do what others do. I want to plough my own furrow.' Why, the only personality a worker has comes from doing things his own way!"

Andalusian Highlights

WITH an area of 87,268 square kilometres, Andalusia constitutes 17 per cent of Spain's total area. Its 6.5 million inhabitants total 17 per cent of the population. Andalusia is one of Spain's 17 autonomous regions. It has its own parliament which meets in Seville. There are eight provinces, each with its special character: Almería, Cádiz, Córdoba, Huelva, Jaén, Málaga, Seville and Granada.

The Sierra Morena divides Andalusia from the plateau of Castile and accents a clear division in everything from architectural style to cultural attitudes. Andalusia was occupied by the Moors longer than any other part of Spain, an historical fact which has left an indelible mark.

Andalucía Baja is the term used for the area around the Guadalquivir river basin, while Andalucía Alta is dominated by the Cordillera Baetica in the south. This range includes the Sierra Nevada, the highest in the peninsula. The range shelters the Mediterranean coast from the cold extremes of the north.

Andalusia is Spain's most important agricultural region, although an increasing number of people now work in service industries, particularly those associated with tourism.

Al-Andalus, an Arabic name, was originally applied by the Moors to the whole peninsula. It is said to mean "the country of the Vandals", which refers to the Germanic tribes which invaded Spain in the 5th century. Modern Andalusia corresponds more or less to the Roman province of Baetica.

GUADALQUIVIR

Wadi al-Kabir (the great river), as the Moors called the Guadalquivir, is Andalusia's lifeline, flowing 660 kilometres from its source in the mountains of Jaén province to its mouth on the Atlantic. On its way, it cuts through five provinces: Jaén, Córdoba, Seville, Cádiz and Huelva. With its more than 800 tributaries, it drains a 57,000-square-kilometre basin and the fertile lands along its banks have been a source of wealth and conflict throughout history. Today it provides much of the region with power, and water for irrigation and drinking. Flooding by the Guadalquivir caused havoc in the past, but a series of dams and irrigation projects has improved control. Constant dredging allows ocean-going vessels to navigate up to Seville, 88 kilometres from the sea. Both the national parks of Cazorla, at the source (see chapter on that area), and Doñana, in the marshes and dunes near the mouth, are rich in wildlife.

HUELVA

Provincial capital: Huelva. Pop. 145,000. Seville 92 km.

Andalusia's westernmost province, on the frontier with Portugal, embraces a wide variety of landscapes in its 10,000 square kilometres, including dunes and marshes near the mouth of the Guadalquivir, large areas of citrus fruit and strawberry farms, and uplands clothed in forest. It was an important source of minerals in ancient times and researchers say the kingdom of Tartessus flourished along its coast. Today, tourism is increasing with developments along the Costa de la Luz (in Cádiz and Huelva provinces) where there are long stretches of pine forests and sandy beaches. Fifty per cent of Huelva is wooded and the northern mountainous zone produces some of Spain's finest cured hams. Palos de la Frontera was the starting point of Columbus's voyage of discovery and provided the crew for his ships.

SEVILLE

Pop. 650,000.

Where Seville stands today was once the heart of the ancient kingdom of Tartessus. The settlement of Hispalis, set on flat land on the banks of the Guadalquivir, was conquered successively by Phoenicians, Greeks, Cathaginians, Romans and Vandals. Julius Caesar proclaimed it a Roman township in 45 BC. Seville became capital of the Visigoth kingdom, was taken by the Moors in 712 and by the 10th century was a rival of Córdoba. In the 11th century, the city became capital of the Almohad kingdom, prospering under the rule of Al Mansur, builder of the Giralda tower. On November 19, 1248, Ferdinand III of Castile ousted the Moors. A carving on the Jerez gate records: "Hercules built me; Caesar surrounded me with walls and towers; the King Saint took me."

The discovery of America introduced a new era of splendour to Seville. Amerigo Vespucci and Magellan were among the navigators who sailed from its port which flourished with trade from the New World. It monopolized trade with America until 1717 when, with the Guadalquivir silting up, the Casa de Contratación (Contracting House), was transferred to its rival, Cádiz. Economic decline followed. This century Seville has revived to some extent. It is Spain's fourth largest city, with sprawling suburbs, an important port and a number of industries, including food processing and aircraft manufacture. It is the capital of the Andalusian autonomous region and houses the Andalusian parliament.

Preparations for Expo '92, the world's fair celebrating Columbus's voyage of discovery 500 years ago, brought an influx of investment both in the creation of a large exhibition site and in urban infrastructure. Seville is a modern city, with high-rise apartment blocks, but has retained old-world charm in its old quarters. Flower-garlanded balconies, secluded plazas, an exuberant populace (particularly in spring when there is a succession of fiestas) make it an attractive place to visit (but visitors should be warned that thefts from tourists and their cars are common). Among Seville's famous sons: St. Isidore, 7th-century historian, the painters Murillo, Velázquez and Zurbarán, and the poets Bécquer and the Machado brothers.

SIERRA MORENA

Running 320 kilometres across northern Andalusia, and embracing the provinces of Jaén, Córdoba, Seville and Huelva, the "Brown Sierra" has no towering peaks but forms a barrier between the region and Castile. Mostly wild country, covered with bushes and trees, it includes many minor ranges between Jaén and the Portuguese border. Mining for copper, silver, lead and coal and raising sheep, pigs and cattle are the main sources of livelihood. Deer and boar hunters flock to the area in winter months. The Valley of Los Pedroches, bordering the range in the north of Córdoba province, is geographically distinct, consisting of an open plateau with granite outcrops.

CORDOBA

Pop. 290,000. Seville 138 km.

Córdoba is one of Spain's oldest cities, probably Carthaginian in origin. Its name is believed to come from Kartuba, Phoenician for "rich and precious city". It flourished in Roman times when it was capital of the province of Baetica and centre of an important farming and mining area. After decline under the Visigoths, in 711 Córdoba was taken by Muslim invaders. Abd ar-Rahman I, of the Umayyad dynasty, founded the Great Mosque, which was expanded by his successors.

Córdoba reached its zenith in the 10th century under Abd ar-Rahman III, who broke with Baghdad and declared himself Caliph of the West. It became Europe's largest city, renowned for culture and wealth. Civil war broke up the caliphate in the 11th century and Córdoba fell under the rule of Seville and then of the intolerant Almoravid and Almohad sects. Ferdinand III captured the city in 1236 and it became a military base in the war against Granada. Losing its cultural and political leadership, Córdoba became a quiet provincial city, known chiefly for its fine leatherwork.

Its famous sons include Roman philosopher Seneca, Lucan the poet, Bishop Hosius who influenced the conversion of the Emperor Constantine, the philosophers Averroës and Maimonides, poets Juan de Mena and Luis de Góngora, and the matador Manolete.

MONTILLA

This area south of the Guadalquivir river, in Córdoba province, is split into two distinct zones: the prosperous Campina, rolling farmland planted with cereals, olive trees and vines, where Baena, Lucena and Montilla are located, and the rugged Penibética, rising to La Tinosa (5,100 feet), with the interesting towns of Cabra and Priego de Córdoba. The sherry-type wines of the Montilla-Moriles region are famous. Medieval castles dot the region, which is traversed by Highway N-331, Córdoba-Málaga.

GUADIX-BAZA

This zone covers an 80-kilometre section in the north-east of Granada province. The main Granada-Murcia highway, route N-342, runs through the area, which includes the foothills of the Sierra Nevada, arid steppe-like plains and spectacular eroded mountains. Guadix, once an important crossroads en route to the port of Almería, was one of the first centres of Christianity in the peninsula. Thousands of people live in man-made cave dwellings in this area.

ALMERIA

Provincial capital: Almería. Pop. 150,000. Seville 427 km.

Almería province in the easternmost part of Andalusia has a climate and terrain more similar to North Africa than the rest of Spain. Its arid landscape and clear skies (more than 3,100 hours of sunshine annually) attracted film-makers in the 1960s. Tourism is growing along a largely unexploited coast, extending 190 kilometres, but facilities are few compared to other areas of the Mediterranean coast. Almería has long been famous for its eating grapes. Modern techniques have brought an agricultural boom to the desert around El Ejido, where cultivation under plastic has created one of Europe's most pro-ductive zones. Almería was known as Urci by the Phoenicians and Cathaginians; Portus Magnus by the Romans and Al-Miriya by the Moors. The provincial capital was an important port during the Caliphate of Córdoba, then capital of an independent emirate and later a haunt of pirates. It was badly damaged in the 1936-39 Civil War.

ALPUJARRAS

Administrative centre: Orgiva. Pop. 5,000. Seville 314 km.

Spectacular region covering southern slopes of Sierra Nevada and the Sierra de la Contraviesa in Granada province and extending into Almería province. More than 40 villages dot this area of alpine pastures, abrupt chasms, terraced fields and woodland, which until recently, was little touched by the 20th century. Silk industry flourished in Moorish times. Scene in the 16th century of bloody Morisco rising, led by Aben Humeya, against the Christian rulers. After it was crushed, the Moriscos were ousted.

GRANADA

Pop. 280,000. Seville 256 km.

Granada, the last stronghold of the Moors in Spain, retains a special character despite all the vicissitudes of history and urban sprawl. The older part of the city meanders over three hills, which have been compared to the opened quarters of a pomegranate (in Spanish a *granada*). The fruit appears on the city coat of arms. Alternatively, the name Granada may derive from the Moorish Karnattah. The altitude, 2,260 feet, gives the city a pleasant, bracing climate for much of the year.

The Iberian settlement of Elibyrge existed here in the 5th century BC, and was renamed Illiberis by the Romans. After the fall of Córdoba to the Christians in the 13th century, thousands of people took refuge in Granada, the last Muslim state in Spain. For 250 years under the Nasrid dynasty, Granada was a brilliant centre of civilization. Among its more than 100,000 inhabitants were wealthy traders, skilled artisans, silk merchants, poets, scientists and landowners. Palace intrigue and months of siege ended Moorish reign in 1492 when the Catholic monarchs, Ferdinand and Isabel, entered the city. Looking back on the city, Boabdil, the last ruler, is said to have been chastised by his mother: "You weep like a woman for what you could not hold as a man." The point, on the Motril road, is known as *El Suspiro del Moro* (the Moor's Sigh).

Expulsion of Jews, Muslims and Moriscos (Muslims converted to Christianity) impoverished Granada and its province, but the city continued to be a centre of art and culture, as the many fine examples of Renaissance architecture testify. The University of Granada was chartered in 1531. The fertile soil of the *vega,* the plain west of the city, which is watered by the Genil river, has contributed to local prosperity. Today, a million or so tourists flock annually to Granada and the Sierra Nevada ski resort has become popular with Spaniards and foreign visitors.

AJARQUIA

Administrative centre: Vélez-Málaga. Pop. 51,000. Seville 243 km.

For a long time, La Ajarquía (it can also be spelt "Axarquía") was a forgotten corner of Málaga province. Poor communications slowed development of this 1,100-square-kilometre zone between the Mediterranean and the province of Granada. Altogether more than 120,000 people live in 30 communities, but the population is growing due to the tourism boom along the 50 kilometres of coast, known as the Costa del Sol Oriental. Unimaginative, at times barbarous, ribbon development and plastic greenhouses offend the eye on the coast, but inland the beautiful mountainous country and immaculately-kept villages retain their charm. Vineyards, almond and olive trees clothe the slopes. Avocado and custard-apple trees, early strawberries, sweet potatoes and tomatoes flourish in irrigated areas.

Traces of Phoenician, Roman and Moorish settlements abound. Some towers dotting the coast were built by the Moors, others were built later to watch out for Barbary pirates. A hilltop near Vélez-Málaga, the administrative centre, is believed to be the site of the Greek city of Mainake. Vélez, the heart of a prosperous agricultural area, was strategically important to the Moorish kingdom of Granada. It fell to the Christians in 1487. The 16th-century Morisco rising spread from the Alpujarras to the Ajarquía and led to the Battle of Frigiliana (1569).

Expulsion of the Moors was followed by the arrival of new settlers from elsewhere in Spain and a general decline of prosperity which lasted centuries. Napoleon's forces were troubled by guerrilla opposition in the Ajarquía, and took merciless revenge. In the Civil War, there was little fighting in this area, but bloody incidents continued in the sierras until 1952 when the last rebels against the Franco regime were wiped out.

ANTEQUERA

Antequera, an ancient crossroads and market town, 1,800 feet above sea-level, sits at the centre of a rich agricultural region in Málaga province. Relics of early man and Roman presence abound in the area. Close at hand are the mysterious dolmens, used as burial tombs more than 4,000 years ago. The Romans established a settlement known as Antikaria. Under the Moors, it remained a strongpoint of the kingdom of Granada, until it fell in 1410. Between Antequera and the Mediterranean coast lie impressive mountain ranges. From Bobadilla, the important railway junction west of Antequera, trains to Málaga weave their way through El Chorro, a particularly spectacular chasm.

MALAGA

Pop. 500,000. Seville 207 km.

Málaga, capital of the Costa del Sol and an important port, was founded by the Phoenicians 2,500 or more years ago. They gave it the name of Malaca, probably derived from malac (to salt) as it was a depot for salting fish. Under the Moors it became one of Andalusia's major cities. For a time it governed an independent kingdom ruled by an emir. Málaga and Almería were the chief seaports for the kingdom of Granada, but the ousting of the Moors heralded sharp decline. Plagues and earth tremors added to Málaga's troubles. Last century it became one of Spain's leading industrial centres, but a variety of factors including the cost of raw materials and the unprofitable railways to Córdoba led to crisis.

The subtropical climate allows figs, grapes, avocados, oranges and lemons to flourish in the province and has encouraged year-round tourism, which has brought a new era of prosperity. Modern Málaga has breweries, fertilizer plants and many service industries. Thanks to the increase in charter flights; its airport is one of the busiest in Europe. The city is renowned for its liberal ideas, and equally for its wine, flamenco singers and fried seafood.

COSTA DEL SOL

An exceptionally mild climate, sandy beaches and good air communications have made Málaga's Sun Coast into one of Europe's most popular year-round playgrounds. In addition, large numbers of expatriates have made their home here. The coast borders the Mediterranean, extending from Granada province into Cádiz province. The stretch east of Málaga is covered under the Ajarquía. This section deals with the 100-km. western section, from Torremolinos to Sotogrande, which has attracted most tourist development. The coast has more than 320 sunny days a year and the annual average day temperature is

22 degrees centigrade. Average day temperature in January, the coldest month, is 16 degrees centigrade. Only on rare occasions do temperatures reach freezing point. Humidity can sometimes make the period between mid-July and mid-August uncomfortable. A wide range of sporting facilities has been installed, including marinas, tennis schools, aquaparks and golf courses. The influx of visitors has also prompted the establishment of some of Spain's finest hotels and restaurants.

RONDA

This craggy region offers some of Andalusia's most dramatic scenery and spectacularly sited towns and villages. It includes the mountains of the western part of Málaga province and the Sierra de Cádiz. Ronda (more than 2,000 feet above sea-level and straddling a 600-foot-deep chasm) is the commercial centre for the area. Roman remains and traces of prehistoric man are to be found nearby. For a time, under the Moors, Ronda ruled an independent kingdom. The difficult terrain long made this area a refuge for smugglers and bandits. A modern highway, the C-339, connects Ronda with San Pedro de Alcántara on the Costa del Sol.

CADIZ

Provincial capital: Cádiz. Pop. 155,000. Seville 123 km.

Capital of this region where many towns carry the name "de la Frontera" because they were on the frontier between Christian and Moorish territory. Located at the end of a narrow peninsula, Cádiz (or Gadir) was founded by the Phoenicians in 1100 BC. After the discovery of America, it became the headquarters of the Spanish treasure fleets. Loss of the colonies in the New World and the disastrous War of Cuba in 1898 led to decline. During the Napoleonic wars it was briefly capital of all Spanish territory not under French control. It is an important port and, with Puerto Real, has large shipyards. An extensive fish-farming industry has been launched around the Bay of Cádiz. The province is important for its wines and fishing; is noted for its fine horses and is a fighting bull breeding centre. Much of the coast is bordered by magnificent, pine-fringed, sandy beaches.

CAZORLA

This area in the north-east of Andalusia embraces the olive groves of Jaén province, where two historic cities, Baeza and Ubeda, are sited, and the sierras of Cazorla and Segura, of which 220,000 hectares have been made a natural park. A paved road runs through the park, which includes some of Andalusia's most attractive mountain scenery, including rushing trout streams, peaks of more than 6,000 feet, lakes and forests. These can be explored on foot or via four-wheel-drive vehicles provided by the guide service. Route N-332, Albacete-Ubeda- Jaén, runs along the northern edge of this area.

DATES

An Historical Chronology of Andalusia

600,000 BC	Primitive man arrives from Africa via Straits of Gibraltar
15000 BC	Stone Age man inhabits many caves in the region, including those of Nerja and of Pileta near Ronda
2500 BC	Dolmens constructed near Antequera
2300 BC	Walled settlement of Los Millares (Almería) flourishes
1100 BC	Phoenician traders establish Gades (Cádiz)
1000-500 BC	Fabled kingdom of Tartessus around Guadalquivir mouth
600 BC	Greeks establish trading settlements, including Mainake (near Málaga)
218-201 BC	Romans oust Carthaginians in Second Punic War
151 BC	Romans create colony at Córdoba
27 BC	Emperor Agustus names region Baetica
AD 313	Christian Council of Illiberis (Elviria, near Granada) decrees celibacy for clergy
409	Vandals overrun Andalusia
412-700	Visigoths take control
711	Moors invade
928	Abd ar-Rahman III declares Andalusia an independent caliphate
936	Construction of Medina Azahara, Córdoba, begins
1031	Collapse of caliphate and disintegration into 26 small warring kingdoms
1086-90	Al-Andalus reunited under Almoravids (Berber invaders)
1126	Córdoba philosopher Averroës born
1146	New invasion by fanatical Almohads from Atlas mountains
1212	Moors crushed at Navas de Tolosa (Jaén)
1248	Ferdinand III, the Saint, captures Seville
1492	Catholic Monarchs conquer last Moorish stronghold, Granada; Columbus sails from Palos (Huelva) to discover New World
1519	Magellan starts global voyage from Seville
1568-70	Morisco rising in Alpujarras (Granada)
1587	Drake raids Cádiz
1588	Spanish Armada defeated
1597	Cervantes detained in Seville jail
1599	Velázquez born, Seville
1609	Moriscos expelled from Spain
1618	Murillo born, Seville

1641	Andalusian independence plot, led by Duke of Medina Sidonia
1704	Britain seizes Gibraltar
1754	Bullfighting maestro Pedro Romero born, Ronda
1805	Nelson's fleet routs Spanish and French navies off Cape Trafalgar
1812	Liberal constitution declared in Cádiz
1834	Andalusia divided into eight provinces
1835	Measures introduced to confiscate church property
1844	Civil Guard founded
1855	Peasant risings begin in Andalusia
1872	Congress of Córdoba forms first anarchist organization
1881	Pablo Picasso born, Málaga; Nobel prize-winning poet Juan Ramón Jiménez born, Moguer (Huelva)
1883	Brutal suppression of Black Hand, alleged secret society
1885	Blas Infante, campaigner for Andalusian nationalism, born, Casares (Málaga)
1898	Birth of Federico García Lorca
1903-5	Anarchist strikes in Andalusia
1929	Iberoamerican Exhibition, Seville
1931	King Alfonso XIII abdicates, Second Republic begins
1933	Massacre of Anarchists at Casas Viejas (Cádiz)
1936-39	Spanish Civil War
1946	Manuel de Falla dies
1950-60	Thousands of Andalusians emigrate
1951	Last rebels wiped out in Andalusian mountains
1960	Tourism boom begins along Mediterranean coast
1975	General Franco dies, monarchy restored
1977	First post-Franco democratic government elected
1980	Andalusia votes for autonomy
1982	Elections for first Andalusian parliament
1983	Andalusian government reveals agrarian reform scheme
1992	World Expo, Seville

VOCABULARY

Spanish Words Used in The Text

A

afición: pastime, interest
aficionado: enthusiast; amateur (player)
aguardiente: highly alcoholic drink, anís seco (dry anise)
alcalde: mayor
alcazaba: castle
alcázar: fortress, royal palace
almadraba: netting trap for tuna
ambiente: atmosphere

B

baile: dance
balneario: spa
bandolero: bandit, highwayman
barranco: ravine
barrio: quarter (of a city)
Bética: Andalusia (literary term)
Betis: Guadalquivir river, name of Seville soccer club
bodega: wine cellar
botijo: earthenware water vessel

C

cacique: local boss
cante hondo: deeply emotional flamenco song
cante chico: light-hearted flamenco song
cantaor: male flamenco singer
campo: countryside, field
carmen: Granada-style villa enclosed by wall
caseta: booth, pavilion
copla: rhyming couplet
corrida: bullfight
cortijo: farmhouse
coto: enclosed pasture, hunting reserve
cura: priest
curandero: healer
chiringuito: beach bar-restaurant
chorizo: petty criminal
churros: fried batter, eaten for breakfast

D

dehesa: ranch, pasture
dominguero: day-tripper
duende: goblin, prankster;
tener duende: to have magic, the soul of flamenco

E

encierro: corralling of bulls, bull-run through streets
echufe: plug, influential connection

F

feria: annual fair
finca: farm
fino: dry sherry
flamenco: gypsy singing and dancing; flashy, cocky

G

gachas: porridge
gitano: gypsy
gracia: charm, attractiveness, wit
gracioso: pleasing, amusing

H

hembra: female
hermano mayor: leader of a (religious) brotherhood (**hermandad**)

J

jamón serrano: mountain-cured ham
jornalero: seasonal worker, landless labourer
juerga: spree

L

latifundio: large estate

M

macho: male
machismo: cult of masculine toughness
maricón: homosexual
matador: killer, bullfighter
migas: dish made from breadcrumbs fried in olive oil
mihrab: ornately-decorated prayer niche in mosque wall facing Mecca
montería: hunting party
Morisco: Muslim converted to Christianity
Mozarab: culture developed by Christians under Muslim rule
Mudéjar: Muslim art in Christian-occupied territory

N

novillero:	novice bullfighter
novio, novia:	fiancé, fiancée

P

pandereta:	tambourine;
de la pandereta:	folkloric
paso:	religious float
Paso, El:	passion play
patio:	courtyard
payo:	non-gypsy
pícaro:	rogue
piropo:	flirtatious compliment
plasticultura:	crop-growing in plastic-covered fields
plaza:	public square
plaza de toros:	bullring
pueblo:	village, town

R

rejoneador:	bullfighter on horseback
romería:	religious pilgrimage

S

saeta:	flamenco-style song praising the Virgin and Christ
Semana Santa:	Holy Week
señorito:	little gentleman, idle rich man's son
sevillana:	lively flamenco song and dance
simpecado:	portrait of the Virgin
sinvergüenza:	scoundrel, shameless person
solera:	blending system for sherry

T

tablao:	flamenco nightclub
taco:	swear-word
tajo:	steep cliff
tapa:	snack; cover, lid
tinto:	red wine
toque:	flamenco guitar-playing
torero:	bullfighter

V

vega:	fertile plain
vendimia:	grape harvest
venencia:	rod used to extract wine from barrel
venta:	inn
verbena:	fiesta or open-air dance
Verdiales:	music from the mountains of Málaga

BIBLIOGRAPHY

Books About Spain and Andalusia

General:

A Guide to Andalusia, Michael Jacobs (Viking, 1990).
Andalucía Sueño y Realidad (including Teoría de Andalucía) María Zambrano and José Ortega y Gasset (Biblioteca de la Cultura Andaluza, Editoriales Andaluzas Unidas).
Andalucía, Tercer Mundo? Antonio Burgos (Ediciones 29, Barcelona, 1971).
A Rose for Winter, Laurie Lee (Penguin, 1983).
As I Walked Out One Midsummer Morning, Laurie Lee (Penguin, 1983).
Enciclopedia de Andalucía, 10 volumes (Promociones Culturales Andaluzas, Seville).
Hacia una Andalucía Libre (Edisur, Seville, 1980).
Handbook for Travellers in Spain, Richard Ford (Centaur Press, 1966).
Historia de los Pueblos de España — Andalucía y Canarias (Editorial Argos Vergara, Barcelona, 1984).
Los Andaluces (Ediciones Istmo, Madrid, 1980).
Or I'll Dress You in Mourning, Larry Collins and Dominique Lapierre (Simon & Schuster).
Spain in the Middle Ages, From Frontier to Empire, 1000-1500, Angus MacKay (MacMillan, 1983).
The Face of Spain, Gerald Brenan (Penguin, 1987).
The Spanish Civil War, Hugh Thomas (Pelican).
The Spanish Labyrinth, Gerald Brenan (Cambridge University Press, 1982).
The Story of Spain, Mark Williams (Lookout Publications).
Travellers in Spain, David Mitchell (Lookout Publications).
White Wall of Spain: The Mysteries of Andalusian Culture, Allen Josephs (Iowa State University Press, 1983).

Relating to particular areas:

Andar por Las Sierras Andaluzas, Manuel Gil Monreal (Penthalón, 1990).
Apuntes Sobre Priego de Córdoba, Manuel Mendoza Carreño (Ediciones El Almendro, Córdoba).
Bernardo de Gálvez, José Rodulfo Boeta (Publicaciones Españolas, Madrid, 1977).
Cazorla and Segura National Reserve, Francisco Rueda Cassinello (Everest).
El Guadalquivir, José Martín Ribes (Caja Provincial de Ahorros, Córdoba).
Guadalquivires (Confederación Hidrográfica del Guadalquivir).
Guerra Civil en Málaga, Antonio Nadal (Arguval, Málaga 1985).
Guerra de Granada, Diego Hurtado de Mendoza (Castalia, Madrid, 1970).
Guía Secreta de Granada, Francisco Izquierdo (Al-Borak, Madrid, 1977).
Guía Secreta de Sevilla, Antonio Burgos (Al-Borak, Madrid, 1974).
Historia de Antequera, Antonio Parejo Barranco (Caja de Ahorros de Antequera, 1987).

La Alpujarra, .Pedro Antonio de Alarcón (Editoriales Andaluzas Unidas, 1983, facsimile reproduction of first 1874 edition).

L'Alpujarra, Secrète Andalousie, Jean-Christian Spahni (La Baconnière, Neuchatel, reprinted 1983 by Granada Provincial Council).

Los Moriscos del Reino de Granada, Julio Caro Baroja (Ediciones Istmo, Madrid, 1985).

Málaga Musulmana, F. Guillen Robles (Ayuntamiento de Málaga, 1957).

Ronda, Emilio Pérez Sánchez (translated by Alastair Boyd, Ronda, 1974).

Sevilla Insólita, Francisco Morales Padrón (Universidad de Sevilla, 1982).

Sierra Nevada and Alpujarra Alta, José Martín Aivar (Everest).

South from Granada, Gerald Brenan (Penguin).

Tales of the Alhambra, Washington Irving (Miguel Sánchez, Granada).

The People of the Sierra, Julian A. Pitt-Rivers (University of Chicago Press, first published in UK by Weidenfeld & Nicolson, 1954).

The Road from Ronda, Alastair Boyd (Collins, 1969).

Specialized themes:

A Way of Life, D.E. Pohren (Society of Spanish Studies, Madrid, 1980).

Cervantes — A Biography, William Byron (Cassell, 1979).

Death's Other Kingdom, Gamel Woolsey (Virago Press, 1988).

El Maquís en España, Francisco Aguado Sánchez (Editorial San Martín, Madrid).

Federico García Lorca: A Life, Ian Gibson (Faber & Faber, 1989).

In Hiding: The Life of Manuel Cortés, Ronald Fraser (Penguin, 1982).

In Search of the Firedance: Spain through Flamenco, James Woodall (Sinclair-Stevenson, 1992).

Leyendas de Andalucía (Editorial Labor, Barcelona, 1984).

Spanish Ballads (Cambridge University Press, 1920).

Spanish Fiestas, Nina Epton (Cassell).

The Art of Flamenco, D.E. Pohren (Society of Spanish Studies, Morón de la Frontera, 1972).

The Assassination of Federico García Lorca, Ian Gibson (Penguin, 1983).

The Pueblo: A Mountain Village in Spain, Ronald Fraser (Pantheon).

The Wines of Spain and Portugal, Jan Read (Faber and Faber).

INDEX - INSIDE ANDALUSIA

The Best of
SPAIN
from Lookout Magazine

Every month *Lookout,* Spain's magazine in English, brings you the best of Spain with features and brilliant colour photographs by international journalists and photographers living in Spain.

Lookout, founded in 1963, covers travel, people, food, wine, Spanish law, property, events, and lots more. *Lookout* is indispensable reading for anyone, anywhere with an interest in Spain… so you owe it to yourself to become a reader!

Lookout is available at news-stands in Spain, or by subscription from Lookout Publications, S.A., Puebla Lucía, 29640 Fuengirola (Málaga), Spain. Tel. (95) 246 0950.

More Great Books
on Spain

Excursions in Southern Spain *by David Baird. 280 pages*
Forty great trips through Andalusia, from the premier travel writer in Spain today. Here, at last, is a handy guided tour of Spain's most fascinating region, packed with practical information, interesting facts, tips on where to eat and where to stay, and clear maps.

The Story of Spain *by Mark Williams. 272 pages*
The bold and dramatic history of Spain, from the caves of Altamira to our day. This is a story of kings and poets, saints and conquistadores, of Torquemada, Picasso, Cervantes, Franco, the Alhambra, the Escorial… Mark Williams has drawn on years of rigorous research to re-create the drama, excitement and pathos of crucial events in the history of the western world. Illustrated in colour.

Gardening in Spain *by Marcelle Pitt. 216 pages*
Your most valuable tool for successful gardening in Spain, from the author of *Lookout* magazines's popular gardening column. How to plan your garden, what to plant, when and how to plant it, how to make the most of flowers, trees, shrubs, herbs. Illustrated with full-colour photographs.

Nord Riley's Spain *by Nord Riley. 272 pages*
The best of popular columnist Nord Riley's writing over 14 years, brought together in the funniest book ever published about expatriate life in Spain. If you're not one of those lucky expats living in Nord Riley's Spain, by the time you've finished this book you'll wish you were.

Travellers in Spain *by David Mitchell. 192 pages (large format)*
Spain through the eyes of famous travellers, from Richard Ford to Ernest Hemingway. This unique survey by David Mitchell, himself a respected observer of Spanish life, is a collection of the most outrageous, admiring, insulting, libellous, passionate, hilarious, thoughtful, bigoted, eloquent remarks ever made about any country. An invaluable key to understanding the Spanish character. Lavishly illustrated in colour and black and white. (Originally published as *Here in Spain.*)

Spanish Property Owners' Handbook
by David Searl. 100 pages
Do you know your rights and obligations as a member of your community of property owners? Here, at last, are the answers! Including full text, in Spanish and English, of the *Ley de la propiedad horizontal*, with comments by legal writer David Searl.

Cooking in Spain *by Janet Mendel. 376 pages*
The definitive guide to cooking in Spain, with more than 400 great Spanish recipes. Plus complete information on Spain's regional specialities and culinary history, how to buy the best at the market, a complete English-Spanish glossary with more than 500 culinary terms, handy conversion guide... all of it illustrated with colour photographs.

The Best of Spanish Cooking *by Janet Mendel. 172 pages*
The top food writer in Spain today invites you to a memorable feast featuring her all-time favourite Spanish recipes. More than 170 tantalizing dishes, so that you can re-create the flavour of Spain in your own home.

A Selection of Wildflowers of Southern Spain *by Betty Molesworth Allen. 260 Pages*
Southern Spain is host to a rich variety of wildflowers in widely diverse habitats, some species growing nowhere else. This book describes more than 200 common plants of the region, each illustrated in full colour with simple text for easy identification and enjoyment.

On sale at bookstores in Spain, or by post from:
Mirador Publications SL,
Puebla Lucía, 29640 Fuengirola (Málaga) Spain